WORLD HEALTH STATISTICS

2017

MONITORING HEALTH FOR THE

SDGs

SUSTAINABLE
DEVELOPMENT GOALS

World health statistics 2017: monitoring health for the SDGs, Sustainable Development Goals

ISBN 978-92-4-156548-6

Design and layout by L'IV Com Sàrl, Villars-sous-Yens, Switzerland.

Printed in France.

CONTENTS

Abbreviations . . . . **v**

Introduction . . . . **vi**

Part 1
Six lines of action to promote health in the 2030 Agenda for Sustainable Development **1**
Overview 1
1.1   Monitoring the health-related SDGs 3
1.2   Health system strengthening for universal health coverage 8
1.3   Health equity – leave no one behind 13
1.4   Sustainable health financing 16
1.5   Innovation, research and development 19
1.6   Intersectoral action for health 21
References 25

Part 2
Status of the health-related SDGs **29**
Overview 29
2.1   Reproductive, maternal, newborn and child health 29
2.2   Infectious diseases 30
2.3   Noncommunicable diseases and mental health 31
2.4   Injuries and violence 32
2.5   Universal health coverage and health systems 32
2.6   Environmental risks 33
2.7   Health risks and disease outbreaks 33
References 34

Part 3
Country success stories **37**
Overview 37
3.1   Ending preventable maternal deaths in Kazakhstan 39
3.2   Reducing the level of malaria in Papua New Guinea 40
3.3   Combating viral hepatitis in Cambodia 41
3.4   Improving health by clearing the air in Ireland 42
3.5   Preventing suicide in the Republic of Korea 43
3.6   Preventing early deaths due to alcohol in the Russian Federation 44
3.7   Fighting the tobacco industry in Uruguay 45
3.8   Strengthening health emergency preparedness in Ghana 46
3.9   Monitoring mortality and cause of death in the Islamic Republic of Iran 47
References 48

Annex A: Summaries of selected health-related SDG indicators **51**

Explanatory notes 51

Indicator 3.1.1   Maternal mortality 52

Indicator 3.1.2   Skilled birth attendance. 53

Indicators 3.2.1/3.2.2   Child mortality 54

Indicator 3.3.1   HIV incidence. 55

Indicator 3.3.2   Tuberculosis incidence 56

Indicator 3.3.3   Malaria incidence 57

Indicator 3.3.4   Hepatitis B incidence 58

Indicator 3.3.5   Need for neglected tropical disease treatment/care 59

Indicator 3.4.1   Mortality due to noncommunicable diseases. 60

Indicator 3.4.2   Suicide mortality rate 61

Indicator 3.5.2   Alcohol use 62

Indicator 3.6.1   Deaths from road traffic injuries 63

Indicator 3.7.1   Family planning. 64

Indicator 3.7.2   Adolescent birth rate 65

Indicator 3.9.1   Mortality due to air pollution. 66

Indicator 3.9.2   Mortality due to unsafe WASH services 67

Indicator 3.9.3   Mortality due to unintentional poisoning 68

Indicator 3.a.1   Tobacco use 69

Indicator 3.b.1   Vaccine coverage 70

Indicator 3.b.2   Development assistance for health 71

Indicator 3.c.1   Health workers. 72

Indicator 3.d.1   IHR capacity and health emergency preparedness 73

Indicator 1.a.2   Government spending on essential services, including health 74

Indicator 2.2.1   Stunting among children. 75

Indicator 2.2.2   Wasting and overweight among children. 76

Indicator 6.1.1   Safely managed drinking-water services 77

Indicator 6.2.1   Safely managed sanitation services 78

Indicator 7.1.2   Clean household energy 79

Indicator 11.6.2   Air pollution 80

Indicator 13.1.1   Mortality due to disasters 81

Indicator 16.1.1   Homicide 82

Indicator 16.1.2   Mortality due to conflicts 83

Indicator 17.19.2   Death registration. 84

Annex B: Tables of health-related SDG statistics by country, WHO region and globally **85**

Explanatory notes 85

Annex C: WHO regional groupings **103**

ABBREVIATIONS

ABV	alcohol by volume
AIDS	acquired immunodeficiency syndrome
AFR	WHO African Region
AMR	WHO Region of the Americas
ART	antiretroviral therapy
COPD	chronic obstructive pulmonary disease
CRVS	civil registration and vital statistics
CVD	cardiovascular disease
DHS	Demographic and Health Survey
EMR	WHO Eastern Mediterranean Region
EUR	WHO European Region
EVD	Ebola virus disease
FCTC	Framework Convention on Tobacco Control
GDP	gross domestic product
GERD	gross domestic expenditure on R&D
GGE	general government expenditure
GGHE	general government health expenditure
GHO	Global Health Observatory
GNI	gross national income
HBV	hepatitis B virus
HBsAg	hepatitis B surface antigen
HIV	human immunodeficiency virus
IDSR	Integrated Disease Surveillance and Response
IGME	Inter-agency Group for Child Mortality Estimation
IHR	International Health Regulations
ITN	insecticide-treated net
JEE	joint external evaluation
LLIN	long-lasting insecticidal net
LMIC	low- and middle-income countries
MDG	Millennium Development Goal
MICS	Multiple Indicator Cluster Survey
MMR	maternal mortality ratio
NCD	noncommunicable disease
NHPSP	National Health Policies, Strategies and Plans
NTD	neglected tropical disease
ODA	official development assistance
OOP	out-of-pocket
PEPFAR	President's Emergency Plan for AIDS Relief
PM	particulate matter
R&D	research and development
RDT	rapid diagnostic test
RMNCH	reproductive, maternal, newborn and child health
SDG	Sustainable Development Goal
SEAR	WHO South-East Asia Region
SRS	sample registration system
TB	tuberculosis
TRIPS	Trade-Related Aspects of Intellectual Property Rights
UHC	universal health coverage
UNAIDS	Joint United Nations Programme on HIV/AIDS
UNDESA	United Nations Department of Economic and Social Affairs
UNICEF	United Nations Children's Fund
WASH	water, sanitation and hygiene
WPR	WHO Western Pacific Region

INTRODUCTION

The World Health Statistics series is WHO's annual compilation of health statistics for its 194 Member States. The series is produced by the WHO Department of Information, Evidence and Research, of the Health Systems and Innovation Cluster, in collaboration with all relevant WHO technical departments.

World Health Statistics 2017 focuses on the health and health-related Sustainable Development Goals (SDGs) and associated targets by bringing together data on a wide range of relevant SDG indicators. In some cases, as indicator definitions are being refined and baseline data are being collected, proxy indicators are presented. In addition, in the current absence of official goal-level indicators, summary measures of health such as (healthy) life expectancy are used to provide a general assessment of the situation.

World Health Statistics 2017 is organized into three parts. In Part 1, six lines of action are described which WHO is now promoting to help build better systems for health and to achieve the health and health-related SDGs. In Part 2, the status of selected health-related SDG indicators is summarized, at both global and regional level, based on data available as of early 2017. Part 3 then presents a selection of stories that highlight recent successful efforts by countries to improve and protect the health of their populations through one or more of the six lines of action. Annexes A and B present country-level estimates for selected health-related SDG indicators.

As in previous years, *World Health Statistics 2017* has been compiled primarily using publications and databases produced and maintained by WHO or United Nations groups of which WHO is a member, such as the UN Inter-agency Group for Child Mortality Estimation (IGME). Additionally, a number of statistics have been derived from data produced and maintained by other international organizations, such as the United Nations Department of Economic and Social Affairs (UNDESA) and its Population Division.

For indicators with a reference period expressed as a range, figures refer to the latest available year in the range unless otherwise noted.

Unless otherwise stated, the WHO regional and global aggregates for rates and ratios are weighted averages when relevant, while for absolute numbers they are the sums. Aggregates are shown only if data are available for at least 50% of the population (or other denominator) within an indicated group. For indicators with a reference period expressed as a range, aggregates are for the reference period shown in the heading unless otherwise noted. Some WHO regional and global aggregates may include country estimates that are not available for reporting.

Unless otherwise stated, all estimates have been cleared following consultation with Member States and are published here as official WHO figures. Where necessary, the estimates provided have been derived from multiple sources, depending on each indicator and on the availability and quality of data. In many countries, statistical and health information systems are weak and the underlying empirical data may not be available or may be of poor quality. Every effort has been made to ensure the best use of country-reported data – adjusted where necessary to deal with missing values, to correct for known biases, and to maximize the comparability of the statistics across countries and over time. In addition, statistical modelling and other techniques have been used to fill data gaps. However, these best estimates have been derived using standard categories and methods to enhance their cross-national comparability. As a result, they should not be regarded as the nationally endorsed statistics of Member States which may have been derived using alternative methodologies.

Because of the weakness of the underlying empirical data in many countries, a number of the indicators presented here are associated with significant uncertainty. It is WHO policy to ensure statistical transparency and to make available to users the methods of estimation and the margins of uncertainty for relevant indicators. However, to ensure readability while covering such a comprehensive range of health topics, the printed and online versions of the World Health Statistics series do not include the margins of uncertainty which are instead made available through online WHO databases such as the Global Health Observatory.[1]

While every effort has been made to maximize the comparability of statistics across countries and over time, users are advised that country data may differ in terms of the definitions, data-collection methods, population coverage and estimation methods used. More detailed information on indicator metadata is available through the Global Health Observatory.

---

1 The Global Health Observatory (GHO) is WHO's portal providing access to data and analyses for monitoring the global health situation. See: http://www.who.int/gho/en/, accessed 18 March 2017.

SIX LINES OF ACTION TO PROMOTE HEALTH IN THE 2030 AGENDA FOR SUSTAINABLE DEVELOPMENT

Overview

The 2030 Agenda for Sustainable Development *(1)* is the world's first comprehensive blueprint for sustainable development. Launched at the end of 2015, this Agenda frames health and well-being as both outcomes and foundations of social inclusion, poverty reduction and environmental protection. From a health perspective, development can be said to be "sustainable" when resources – natural and manufactured – are managed by and for all individuals in ways which support the health and well-being of present and future generations *(2)*.[1]

In addition to acting as a stimulus for action, the 2030 Agenda provides an opportunity to build better systems for health – by strengthening health systems per se to achieve universal health coverage (UHC), and by recognizing that health depends upon, and in turn supports, productivity in other key sectors such as agriculture, education, employment, energy, the environment and the economy.

To help build better systems for health and to achieve the Sustainable Development Goals (SDGs) WHO is promoting

the six main lines of action shown in Table 1.1. Recognizing that the SDGs embrace all aspects of health, these actions are intended to encourage not only the realigning of present efforts in relation to the 2030 Agenda, but also the investigating of new ways of accelerating gains already made in improving health and well-being. For each of the six lines of action expanded upon in more detail in subsequent sections of this report (see sections 1.1–1.6) there are a number of opportunities and challenges.

First, the monitoring and evaluation of progress made towards defined targets was a major strength of the Millennium Development Goals (MDGs) – both in terms of measuring progress and fostering accountability. In the SDG framework, health both contributes to and benefits from all the other goals. As a result, the measurement of progress must traverse the whole framework. In addition to the 13 specific health targets of SDG 3, a wide range of health-related targets are incorporated into the other goals. Examples include SDG 2 (End hunger, achieve food security and improved nutrition and promote sustainable agriculture); SDG 6 (Ensure availability and sustainable management of water and sanitation for all); SDG 7 (Ensure access to affordable, reliable, sustainable and modern energy for all); SDG 8 (Promote sustained, inclusive and sustainable economic growth, full and productive employment and decent work for all); SDG 11 (Make

---

[1] This definition, oriented towards health, builds upon the general definition of sustainable development given in: Our common future. Report of the United Nations World Commission on Environment and Development. Geneva: United Nations World Commission on Environment and Development (www.un-documents.net/our-common-future.pdf, accessed 13 March 2017).

cities and human settlements inclusive, safe, resilient and sustainable); SDG 12 (Ensure sustainable consumption and production patterns); SDG 13 (Take urgent action to combat climate change and its impacts); and SDG 16 (Promote peaceful and inclusive societies for sustainable development, provide access to justice for all and build effective, accountable and inclusive institutions at all levels).

Health research, and monitoring and evaluation activities have been boosted in recent years by rapid technological advances that allow for the collection and management of increasingly large volumes of primary data – disaggregated to reveal the individuals and populations most in need. The advent of "big data" is a motivation to build links between databases in different sectors, to provide greater access to data and to develop new analytical methods that will lead to a better understanding of disease and open up pathways to new interventions.

Efforts to compile health statistics – including for the WHO World Health Statistics series – have prompted reflection on how best to measure health as both an outcome and determinant of sustainable development. In order to monitor progress towards the overall SDG 3 goal (Ensure healthy lives and promote well-being for all at all ages), WHO has considered several overarching indicators. These include "life expectancy"; "healthy life expectancy"; and "number of deaths before age 70" (3). Such indicators are affected not only by the progress made towards the SDG 3 targets but also towards the health-related targets in other goals. They therefore reflect the multisectoral determinants of health. Current estimates of life expectancy and healthy life expectancy are included in this report as summary indicators of health throughout the life-course (see Annexes A and B). The development and monitoring of comparable indicators of health-state distributions, disability and well-being in populations will require further research, along with the implementation of standardized survey instruments and methodologies.

During the period 2000–2015, the MDGs focused on programmes tailored to specific health conditions – mainly in relation to maternal and child health, and communicable diseases (notably HIV/AIDS, malaria and tuberculosis). Far less attention was given to the performance of whole health systems, including health services, with the result that the potential benefits of doing so were neglected. The SDGs remedy this situation by emphasizing the crucial need for UHC, including full access to and coverage of health services, with financial risk protection, delivered via equitable and resilient health systems. UHC is not an alternative to the disease-control programmes of the MDG era – rather it embraces these programmes so that increased population coverage can be sustained within a comprehensive package of health services. The SDGs also encompass the provision of services for noncommunicable

diseases (NCDs), mental health and injuries, while fostering practical ways of implementing health interventions through already established international and other mechanisms. Such mechanisms include the WHO Framework Convention on Tobacco Control (4) which is now considered to be an instrument capable of promoting not only health but development more broadly.

The persistence of profound social and economic inequities not only compromises the freedoms and entitlements of individuals but directly contravenes the principle, clearly set out in the WHO Constitution, that the right to the highest attainable standard of health is a fundamental right of every human being. As well as being an objective in its own right, health equity is a key enabling factor, for example in working towards UHC. In seeking health equity, there are mutual synergies to be harnessed between activities aimed at achieving the SDG 3 targets and those that promote gender equality (SDG 5), equality within countries more generally (SDG 10) and transparency, accountability and non-discriminatory laws (SDG 16). However, to make the movement towards equity a real force for change, specific programmes of work are needed to identify objectively who is being left behind, and to develop and implement effective solutions.

Sustainable financing underpins any system that aims to improve health. One unintended consequence of the focus on disease-control programmes during the MDG era was the creation of parallel financial flows and the duplication of health system functions, such as those for information gathering and procurement. It is intended that inclusion of the concept of UHC within SDG 3 will lead to a more comprehensive approach to health financing.

New priorities for health financing have now been set out in the Addis Ababa Action Agenda (5). One point of agreement is that each country has the primary responsibility for its own economic and social development. In that context, the guiding principles of health financing include, for example, enhancing domestic tax administration and reducing tax avoidance to increase the overall capacity for public spending, including on health. In addition to the principles outlined in the Addis Ababa Action Agenda, good practice also involves reducing the fragmentation of financial flows and pooling health revenues so as to maximize redistributive capacity and better match funds to priority health services and populations.

Research and innovation are further prerequisites for achieving the SDGs. Here, innovation refers not only to the invention and development of new technologies but also to finding novel means of implementation that would include legal and financial instruments, health workforce expansion outside the medical profession, and the use of common platforms for health delivery. Without continuous

Table 1.1
New opportunities provided by the 2030 Agenda with reference to six main lines of action

	Six main lines of action	Opportunities provided by the 2030 Agenda
Building better systems for health	Intersectoral action by multiple stakeholders (see section 1.6)	Placing health in all sectors of policy-making; combining the strengths of multiple stakeholders
	Health systems strengthening for UHC (see section 1.2)	Disease-control programmes embedded in a comprehensive health system that provides complete coverage through fully staffed and well-managed health services, with financial risk protection
Enabling factors	Respect for equity and human rights (see section 1.3)	Improving health for whole populations by including all individuals ("leave no one behind") and empowering women
	Sustainable financing (see section 1.4)	Attracting new sources of funding; emphasizing domestic financing, with alignment of financial flows to avoid duplication of health system functions
	Scientific research and innovation (see section 1.5)	Reinforcing research and innovation as foundations for sustainable development, including a balance of research on medical, social and environmental determinants and solutions
	Monitoring and evaluation (see section 1.1)	Exploiting new technologies to manage large volumes of data, disaggregated to ascertain the needs of all individuals; tracking progress towards SDG 3 and all other health-related targets

investment in research and innovation in new technologies and health service implementation many of the ambitious SDG targets simply will not be achieved.

It is clear that responsibility and accountability for health in the context of sustainable development extend well beyond the health sector. The 2030 Agenda now provides a real opportunity to place health in all domains of policy-making, to break down barriers and build new partnerships, and to bring coherence to policies and actions. Among the many examples of key synergies that characterize the SDGs, health stands on common ground with social inclusion and poverty alleviation, and efforts to move towards UHC contribute directly to public security. In addition, ending hunger and achieving food security and improved food safety and nutrition are vital for health and development, while the provision of clean water and sanitation could substantially reduce the hundreds of thousands of deaths each year caused by diarrhoeal diseases.

The six lines of action shown in Table 1.1 and individually discussed in more detail in sections 1.1–1.6 below are not intended to be comprehensive and exclusive. Rather, their purpose is to highlight the core values that underpin sustainable development, and to identify some of the crucial factors that will need to be addressed in building better systems for health and well-being, and in achieving the ambitious goals and targets set by the international community.

1.1 Monitoring the health-related SDGs

One key element in fostering accountability around the MDGs was the increased emphasis placed on monitoring progress. In the SDG era this focus on monitoring progress continues, with countries proposing a country-led follow-up and review framework (6). One of the framework's guiding principles is that the monitoring process will be voluntary and country-led, and that national official data sources will provide the foundation for both regional and global-level reviews. Countries have affirmed their resolve to implement robust monitoring strategies in order to ensure accountability to their citizens. For many countries, this would imply new and improved data-collection efforts. Disaggregation by all relevant inequality dimensions is another key guiding principle that will have important implications for data gathering (see section 1.3).

The SDGs also represent new directions in terms of the health and health-related indicators chosen. In addition to the 13 explicit health targets of SDG 3 there are numerous health-related targets in the other 16 goals (Table 1.2). In addition, in contrast to the MDG focus on maternal and child health and priority infectious diseases, the SDGs are broader and more comprehensive, and include indicators for NCDs, mental health and injuries. The use of mortality indicators to monitor the health of populations has also increased. Around one third of the selected health-related indicators shown in Table 1.2 require information on total or cause-specific mortality. Countries will face new challenges in building or improving systems for monitoring mortality by cause.

Data for monitoring the health-related SDGs

Currently, very few of the 42 selected health-related SDG indicators listed in Table 1.2 are adequately measured in most countries – with the result that high-quality data are not routinely collected with sufficient detail to allow for regular computation of national levels and trends, or for disaggregation across key dimensions of inequality. In addition, whereas many countries have established monitoring systems for some indicators that can be strengthened, other indicators are new and hard to measure, and further investment and development will be required before sufficient country-level data are available. Countries will need strong health information systems that use multiple data sources to generate the statistics needed for decision-making and for tracking progress towards the SDG targets.

Table 1.2
SDG 3 indicators and other selected health-related indicators[a] by data source

Indicator	Indicator area	CRVS[b]	Survey[c]	Facility records[d]	Other common data sources	Key definitional or methodological challenges
3.1.1	Maternal mortality	●	●		Specialized study; (census)	Reporting of pregnancy-related deaths in surveys; under-reporting of maternal deaths in CRVS systems
3.1.2	Skilled birth attendance		●	●		Need for consistent definition of skilled cadres across countries and data sources
3.2.1	Under-five mortality rate	●	●		(Census)	Under-reporting of neonatal deaths; age misstatement
3.2.2	Neonatal mortality rate	●	●			Under-reporting; age misstatement; misclassification with stillbirths
3.3.1	HIV incidence	●	●	●		Models needed to infer incidence from observed prevalence and antiretroviral therapy (ART) coverage data
3.3.2	Tuberculosis incidence	●	●	●	Case notifications	Determining rate of under-reporting of cases from facility data and/or routine surveillance systems
3.3.3	Malaria incidence		●	●	Case notifications	Incompleteness of case notifications in high-burden areas; prediction of incidence from parasite-prevalence surveys
3.3.4	Hepatitis B incidence		●			Need to survey large number of five-year-olds once vaccination is at scale
3.3.5	Need for neglected tropical disease treatment/care		●	●	Case notifications	Under-reporting of cases; aggregation across diseases
3.4.1	Mortality due to NCD	●	●			Quality of cause-of-death assignment
3.4.2	Suicide mortality rate	●	●		Police/coronial data	Determination of intent; under-reporting due to stigma, economic or legal concerns
3.5.1	Treatment for substance use disorders			●		Lack of agreed indicator definition
3.5.2	Alcohol use				Industry/government sales records	Estimating tourist consumption and home production
3.6.1	Deaths from road traffic injuries	●	●		Police/coronial data	Definitional differences across death registration data, surveillance systems and police data
3.7.1	Family planning		●	●		Unmarried women are typically excluded
3.7.2	Adolescent birth rate	●	●		(Census)	Age misstatement
3.8.1	UHC coverage index		●	●		Asynchronous data collection across tracer indicators; lack of disaggregation variables for some tracer indicators
3.8.2	Financial protection		●			Lack of standard survey instrument
3.9.1	Mortality due to air pollution	●	●		Air-quality monitors/ satellite data	Uncertainty around assumptions used to attribute deaths to poor air quality
3.9.2	Mortality due to unsafe WASH services	●	●		Hand-washing observation studies	Uncertainty around assumptions used to attribute deaths to unsafe WASH
3.9.3	Mortality due to unintentional poisoning	●	●			Deaths from alcohol and illicit drug use are often assigned to unintentional poisoning with an unspecified substance
3.a.1	Tobacco use		●			Inconsistent indicator definition measured across surveys
3.b.1	Vaccine coverage		●	●		Reconciliation of household survey and administrative data sources
3.b.2	Development aid for health research				Official government report	Incomplete reporting
3.b.3	Essential medicines				Health-facility survey	Establishing sampling frame of public and private facilities; confirming quality of medicines in stock
3.c.1	Health workers		●	●	Census	Inconsistent definitions across sources
3.d.1	IHR capacity and emergency preparedness				Country self-assessment and/or key informant survey	Consistency and accuracy of reported assessments

Table 1.2, continued

Indicator	Indicator area	CRVS[b]	Survey[c]	Facility records[d]	Other common data sources	Key definitional or methodological challenges
1.a.2	Proportion of government spending on essential services, including health				Government budget data	Difficulty accessing expenditures that are not centrally available or are off-budget
2.2.1	Stunting among children		●	●		Proper measurement requires trained anthropometrist; age misreporting
2.2.2	Wasting and overweight among children		●	●		Accuracy and precision of the scale used to weigh the child; age misreporting
5.2.1	Intimate partner violence against women		●			Definitional issues and comparability of self-reporting across countries
5.3.2	Female genital mutilation		●			Reliability and validity of self-reporting is not known
6.1.1	Safely managed drinking-water services		●		Supplementary data on quality of water services	Obtaining data on water availability and quality in households
6.2.1	Safely managed sanitation services		●		Supplementary data on excreta management	Obtaining data on excreta management
7.1.2	Clean household energy		●			Survey modules must be revised to monitor clean energy
8.8.1	Occupational injury mortality	●			Occupational surveillance systems	Definitions vary across countries
11.6.2	Air pollution				Air-quality monitors; satellite data	Placement of air-quality monitors; calibration of satellite data to match ground measurements
13.1.2[e]	Mortality due to disasters	●	●		Estimates by governments, aid agencies, NGOs, academics and the media	Defining end of disaster event and attributing deaths to the disaster
16.1.1	Homicide	●	●		Police/coronial records	Under-reporting and misreporting in death registration data; under-reporting and inconsistent definitions in criminal justice data sources
16.1.2	Mortality due to conflicts	●	●	●	Estimates by governments, aid agencies, NGOs, academics and the media	Civil registration and vital statistics (CRVS) systems are likely to break down during large-scale conflicts; definitional issues; under-reporting, double counting and biased reporting
16.1.3	Population subject to violence		●	●		Operational definition of psychological violence; data collection among children
17.19.2	Birth and death registration	●	●		Census	Imprecise demographic methods used to determine completeness

Note: Use of ● indicates preferred data source; ● or ( ) indicate a lower-quality, or non-preferred data source.

[a] Indicators outside the health goal (SDG 3) were selected from indicators of health outcomes, proximal determinants of health, health-service provision or health information systems; in cases where several indicators cover the same area, only a subset are shown above. Other health-related indicators within scope include: 2.1.1 (undernourishment); 4.2.1 (children developmentally on track); 5.2.2 (non-intimate partner sexual violence against women); 5.3.1 (child marriage); 5.6.1 (women making informed decisions on reproductive health); 6.3.1 (wastewater treatment); 11.6.1 (urban waste management); 12.4.2 (hazardous waste management); 16.2.1 (children subject to physical punishment/caregiver aggression); 16.2.3 (youths experiencing sexual violence); and 16.9.1 (birth registration).

[b] Predominantly referring to death registration with medical certification of cause of death.

[c] This category comprises a wide variety of population-based surveys, including demographic and health surveys, general health examination surveys, disease-specific biomarker surveys and living-standard surveys.

[d] Data based on facility contacts, at the primary, secondary or tertiary level.

[e] Indicator 13.1.2 is the same as indicators 1.5.1 and 11.5.1 (all include deaths from natural disasters).

Effective monitoring of SDG indicators requires well-functioning country health information systems that include data from sources such as civil registration and vital statistics (CRVS) systems, household and other population-based surveys, routine health-facility reporting systems and health-facility surveys, administrative data systems and surveillance systems (Table 1.2). Some indicators also rely on non-health-sector data sources. For several indicators, multiple data sources potentially exist. For example, in countries without a well-functioning CRVS system to record births, deaths, and causes of death, household surveys (and sometimes health-facility data) can be used. Sample registration systems (SRS), such as those used in China and India, can also provide valuable information by recording vital events in a subset of the national population, and can serve as a platform for transitioning to a complete CRVS system.

The predominant data sources needed to monitor the health-related SDGs are household surveys and CRVS systems, specifically death registration data (Table 1.2). Household surveys such as Demographic and Health Surveys (DHS) and Multiple Indicator Cluster Surveys (MICS) are routinely carried out in many low- and middle-income countries (LMICs) every 3 to 5 years. However, data for some of the SDG indicators that could be measured by household surveys are not routinely collected, such as NCD service coverage indicators in the UHC coverage indicator 3.8.1. In addition, due to their focus on reproductive, maternal, newborn and child health (RMNCH), DHS and MICS may not interview important segments of the population, such as unmarried men or older adults. National health examination surveys carried out in some high- and middle-income countries – such as the National Health and Nutrition Examination Survey (NHANES) in the United States of America – are more comprehensive. All countries should consider implementing routine, comprehensive health examination surveys, with the periodic inclusion of specific in-depth modules, in order to monitor all the relevant indicators efficiently, without overburdening survey respondents. WHO, the World Bank, and the International Household Survey Network (IHSN) are developing a set of standardized short and long survey modules for collecting data on health and health-related SDG indicators as a resource for countries. These modules will be linked to the Survey Solutions tool of the World Bank to enable end-users to build a survey questionnaire that can be implemented in a Computer Assisted Personal Interview (CAPI) platform.

For mortality data, death registration data from CRVS systems are the preferred source. However, in almost all low-income countries, and some middle-income ones, CRVS systems do not function well enough to produce data for monitoring (Table 1.3). Instead, population censuses and household surveys are the main data sources currently available in most LMICs. Population censuses can provide data on levels of mortality by age and sex, and by subnational unit, particularly if specific mortality questions are included. Household surveys, in particular DHS and MICS, are an important source of mortality data for children through birth histories, and – in some surveys, with greater uncertainty – adults through sibling survival histories.

Although data on cause-specific mortality (for example, due to NCDs) can be obtained from household surveys through verbal autopsy, their accuracy and precision are major problems. In general, verbal autopsy modules in national household surveys can provide a general idea of causes of death but do not generate data of sufficient quality to allow for the monitoring of trends over time. Mortality due to some specific injury categories (such as road traffic injury) may be better measured by verbal autopsy, but important biases remain for any injury mortality associated with stigma, such as suicide. Repeated use of a consistent verbal autopsy instrument, sampling method and analysis method to assign cause of death maximizes the utility of verbal autopsy data for monitoring purposes.

Given the limitations of surveys and censuses, well-functioning CRVS systems are ultimately needed to properly monitor mortality and related indicators. However, efforts to strengthen CRVS systems, although crucial, are unlikely to improve statistics in the short term as it generally takes more than a decade to implement a fully functioning system. Developing SRS, with verbal autopsy for community deaths, in conjunction with CRVS strengthening will therefore be essential in bridging the current gap. Examples of countries currently implementing or working towards SRS include Indonesia and Mozambique, while both China and India have long-term positive experience of using of such systems.

Data for SDG monitoring: the case of death registration data

Death registration data, including with medical certification of the cause of death and cause of death coded using ICD, are the preferred source of information for monitoring mortality by cause, age and sex. However, there are major gaps in the coverage of death registration and persisting quality issues in death registration data. The two main dimensions of quality which impede the use of death registration data for public health monitoring are: (a) failure to register some deaths; and (b) missing, incomplete or incorrect information on cause of death. Completeness – defined as the percentage of all deaths in a geographic area that are registered – is a measure of the reach of a death registration system. The cause-of-death information given on the death certificate may be incorrect, incomplete or missing, reducing the utility of the data for public health monitoring purposes. The percentage of deaths certified to one of a short list of leading garbage codes – that is, a cause which is not a valid underlying cause of death or is ill-defined – is an indicator of the quality of cause-of-death information. If too few deaths are registered, or the quality

Figure 1.1
Number of global deaths in 2015, by expected registration/reporting status[a]

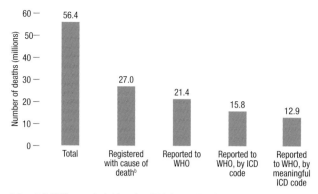

[a] Reports to WHO are projected based on 2010 data to allow for reporting lag.
[b] Local death registration, in the absence of a state or national system to compile data, is excluded, as is registration with cause of death based on verbal autopsy. The discrepancy between deaths registered and deaths reported to WHO is primarily due to China reporting only SRS data.

of cause-of-death information is too poor, death registration data cannot be used to reliably monitor mortality by cause.

In 2015, nearly half of all deaths worldwide were registered in a national death registration system with information on cause of death (Figure 1.1), an increase from around one third in 2005. However, only 38% of all global deaths are currently reported to the WHO Mortality Database (7) – which collects information on registered deaths and their causes from WHO Member States. In addition, some countries report their data to WHO using a condensed cause list, thereby limiting assessment of the quality of cause-of-death information. Only around 28% of all global deaths are reported to WHO by ICD code (regardless of ICD revision), and even then many

such deaths are assigned a garbage code,[1] leaving just 23% of deaths reported to WHO with precise and meaningful information on their cause.

Figure 1.2 shows the proportion of deaths assigned to garbage codes by age (7). The proportion of deaths assigned to garbage codes increases sharply for older age groups. Overall and at all ages over 5 years of age, a larger proportion of male deaths had precise and meaningful information on cause of death than female deaths.

Completeness of death registration and quality of cause-of-death information vary widely between countries, with some countries having high completeness and low use of garbage codes and others vice versa (Figure 1.3) (7, 8). In order to assess the overall quality of death registration data, WHO has developed the concept of "usability" (9), which is defined as the percentage of all deaths which are registered with meaningful cause-of-death information.[2] Usability is a key indicator of the utility of the data generated by national death registration systems in monitoring mortality rates (Figure 1.3). Together with information on reporting status, WHO has used data on usability to categorize national death registration data reported to WHO as very low, low, medium or high quality (Table 1.3).

---

[1] A selected set of ICD-10 garbage codes were considered in this analysis: A40–A41 (streptococcal and other septicaemia); C76, C80, C97 (ill-defined cancer sites); D65 (disseminated intravascular coagulation [defibrination syndrome]); E86 (volume depletion – for example, dehydration); I10, I26.9, I46, I47.2, I49.0, I50, I51.4–I51.6, I51.9, I70.9, I99 (ill-defined cardiovascular); J81, J96 (ill-defined respiratory); K72 (ill-defined hepatic failure); N17–N19 (ill-defined renal failure); P28.5 (respiratory failure of newborn); Y10–Y34, Y87.2 (injuries of undetermined intent); R00–R94, R96–R99 (signs and symptoms not elsewhere classified). Equivalent ICD-9 codes were extracted when available. WHO plans to review and update a list of leading garbage codes for the assessment of death registration data quality.

[2] Usability is calculated as completeness multiplied by the proportion of registered deaths that are assigned a meaningful cause of death. (Usability (%) = Completeness (%) x (1-Deaths assigned to a garbage code (%)).

Figure 1.2
Proportion of deaths assigned to selected garbage codes by age and sex, 2005-2015[a]

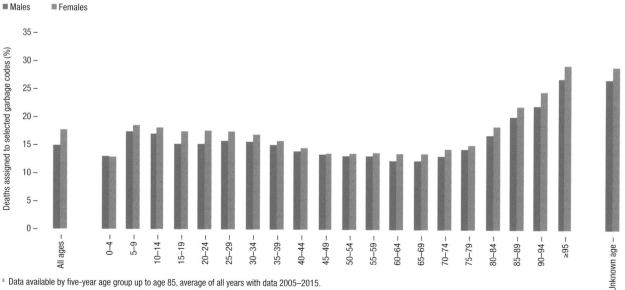

[a] Data available by five-year age group up to age 85, average of all years with data 2005–2015.

Figure 1.3
Percentage of deaths assigned to a garbage code against completeness, and resulting WHO usability category, selected countries

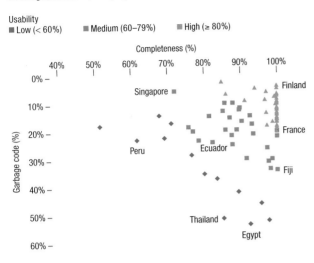

Usability
■ Low (< 60%)　■ Medium (60–79%)　■ High (≥ 80%)

Table 1.3
Quality of death registration data reported to WHO by Member States, assessed for the period 2005–2015, by WHO region[a]

WHO region	High quality	Medium quality	Low quality	Very low quality or no data	Total
AFR	1	2	1	43	47
AMR	10	18	4	3	35
SEAR	0	0	3	8	11
EUR	33	12	8	0	53
EMR	0	1	7	13	21
WPR	5	5	3	14	27
Global (percentage)	**49 (25%)**	**38 (20%)**	**26 (13%)**	**81 (42%)**	**194**

[a] "High quality" refers to countries reporting at least 5 years of data to WHO, reporting latest year of data by ICD code, and with average usability during this period ≥ 80%. "Medium quality" refers to countries reporting at least 5 years of data to WHO, reporting latest year of data by ICD code, and with average usability ≥ 60% and < 80%; or to countries reporting at least 5 years of data to WHO, reporting with a condensed cause list, and with average usability ≥ 80%. "Low quality" refers to countries reporting any data by ICD code with average usability ≥ 40% and < 60%; or to countries reporting any data with a condensed cause list with average usability ≥ 60% and < 80%. All other countries reporting death registration to WHO are considered to have very low quality data.

A number of countries have now made major improvements in both completeness and quality of cause-of-death assignment in death registration data, and two examples are highlighted later in this report. In Kazakhstan, a confidential audit of deaths among reproductive-age women was implemented to identify all maternal deaths. This then resulted in the correction of death registration data when new maternal deaths were identified (see section 3.1). In the Islamic Republic of Iran, the recording of deaths with detailed cause-of-death information was scaled-up from 5% in 1999 to 90% in 2015 (see section 3.9). These and other success stories have very clearly demonstrated that a long-term strategy of investment in CRVS systems, including regular assessment of the quality of cause-of-death data, can bring about substantial improvements in the data used for monitoring. This in turn allows for more targeted investments in health-system strengthening, and ultimately leads to significant improvements in population health.

1.2 Health system strengthening for universal health coverage

SDG Target 3.8 on achieving universal health coverage (UHC) lies at the centre of SDG 3 on health. Making progress towards UHC is an ongoing process for every country as they work to ensure that all people receive the health services they need without experiencing financial hardship. The health-related targets of the SDGs cannot be met without making substantial progress on UHC (Figure 1.4) *(10)*. Achieving UHC will, in turn, require health system strengthening to deliver effective and affordable services to prevent ill health and to provide health promotion, prevention, treatment, rehabilitation and palliation services. Health system strengthening requires a coordinated approach involving improved health governance and financing to support the health workforce, and provide access to medicines and other health technologies, in order to ensure delivery of quality services at the community and individual levels. As part of this, health information systems will be vital in informing decision-making and monitoring progress. Investments in these areas, financial and otherwise, should seek to increase responsiveness, efficiency, fairness, quality and resilience, based on the principles of health service integration and people-centred care.

The broad focus of the SDGs offers an opportunity to reset and refocus health strategies and programming to strengthen health systems. The MDGs provided an important impetus for making progress in a selected set of health areas – namely reproductive, maternal and child health, and HIV/AIDS, malaria and tuberculosis. However, far less attention was given to the performance of whole health systems, including health services, with the result that the benefits of doing so were not sufficiently emphasized. Many countries lack sound health financing, leading to high out-of-pocket (OOP) payments and financial catastrophe or impoverishment for families. Many countries also have major inadequacies in terms of their health workforce and infrastructure (especially in rural areas), medical products, service quality, information systems and accountability. Weak health systems also leave major gaps in national, regional and global defences against outbreaks of infectious diseases, such as Ebola virus disease and novel strains of influenza.

Since the SDGs expand well beyond the MDGs to embrace NCDs, mental health and injuries, and explicit targets on implementing health services, strengthening health systems becomes the only realistic way of achieving the health-related SDG targets. The platform for achieving all of this is UHC, which requires that effective health services are provided to all who need them, while ensuring that accessing such services does not expose users to financial hardship.

Figure 1.4
Health system strengthening, universal health coverage and the SDGs

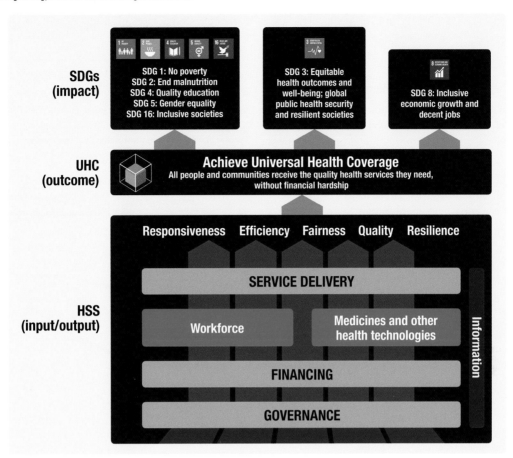

The International Health Partnership for UHC 2030 is an initiative coordinated by WHO and the World Bank to enable multi stakeholder action in building and expanding robust and resilient health systems, and ensuring accountability for the progress made towards UHC as a vital part of achieving the health-related SDGs *(11)*. Effective and efficient health system strengthening will require new approaches – such as ensuring a capable and motivated health workforce as outlined by the *WHO Global strategy on human resources for health: Workforce 2030 (12)*. Coordination will also be needed across the wide range of topic-specific initiatives that will all share the benefits of improved health systems. These include global strategies and plans in the areas of women, children and adolescent health *(13)*, HIV, viral hepatitis and sexually transmitted infections *(14)*, and the prevention and control of NCDs *(15)*. In addition, coordinating efforts to improve health information systems will require the support of initiatives such as the Health Data Collaborative *(16)*.

The challenge of monitoring progress in all of the above strategies and other initiatives to strengthen aspects of health systems can seem overwhelming. However, by selecting a small, representative set of tracer indicators of health service coverage, along with indicators of financial hardship experienced by those accessing health services, a concise summary can be produced of the extent to which health systems are progressing towards the delivery of UHC.

Monitoring progress

In response to the calls of governments for technical support on UHC monitoring, WHO and the World Bank have developed a UHC monitoring framework. This framework is based on a series of country case studies and technical reviews, and on consultations and discussions with country representatives, technical experts, and global health and development partners. The framework focuses on the two key components of UHC – coverage of the population with quality essential health services and coverage of the population with financial protection. This work led to the adoption of two indicators for UHC within SDG Target 3.8.[1] The United Nations recognizes WHO as the custodian agency for both of these indicators with the World Bank as a partner agency for SDG indicator 3.8.2.

The UHC SDG indicators, supplemented with others, will enable countries to monitor progress in health system strengthening towards UHC at national and subnational levels. WHO has summarized the currently available data in a recently launched UHC data portal *(17)*. Beyond these global assessments, efforts are ongoing across all WHO regions to contextualize UHC monitoring to better reflect

---

[1] **SDG indicator 3.8.1:** Coverage of essential health services (defined as the average coverage of essential services based on tracer interventions that include reproductive, maternal, newborn and child health, infectious diseases, noncommunicable diseases and service capacity and access, among the general and the most disadvantaged population; and **SDG indicator 3.8.2:** Proportion of population with large household expenditures on health as a share of total household expenditure or income.

specific health system challenges in each region and at country level *(18–21)*. The following sections summarize the methodologies and data used for monitoring the UHC SDG indicators of essential health service coverage and financial protection coverage.

Coverage of essential health services

SDG indicator 3.8.1 is measured using an index of 16 tracer indicators of health services (Table 1.4). These indicators were selected based on epidemiological and statistical criteria, and following several years of consultation with country representatives, academics and international agencies. The indicators draw on a variety of different data sources, the most important of which are household surveys. Many of the indicators are well studied with United Nations estimates available for Member States.

As shown in Figure 1.5 *(17)*, global coverage of tracer interventions against HIV, TB and malaria have increased substantially since 2000, which is consistent with the massive increase in resources devoted to these disease areas through the Global Fund and the President's Emergency Plan for AIDS Relief (PEPFAR). Coverage of tracer interventions for maternal, newborn and child health

have seen more modest but steady increases – with some being more rapid, such as DTP3 coverage in the WHO African Region, where an almost 50% increase since 2000 was presumably driven at least in part by GAVI, United Nations agency and donor funding. Antenatal care coverage has increased by 30–60% across regions outside of Europe and the Americas.

Figure 1.5
Trends in global coverage of tracer indicators of essential health services, 2000–2015

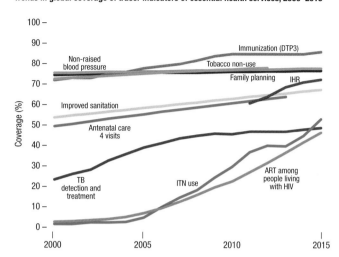

Table 1.4
Tracer indicators of the coverage of essential health services

Tracer area	Tracer indicator	Key definitional or methodological challenges
Reproductive, maternal, newborn and child health		
a. Family planning	Demand satisfied with a modern method among women aged 15–49 years (%)	Unmarried women are typically excluded
b. Pregnancy and delivery care	Antenatal care – four or more visits (%)	Quality of antenatal services not captured
c. Child immunization	One-year-old children who have received three doses of a vaccine containing diphtheria, tetanus and pertussis (%)	Does not capture all vaccines in national schedule
d. Child treatment	Care-seeking behaviour for children with suspected pneumonia (%)	Small sample sizes and respondent errors
Infectious diseases		
a. TB treatment	TB cases detected and treated (%)	Determining rate of under-reporting of cases from facility data and/or routine surveillance systems
b. HIV treatment	People living with HIV receiving ART (%)	Mixture of different data sources on HIV prevalence and people receiving ART
c. Malaria prevention	Population at risk sleeping under insecticide-treated bed nets (%)	Defining at-risk population
d. Water and sanitation	Households with access to improved sanitation (%)	"Improved" facilities may not be safely managed
Noncommunicable diseases		
a. Treatment of cardiovascular diseases	Prevalence of non-raised blood pressure (%)	Not specific to health system response – conditional on background prevalence
b. Management of diabetes	Mean fasting plasma glucose (FPG) (mmol/l)	Not specific to health system response – conditional on background FPG levels
c. Cervical cancer screening	Cervical cancer screening among women aged 30–49 years (%)	Does not capture whether effective treatment is available
d. Tobacco control	Adults aged ≥ 15 years not smoking tobacco in last 30 days (%)	Inconsistent indicator definition measured across surveys
Service capacity and access		
a. Hospital access	Hospital beds per capita (in relation to a minimum threshold)	Optimal level unclear and may vary depending on health system structure
b. Health worker density	Health professionals per capita (in relation to a minimum threshold): physicians, psychiatrists and surgeons	Nurses/midwives should be included but hard to measure and define comparably across countries
c. Essential medicines	Proportion of health facilities with basket of essential medicines available	Establishing sampling frame of public and private facilities; confirming quality of medicines in stock
d. Health security	IHR core capacity index	Key informant data

Several tracer indicators of services targeting diseases outside the focus of the MDGs suggest that broader health system strengthening is needed in many countries. For example, the prevalence of hypertension, a key tracer indicator of health services for cardiovascular diseases, has not declined in many low-income countries in Africa and Asia since 2000 – despite the existence of effective and inexpensive treatment that has led to substantial reductions in higher-income countries. Limited data on access to essential medicines during the period 2007–2014 indicate that the median availability of selected essential medicines was only 60% and 56% in the public sector of low-income and lower-middle-income countries (22). Available data for 2005–2015 also indicate that around 40% of countries have less than one physician per 1000 population (23) and less than 18 hospital beds per 10 000 population (17).

The state of health service coverage can be summarized using an index, which averages the coverage values of the tracer indicators. One challenge in working with an index, particularly when tracking progress over time, is the asynchronous timing of data collection for the different indicators both within and across countries. Based on the underlying data sources available since 2010 for each of the tracer indicators (that is, ignoring estimates and projections), the average proportion of indicators used to compute the UHC service coverage index is around 70% across countries globally, with the following WHO regional breakdown:

African Region	74%
Region of the Americas	72%
South-East Asia Region	71%
European Region	65%
Eastern Mediterranean Region	63%
Western Pacific Region	67%

Although other data systems, such as CRVS systems, are typically incomplete in the WHO African Region and WHO South-East Asia Region, data availability for monitoring the coverage of essential health services is relatively high compared to other WHO regions because of the widespread implementation of standardized household health surveys. However, even with available data, many of the tracer indicators shown in Table 1.4 are imperfect proxies of the *effective* coverage of health interventions and services, meaning that they only capture data on access to a particular service – not on whether or not that service is of sufficient quality to improve health.

Summarizing service coverage across key inequality dimensions presents a further challenge because the same disaggregation variables are not collected for all tracer indicators. However, coverage indicators for reproductive, maternal, newborn and child health services for 39 LMIC with available data show reductions in inequality by household wealth quintile between 1995–2004 and 2005–2014 in the median value for average coverage across

indicators. Although coverage levels increased for both the poorest and wealthiest quintiles, the increase was almost three times larger for households in the poorest quintile (24). Thus, there is evidence that progress can be made in reducing inequalities in the coverage of health services. Nevertheless, large inequalities still remain apparent for many indicators, with lower coverage among disadvantaged populations.

Financial protection

The primary objective of the health-financing system is to promote financial protection in health. At a global level, WHO support for monitoring financial protection is underpinned by the World Health Assembly resolution WHA58.33 on sustainable health financing, universal coverage and social health insurance (25). SDG indicator 3.8.2 focuses on financial protection – and is defined as: proportion of population with large household expenditures on health as a share of total household expenditure or income.[1] Large household expenditures on health are defined in terms of two thresholds: 10% and 25% of total household expenditure or income. This definition was chosen following a consultative two-year process led by the Inter-agency and Expert Group on SDG Indicators and is often referred to as "catastrophic health expenditures".

SDG indicator 3.8.2 aims to identify people that must devote a substantial share of their wealth or income to pay for health care. The focus is on payments made at the point of use to receive any type of treatment, from any type of provider, for any type of disease or health problem. These payments – also known as out-of-pocket (OOP) payments – exclude any reimbursement by a third party such as the government, a health insurance fund or a private insurance company (26). OOP payments are the least equitable way to finance the health system as they only grant access to the health services and health products that individuals can pay for, without solidarity between the healthy and the sick. And yet OOP payments remain the primary source of funding in many LMIC, where risk-pooling and pre-payment mechanisms both tend to play a limited role (Figure 1.6) (27, 28).

OOP payments on health care can be a major cause of impoverishment. This can be monitored by measuring changes in the incidence of poverty[2] and severity of poverty[3] due to OOP payments using a poverty line of US$ 1.90 per person per day. Such analyses of "impoverishing

---

[1] Total household expenditure is the recommended measure of household monetary welfare. Income is to be used only if there is no household survey with information on both total household expenditure on health and total household expenditures.

[2] The incidence of poverty is measured by the poverty headcount ratio which simply counts the number of people whose total household expenditure or income is below a given poverty line. Changes in the incidence of poverty due to OOP payments are measured as the difference in poverty headcount ratios due to household expenditure or income gross of OOP payments above a poverty line but household expenditure or income net of OOP payments below a poverty line.

[3] The severity of poverty is measured by the poverty gap ratio, which is the average amount by which total household expenditure or income falls short of the poverty line as a percentage of that line (counting the shortfall as zero for those above the poverty line). It lies between 0% when no one in a country is poor and 100% when everyone has zero consumption expenditure or income and the poverty line is positive.

Figure 1.6
Out-of-pocket expenditures as a fraction of total health expenditures,[a] 2014

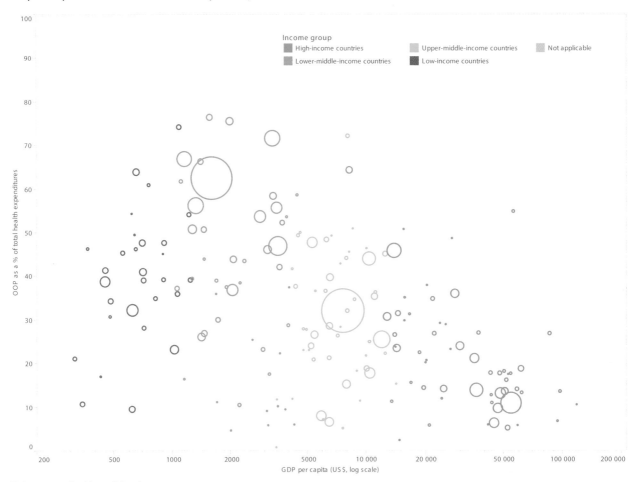

health expenditure" demonstrate the interdependency between different SDG targets – specifically, eradicating extreme poverty (SDG Target 1.1) and achieving UHC (SDG Target 3.8).

The primary source of data for estimating levels of both catastrophic and impoverishing health expenditure is a household survey with information on both household expenditure on health and total household expenditures, as routinely conducted by national statistics offices. Based on information available to WHO in February 2017, the extent of data availability is fair, with about half of all WHO Member States having at least one data point since 2005, with the following WHO regional breakdown in terms of proportion of countries having such data:

African Region	62%
Region of the Americas	37%
South-East Asia Region	82%
European Region	59%
Eastern Mediterranean Region	43%
Western Pacific Region	37%
All WHO Member States	52%

Based on the latest available household expenditure survey data for 117 countries as of March 2017 (median year 2008), around 9.3% of the population on average faced OOP payments in excess of 10% of their budget (total household expenditure or income), including on average 1.8% of the population who spent 25% or more of their budget on health care.[1]

Across 106 countries with data (median year 2009) the average incidence of poverty was about 0.65 percentage points higher than it would have been without OOP payments for health care, based on a US$ 1.90 per capita per day poverty line. This means an additional 4.6% of the population ended up with less than US$ 1.90 per capita per day after paying for health care. Looking at the extent to which total expenditure or income fell short of the poverty line, the severity of poverty as measured by the poverty gap[2] was 7.5% higher than it would have been without any OOP payments for health care. As shown in Figure 1.7, OOP health payments exacerbate the severity of poverty the most among the poorest and those living in rural areas.

---

[1] Average figures are unweighted.

[2] The poverty gap is the average amount by which total household expenditure or income falls short of the poverty line as a percentage of that line (counting the shortfall as 0 for those above the poverty line).

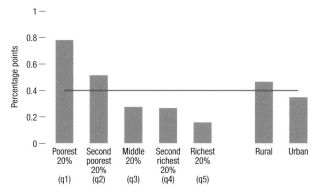

Figure 1.7
Average changes in the poverty gap due to OOP payments, by quintiles of daily per capita total household expenditure or income, and by rural or urban location, 1991–2015 (median year 2009)[a]

[a] Analysis based on a US$ 1.90 per capita per day poverty line, from the latest available survey for 106 countries with available estimates as of February 2017. The horizontal line indicates the average change across the 106 countries.

Progressive realization

Despite health system reforms, all countries struggle to extend the coverage of quality services with financial protection, including high-income countries with long-established institutional arrangements for health systems that may, for example, be working to maintain their levels of coverage in the face of rising costs. Demographic and epidemiological changes play an important role along with technological advances and changes in patterns of service utilization. Meeting the health-related SDG targets will therefore require a progressive realization of UHC, through significant efforts to strengthen health systems. This can only be achieved through committed and coordinated investments in health governance and financing; health workforce, medicines and other health technologies; and health information systems. The key to delivering high-quality, people-centred and integrated health services is to: (a) establish efficient, decentralized and integrated health systems staffed by motivated and well-trained professionals; and (b) provide – and ensure appropriate use of – the full range of quality-guaranteed essential medical products, financed in ways that guarantee predictable and adequate funding for the system while at the same time offering financial protection to its users.

1.3 Health equity – leave no one behind

The 2030 Agenda for Sustainable Development emphasizes the need for monitoring to go beyond the measurement of aggregate performance to ensure that no one is left behind. This means that data for health-related SDG targets should be disaggregated for key disadvantaged subgroups within countries and health inequality measures calculated. In keeping with the mutually reinforcing nature of the SDGs, progress towards this end will not only contribute to the achievement of the health-related targets themselves but also to SDG 5 on achieving gender inequality, SDG 10 on reducing inequalities and to SDG target 17.18.1 on data disaggregation.

As evidenced by recent WHO reports (29, 30), health inequalities within and between countries can be substantial. It is therefore now crucially important to reinforce and reform national health information systems to ensure that they have the capacity to collect, analyse and report equity-relevant data, and to support the systematic integration and use of such data in decision-making and in ongoing national and subnational planning, programming, monitoring, reviewing and evaluation.

Trends in health inequality

WHO *World Health Statistics 2013* examined the health gaps between countries and concluded that concerted efforts to achieve the MDGs and other health goals had led to their reduction, at least in absolute terms, between high-resourced and low-resourced countries (31). It is harder to assess trends in within-country health inequality due to a lack of comparable and relevant data across health indicators in a large number of countries. It is important here to distinguish between the concepts of health inequality – differences in health indicators among population subgroups – and income or wealth inequality. Although there has been an average increase in income inequality in both developing countries and many high-income countries in recent decades (32), health inequalities have not necessarily followed the same pattern.

Recent WHO global health inequality reports (29, 30) and a number of recent studies (33, 34) have indicated that overall, and in most countries with data available, health inequalities have been decreasing in terms of reproductive, maternal and child health intervention coverage (Figure 1.8) (24), and child mortality. On the other hand, trends in child malnutrition inequalities are mixed, with no overall increase or reduction at the global level (29, 35).

There are currently no comparable cross-national studies of trends in adult mortality, life expectancy, NCDs or injuries. There is, however, evidence of widening health inequalities in some high-income countries. For example, several studies found widening inequalities in life expectancy in the United States of America – with falling life expectancy among non-Hispanic white Americans, particularly those of lower socioeconomic status (36–38). Suicide, drug poisoning and violence were major contributors to increased mortality. Conversely, one study of health outcomes for 45 English subregions grouped into quintiles of average deprivation (39) found that between 1990 and 2013, the range in life expectancy remained 8.2 years for men and decreased from 7.2 years in 1990 to 6.9 years in 2013 for women. Trends in NCD risk factor inequalities are likely to vary depending on the country and risk factor, with a lack of comparable data precluding any global understanding of these (40).

Figure 1.8
Composite coverage index of reproductive, maternal and child health interventions: change over time in national average, and in poorest and richest quintiles, in 39 LMIC[a]

WHO region
■ AFR   ■ AMR   ■ SEAR   ■ EUR   ▨ EMR   ■ WPR

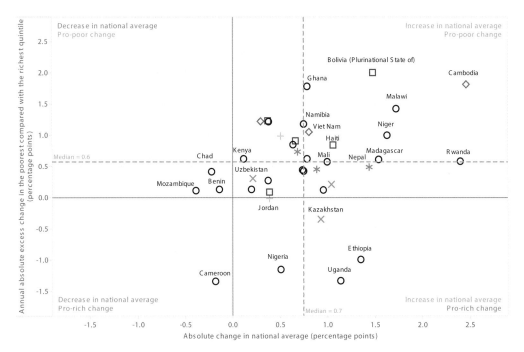

[a] Data taken from DHS and MICS 1995–2004 and 2005–2014. Each country is represented by the shape corresponding to its WHO region. Dashed orange lines indicate the median values (middle points). Blue and red text indicates desirable and undesirable scenarios, respectively. For each study country, annual absolute change in national average was calculated by subtracting the national coverage in survey year 1 (conducted in 1995–2004) from the coverage in survey year 2 (conducted in 2005–2014) and dividing by the number of intervening years. Annual absolute excess change was calculated by subtracting the annual absolute change in quintile 5 from the annual absolute change in quintile 1.

Health inequality monitoring

Monitoring health inequality helps to identify the health "gap" for disadvantaged population subgroups, and to ensure that policies, programmes and practices are successful in reaching the most vulnerable. Additional information on the reasons behind the differences in health provides decision-makers with the information they need to more effectively understand the barriers to health and to design interventions and approaches to overcome them.

Developing equity-oriented health information systems entails country capacity-building to support the collection, analysis and reporting of data for the SDG health and health-related indicators by population subgroups. Disadvantaged groups may be defined in terms of their economic status,

educational level, sex, age, place of residence, ethnicity, migrant status, disability status, and other characteristics appropriate to the country context, such as caste.

Table 1.5 lists potential ways of improving data sources for health inequality monitoring (41). Household surveys and population censuses allow for the collection of a range of inequality dimensions at individual and household level, including socioeconomic variables, minority population status and disability status. Household survey programmes such as DHS and MICS currently offer comparable data across a large number of developing countries (42, 43) and are usually repeated over time. The main disadvantage of household surveys for inequality monitoring is the requirement for relatively large sample sizes to allow

Table 1.5
Improving data sources for health inequality monitoring

Population census	CRVS	Household survey	Institution-based records	Surveillance system
		Data source		
		Potential means of improvement		
• Include individual or small area identifiers	• Expand coverage • Include individual or small area identifiers • Include at least one socioeconomic indicator (for example, educational level) • Include cause of death, birth weight and gestational age (if not included)	• Repeat surveys regularly • Harmonize survey questions over time • Increase sample sizes • Include individual or small area identifiers • Include a comprehensive list of relevant inequality dimensions	• Standardize electronic records across institutions • Include individual or small-area identifiers	• Integrate surveillance functionality into the national health information system • Include individual or small area identifiers

meaningful subgroup comparisons, while population censuses are infrequent (typically conducted once every 10 years) and do not usually cover as many topics as household surveys. CRVS systems usually include data on place of residence and may also collect individual measures of socioeconomic disadvantage. In the case of death registration, there are concerns about the accuracy of individual measures obtained from registration informants. Even so, well-functioning registration systems and health information systems enable some countries to report comprehensively on health indicators disaggregated by relevant inequality dimensions. Health-facility data can be used at lower administrative levels such as districts, but fragmentation and poor quality may hinder their wider use. In addition, health-facility data exclude people not using facility services, who are also likely to be the most disadvantaged.

In many countries substantial investments will be required to build capacity for health inequality monitoring. This will include investments in developing and strengthening data-collection practices for different data sources, including household health surveys, censuses, CRVS systems and health-facility records. For example, household health surveys can be expanded to cover topics for which data are often unavailable, such NCDs and injuries. Countries are also urged to move towards the implementing of standardized electronic facility-reporting systems, which enable more efficient data processing compared to the pen-and-paper method. Further improvement opportunities include allowing for the linking of different data sources through the integrating of small-area identifiers such as postal codes, or individual identifiers such as personal identification numbers, into data-collection processes. Particular attention should be given to ensuring adequate personal identity protection measures and safe data storage. In addition, ethical safeguards such as the Fundamental Principles of Official Statistics or the Declaration on Professional Ethics of the International Statistical Institute should be adopted and enforced with a view to creating an institutional framework that helps to prevent the misuse of data (44). In addition to the improvements in data collection mentioned above, many countries also need to enhance technical expertise in health inequality analysis and reporting.

National health inequality monitoring is the foundation of global health inequality monitoring, which will require comparable data and indicators both within and across countries to track the progress made in international initiatives such as the SDGs and UHC. The WHO Health Equity Monitor (45) is an example of a global database that provides disaggregated and comparable data on RMNCH. WHO has also developed other tools and resources to assist its Member States in monitoring health inequality (Box 1.1) and has conducted training workshops in a number of regions.

Box 1.1
Selected WHO tools and resources for health inequality monitoring[a] and data use

The WHO Health Equity Monitor data repository and theme page provide comparable and disaggregated RMNCH data. Aiming to serve as a platform for both global and national health inequality monitoring, the Health Equity Monitor data repository covers over 30 RMNCH indicators, with data from more than 280 DHS and MICS across 102 countries. The theme page supports the analysis and interpretation of disaggregated data by highlighting key messages and demonstrating innovative reporting approaches.
• The theme page can be accessed at: www.who.int/gho/health_equity/en/
• The data repository can be accessed at: http://apps.who.int/gho/data/node. main.HE-1540?lang_en

The WHO Handbook on health inequality monitoring: with a special focus on low- and middle-income countries is a resource designed to support the development and strengthening of health inequality monitoring systems at national level. The handbook provides an introduction to health inequality monitoring concepts, and describes a step-wise approach to monitoring, drawing from examples from LMIC.
• The handbook is available at: www.who.int/gho/health_equity/handbook/en/

The WHO Health inequality monitoring eLearning module is based on the content and organization of the Handbook on health inequality monitoring: with a special focus on low- and middle-income countries. The eLearning module allows the learner to build up a theoretical understanding of health inequality monitoring through self-directed progressing through the material. Learner engagement is encouraged through discussion points, application exercises, quiz questions and suggested readings.
• The eLearning module is available at: extranet.who.int/elearn/course/category. php?id

The WHO Health Equity Assessment Toolkit (HEAT) was developed as an online tool for health inequality analysis. HEAT enables users to perform health inequality summary measure calculations using an existing database of disaggregated data, and to create customized visuals based on disaggregated data or summary measures. A new edition of the software package – HEAT Plus – is currently under development and will allow users to upload and work with their own database.
• HEAT can be accessed at: http://www.who.int/gho/health_equity/assessment_ toolkit/en/

The WHO Innov8 approach for reviewing national health programmes is intended to support operationalization of the SDG commitment to "leave no one behind". Innov8 is an eight-step analytical process undertaken by a multidisciplinary review team. This then leads to recommendations for improving programme performance through concrete action to address health inequities, support gender equality and bring about the progressive realization of UHC and the right to health, and address crucial social determinants of health.
• Innov8 materials can be accessed at: http://www.who.int/life-course/partners/ innov8/en/

[a] Extracted from: State of inequality: childhood immunization. Geneva: World Health Organization; 2016.

Understanding the "why" behind inequalities

Health inequality monitoring identifies where inequalities exist and how large they are. It is also important to understand why these inequalities exist. Quantitative studies help to identify the relationships between potential determinants and the health indicators of interest. There are also more specific analytical techniques to further break down the determinants of health inequalities. It is also important that national health information systems have the capacity to link with, and track data from, other sectoral domains to evaluate other factors (such as social protection or environmental determinants) that influence health and health inequalities.

Additional qualitative data and participatory analysis may enable the "unpacking" of the drivers behind health inequalities at national and subnational levels. For example, informant interviews can be carried with health professionals to discuss bottlenecks in system performance that may influence inequalities. Focus groups can also be conducted with the target population for health interventions, and should include people who access and complete treatment and, importantly, those who do not access or do not complete treatment. Focus groups can provide information on demand-side issues that more disadvantaged subpopulations disproportionately face – often linked to adverse social and environmental determinants as well as gender norms, roles and relations. Other measures include community monitoring efforts, such as community scorecards, and reflect a human-rights-based approach to planning and implementation. Joint stakeholder meetings – at which decision-makers, providers, communities and partners meet to review the quantitative and qualitative findings on who is being left behind and why – provide vital inputs needed to review plans and redesign services and financial protection measures.

Strengthening use of data on who is being left behind and why

Data collection, analysis and reporting on health inequalities and their drivers will not be sufficient, in themselves, to ensure that no one is left behind during progress towards the SDGs. A crucial next step is data use. Making changes in policies, programmes and budgetary allocations will require a systematic approach to demand-generation for data, informed by a mapping of the most strategic entry points across all levels of the health system and at cross-governmental level.

One such entry point will be National Health Policies, Strategies and Plans (NHPSP) *(46)*, many of which will be renewed in the coming years and can be adapted to further synergize with the SDGs. In support of policy-making and programming that incorporate a leave-no-one-behind focus, WHO launched its *Strategizing national health in the 21st century: a handbook (47)* that includes a cross-cutting focus on equity. In NHPSP and associated subnational plans, data on health inequalities can be incorporated into situation assessments, priority setting/prioritization processes, and monitoring, evaluation and review approaches. It is then essential that corresponding measures and approaches to address inequities feature in the main implementation lines of the NHPSP and in budgeting. Such measures could include closing remediable and unjust coverage gaps between sexes, by rural/urban area or by income quintiles, as well as improving health information systems to be more equity responsive. The NHPSP can, along with cross-governmental development strategies, also incorporate a strengthened focus on intersectoral action for health and equity *(47)*. Generating and using data on the social and environmental determinants of health will be important for this.

NHPSP may include targets linked to the strategic directions and key objectives of the health sector. There will thus be opportunities to develop targets in support of the concept of progressive universalism *(48)*. Under this concept, the more disadvantaged subpopulations benefit at least as much as more advantaged subpopulations in reforms aimed at achieving UHC.

It is also important that national health information strategies include an appropriate focus on health inequality monitoring, with related strengthening of data sources, analysis capacity, reporting and dissemination, and the linking of data across sectoral domains. National health information strategies, if sufficiently equity-oriented, can be important mechanisms for generating data demand, and hence ensuring accountability for leaving no one behind in the context of the SDGs.

A further entry point for using data on health inequalities and their drivers occurs during the regular and ongoing review of health programmes. Data on the subpopulations not accessing programme services, not obtaining effective coverage and/or experiencing financial hardship as a result of service usage can feed into programme performance reviews. This information can inform adjustments to programming that help close coverage gaps and reduce inequities. The WHO *Innov8 approach for reviewing national health programmes to leave no one behind (49)* (Box 1.1) can help to generate demand for the use of data on health inequalities and their drivers.

1.4 Sustainable health financing

Sustainable health financing means that the obligations that a health system has with respect to what a population is entitled to receive – as a country seeks to progress towards UHC – are balanced with its ability to meet those obligations given available resources *(50)*. Following a brief summary of recent trends in health financing, this section focuses on the approach countries can take to financing health in the SDG era.

Trends

Across income levels – on average, as economies grow then total health expenditure per capita increases. This overall increase in the level of total health expenditure masks shifting dynamics with respect to the source of funds. As countries move from low-income to lower- and upper-middle income status, both external (that is, donor) sources and out-of-pocket (OOP) sources[1] as a proportion of total health expenditure tend to decline, with the proportion of total health expenditure coming from public (that is, government) sources tending to rise. However, these trends do not all happen at the same pace. The decline in the proportion of total health expenditure coming from external sources tends to happen at an average lower country income level than the decline in that coming from OOP sources (Figure 1.9) *(27, 28, 51)*.

---

[1] OOP sources refers to payments made by patients at the point of use to receive any type of service, from any type of provider, for any type of disease of health problem. See section 1.2 for more discussion on OOPs.

Figure 1.9
Health financing patterns across income levels, 2014[a]

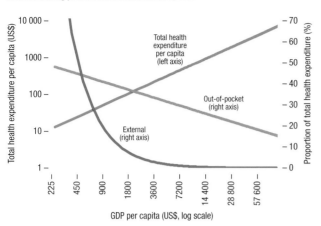

Across time – between 1995 and 2014 there was a general slight increase in the level of health spending from public sources both globally and in low-income countries (Figure 1.10) and a slight decline in the proportion derived from OOP sources (Figure 1.11) (27). The proportion of total health expenditure in low-income countries coming from OOP sources during this same period was higher than the global average (Figure 1.11), while the proportion coming from public sources was lower than the global average (Figure 1.12) (27).

Figure 1.10
Public expenditure on health as a percentage of GDP, 1995–2014

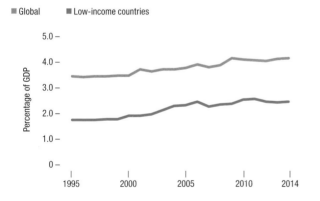

Figure 1.11
Out-of-pocket spending as a percentage of total health expenditure, 1995–2014

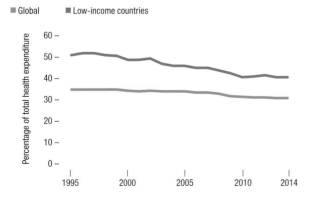

Figure 1.12
Public expenditure on health as a percentage of total health expenditure, 1995–2014

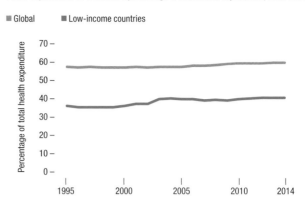

Despite a strong political push at both the global and regional levels to prioritize public spending on health to support progress toward UHC, health as a share of total government spending on average increased only modestly worldwide (Figure 1.13) (27). Furthermore, following large increases in the proportion of total health expenditure derived from external sources in the 2000s in low-income countries there are now indications that the rate of increase is now slowing or even reversing (Figure 1.14) (27).

Figure 1.13
Public expenditure on health as a percentage of general government expenditure, 1995–2014

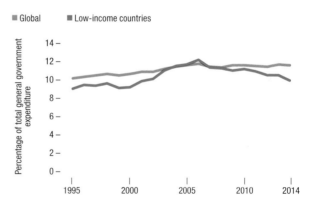

Figure 1.14
External sources as a percentage of total health expenditure, 1995–2014

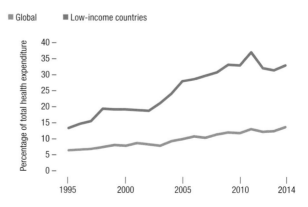

Such trends underscore the challenge of implementing financial protection measures, particularly in low-income countries where continued concerted efforts are required to address persistently high OOP spending levels.

Health financing in the SDG era

UHC stresses that all programmes and priority interventions fall within the overall health system and are part of coverage objectives (1). Unlike the MDG era, during which a fragmented approach to financing specific diseases or interventions was often taken, the focus now is on how to sustain increased effective coverage of priority interventions not simply specific programmes. UHC brings these and other issues together under a common umbrella with a system-wide focus that is needed to tackle the challenges of sustainability (52).

One such important challenge is ensuring an increased emphasis on domestic public sources of revenue for the health sector. Data obtained in a number of countries demonstrate clearly that, on average, greater public spending on health is associated with a lower dependence of health systems on potentially impoverishing OOP payments (53). Due to the current global economic climate, and as countries transition away from donor support as their economies grow, there is now a greater emphasis being placed on domestic public sources of revenue to finance the health system (54, 55). This requires concerted efforts by governments to provide public funding for health services derived from general taxes (56). In particular, many countries have explicitly used general budget revenues to expand coverage of health interventions for the poor, for people in the informal sector or for the entire population. This shift requires donors and countries alike to refine the ways in which aid is targeted, while requiring governments to improve overall domestic resource-generation efforts through improved national taxation systems that are both equitable and efficient (57).

Another important challenge is to develop comprehensive approaches that go beyond framing sustainability as a revenue issue alone, and which also address system inefficiencies and expenditure management problems (58). Sustaining current and improved levels of health service coverage will require efforts to address the ways in which currently available resources are allocated and used. The crucial importance of such a dual "revenue-expenditure" focus is underscored by recent evidence that shows wide variations in key measures of health service coverage and financial protection at very low levels of public spending on health (< PPP$ 40 per capita). It has been noted that some countries achieve coverage levels more than double those observed in other countries with similar levels of spending (59). Such results emphasize that ensuring sustainability is not about meeting a specific spending target or advocating for funding streams for a particular programme, because progress towards UHC will not depend simply on the level of health spending. In all countries, addressing existing system bottlenecks, constraints and inefficiencies is essential for sustaining progress towards achieving UHC (59).

Strategic priorities

While there is no single "best model" of health financing, there exist a number of key strategic priorities for sustaining progress towards UHC that are applicable across country contexts.

- **Continued importance of the fundamentals of good health financing policy** – while specific systems will vary, there is now convergence around the desirable attributes of national health financing arrangements needed to make progress towards UHC. These include: (a) moving towards a predominant reliance on compulsory (that is, public) funding sources for the health system (60); (b) reducing fragmentation in pooling to increase the ability of the health system to redistribute available prepaid funds to meet health needs and protect against the financial risk of paying for care (61–64); and (c) increasingly link the payment of providers to information on their performance and to the health needs of the populations they serve ("strategic purchasing") (54).

- **Increasing overall government budget revenues** – this is central to mobilizing resources for the health sector. As outlined in the Addis Ababa Action Agenda, revenue-raising involves enhancing revenue administration through progressive tax systems, improved tax policy, more efficient tax collection and reduced illicit financial flows (65). These key elements underpin strong fiscal capacity, which in turn is essential for health financing. Without them, systems will be more dependent upon private funding sources, such as OOP spending and voluntary health insurance – high levels of which are associated with inequity and poor financial protection.

- **Productive dialogue between the health sector and finance authorities tasked with allocating government resources** – this should be done at the sectoral level (not at the level of a single programme or disease intervention) and should focus on the overall level of funding for health. Such communication channels are important in aligning health-financing reform strategies with public financial management rules, and enable health systems to take real steps towards results-oriented accountability rather than merely focusing on input control and budget implementation.

- **Move away from silos** – this will require tackling the issues of how resources for health are apportioned and how the overall health system is designed and organized. At present, externally financed vertical health programmes are often in place, and frequently operate independently of the rest of the health system so as to focus resources on a single disease or intervention. The rationale for such a narrow organizational approach may no longer make sense when these programmes are domestically financed. Rather, in the context of overall health system strengthening efforts, the efficiency and general effectiveness of programmes might be improved if certain key aspects were better integrated or coordinated with the rest of the health system. For example, the unifying of previously duplicative and uncoordinated information and data systems can result in important benefits in terms of both the efficiency and coherence of the overall system. More generally, the sustainability challenge needs to be reframed away from programmes per se and towards increased effective coverage of priority health services.

1.5 Innovation, research and development

The health-related SDGs include daring and audacious targets, such as the SDG Target 3.2 to end preventable child mortality and SDG Target 3.3 to end the epidemics of AIDS, tuberculosis, malaria and neglected tropical diseases (NTDs) by 2030. These aims will not be achieved in all countries simply by continuing past improvements. Instead, innovation will be needed, both in technologies and in the means of implementation of activities. The WHO Global Observatory on Health Research and Development (R&D) (66) (hereafter referred to as "the Observatory") maps and analyses data on health R&D, including on funding streams for innovation in health technologies, with the goal of improving access to these technologies through better coordination of new R&D investments based on public health needs.

Health R&D – innovation and access to medicines

Health R&D is vital not just in ensuring the availability of appropriate health technologies but also in ensuring access by all affected populations. Ensuring access to health technologies is vital for the protection and promotion of health. However, despite improvements in recent decades, innovation for new products remains focused away from the health needs of those living in the poorest countries. For example, as little as 1% of all funding for health R&D is allocated to diseases that are predominantly incident in developing countries, such as malaria, TB and NTDs, despite these diseases accounting for more than 12.5% of the global burden of disease (67, 68). The result is diseases which are considered to be "neglected", with insufficient incentives to stimulate market-driven investments. These equity concerns exist not only on an international level, but also within countries, with inequities in availability, affordability and acceptability – the three dimensions of access to health technologies and services.

New health technologies, such as medicines, vaccines and diagnostics, are also becoming increasingly expensive. WHO collaborates with key partners – including the World Trade Organization, the World Intellectual Property Organization and other relevant intergovernmental organizations – on public health, intellectual property and trade-related issues, and in particular on the key role of intellectual property

rights in promoting innovation and its impact on access to medicines. This includes efforts to increase transparency in the patenting of essential medicines and to promote access to medicines through different means, including through the use of Trade-Related Aspects of Intellectual Property Rights (TRIPS) "flexibilities" and de-linking the cost of developing technologies from their market price.

The establishment of the WHO Global Observatory on Health R&D

In May 2013, the Sixty-sixth World Health Assembly specifically mandated the establishment of the Observatory in resolution WHA66.22 to:

...consolidate, monitor and analyse relevant information on health research and development activities...with a view to contributing to the identification and the definition of gaps and opportunities for health research and development priorities, and supporting coordinated actions on health research and development.

The Sixty-ninth World Health Assembly in May 2016 then re-emphasized the central role of the Observatory and requested the establishment of an expert committee on health R&D to set priorities for new investments based on information primarily provided by the Observatory. The Observatory was launched in January 2017 after feedback on a demonstration version released in 2016. This global-level initiative aims to achieve the goals set out in resolution WHA66.22 by:

* consolidating, monitoring and analysing relevant information on the health R&D needs of developing countries
* building on existing data-collection mechanisms
* supporting coordinated actions on health R&D.

By doing so, the Observatory will contribute towards achieving the SDG targets, specifically SDG Target 3.b and SDG Target 9.5 (Box 1.2).

Box 1.2
SDG targets and indicators related to health R&D

• SDG Target 3.b

Support the research and development of vaccines and medicines for the communicable and noncommunicable diseases that primarily affect developing countries, provide access to affordable essential medicines and vaccines, in accordance with the Doha Declaration on the TRIPS Agreement and Public Health, which affirms the right of developing countries to use to the full the provisions in the Agreement on Trade-Related Aspects of Intellectual Property Rights regarding flexibilities to protect public health, and, in particular, provide access to medicines for all

SDG indicator 3.b.2: Total net official development assistance to medical research and basic health sectors

• SDG Target 9.5

Enhance scientific research, upgrade the technological capabilities of industrial sectors in all countries, in particular developing countries, including, by 2030, encouraging innovation and substantially increasing the number of research and development workers per 1 million people and public and private research and development spending

SDG indicator 9.5.1: Research and development expenditure as a proportion of GDP

SDG indicator 9.5.2: Researchers (in full-time equivalent) per million inhabitants

Mapping and analysis of health R&D data for coordinated priority setting of new investments

The process of meeting the health R&D needs for achieving the SDGs can be broken down into three stages (Figure 1.15).

Figure 1.15
Three stages for an informed and coordinated priority-setting process for new R&D investments based on public health needs

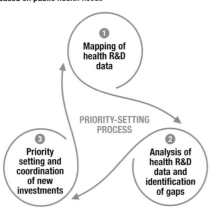

Implementation of these stages will lead to the rational allocation of R&D resources to meet priorities based on population needs. The Observatory was developed to work across all three stages – in the case of stage 3, through its close interaction with the newly established WHO Expert Committee on Health R&D.

The content of the Observatory – and how it can be used

The Observatory is structured around the following six areas:

- **Monitoring** – bringing together data from global data sources that allow health R&D activities to be monitored, with a description of the scope and limitations for each set of data. Examples include R&D inputs such as funding flows or availability of human resources; R&D processes such as clinical trials or tracking of health technologies in the pipeline for new product development; and R&D outputs such as research publications.
- **Benchmarking** – comparing health R&D activities and performance across countries – for example, in terms of expenditures on, or research capacity for, health R&D relative to other criteria such as the disease burden.
- **Indicators** – tracking indicators that are closely linked to the SDG targets relating to health R&D, for example, SDG indicators 3.b.2, 9.5.1 and 9.5.2.
- **Analysis** – identifying strategic R&D needs, priorities and gaps for specific diseases through expert assessment, with preliminary analyses currently available for TB, malaria and leishmaniasis.
- **Databases and resources** – providing users with access to a range of health R&D-related information.
- **Classifications and standards** – providing data classification standards used by the Observatory as a step towards catalysing and promoting increased uniformity in the collecting and sharing of R&D data.

SDG monitoring data available from the Observatory

Data for monitoring SDG indicator 3.b.2 and the health-related component of SDG indicator 9.5.1 are available from the Observatory, and are summarized below. Figure 1.16 *(69)* shows the official development assistance (ODA) for

Figure 1.16
ODA for medical research and basic health sectors as a percentage of GNI and of total ODA, by donor country, 2010–2015ᵃ

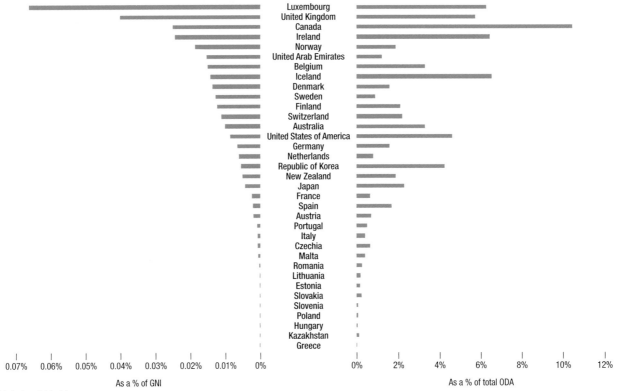

ᵃ Latest available data.

medical research and basic health sectors as a percentage of gross national income (GNI) (left chart), and as a percentage of total ODA (right chart), across 35 donor countries with available data since 2010. ODA for medical research and basic health sectors as a percentage of GNI ranges from less than 0.01% in some countries to 0.07% in Luxembourg. ODA for medical research and basic health

sectors as a percentage of total ODA ranges from less than 1.0% in some countries to 10.4% in Canada. ODA for medical research and basic health sectors per capita by recipient country are presented in Annex A and Annex B.

Figure 1.17 (27, 70) shows gross domestic expenditure on R&D in the field of health and medical sciences (health GERD) as a percentage of gross domestic product (GDP), across 62 countries with available data since 2010. Values range from 0.01% or less in some countries to 0.51% in the Republic of Korea.

These analyses provide baseline information for benchmarking progress in SDG indicator 3.b.2 and the health-related component of SDG indicator 9.5.1. Other analyses available from the Observatory relevant to these SDG indicators include health GERD as a percentage of total gross domestic expenditure on R&D (total GERD), and number of researchers in the field of health medical sciences per million population and as a percentage of all researchers. In addition, a wide range of detailed data analyses and visualizations are available to monitor and benchmark specific health R&D areas of interest, including those with specific focus on neglected diseases.

Expansion of the Observatory

The Observatory will continue to expand the scope, types and sources of data used for the mapping and analysis of health R&D. It will also continue to contribute to existing efforts to improve data quality and classification standards in order to improve information sharing and the knowledge base in this area.

1.6 Intersectoral action for health

The SDGs provide the first comprehensive blueprint for human development, within which population health plays a central role as a precondition, outcome and indicator of sustainable development (1). Health contributes to, and is influenced by, the actions taken to achieve all the SDGs and SDG targets. This presents the health sector with new opportunities. By addressing the policies and decision-making processes of other sectors through intersectoral action, it is possible to strengthen both health care and the broader systems for promoting population health and well-being.

Intersectoral action broadly refers to the alignment of intervention strategies and resources between actors from two or more policy sectors in order to achieve complementary objectives (71). Systems for promoting health and well-being are constrained wherever sectoral policies are unaligned, as much of the disease burden worldwide is caused by modifiable health determinants. For example, it is estimated that more than 15% of all deaths are caused by environmental risks, 22% by dietary risks,

Figure 1.17
Gross domestic expenditure on R&D in health and medical sciences (health GERD) as a percentage of GDP, 2010–2014[a]

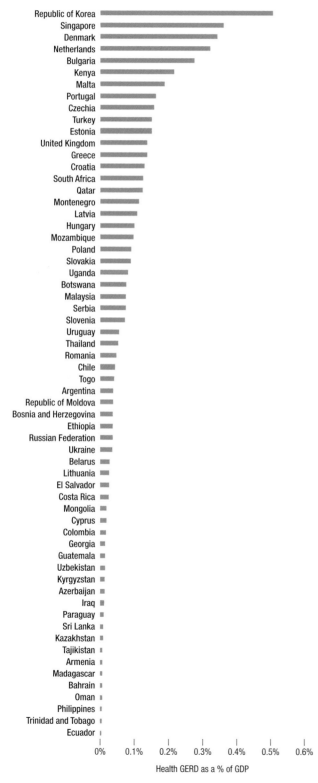

Health GERD as a % of GDP

[a] Latest available data.

3% by low physical activity levels and 3% by maternal and childhood undernutrition *(72–73)*. A large percentage of these deaths can be prevented, and many of the most cost-effective interventions are intersectoral.

During the MDG era, important strides in relation to health determinants were made – with increased coverage of access to improved water sources and decreased HIV/AIDS stigma being two key achievements. The last decade in global health has also seen the WHO Framework Convention on Tobacco Control and the International Health Regulations improving policy alignment between the finance, trade, agriculture, industry and education sectors, among others. In addition, the United Nations Road Safety Collaboration and the Conference of the Parties for Climate Change have reinforced collaboration with the transport and environment sectors. However, all intersectoral efforts also present challenges, requiring constant attention, for example, to improving interdisciplinary understanding, to recognizing and addressing conflicts of interests, to identifying and revamping outdated health legislation, and to generating rewards for health promotion and disease prevention. The health sector will need to demonstrate strong public health leadership in stewarding health in the SDG era *(74)*, while developing sustained, overarching systems supporting health governance.

Opportunities for action

There are many opportunities for improving health via intersectoral action *(75)*. Foremost among these are actions to reduce harmful exposures which are predominantly determined by the policies of sectors other than health (Table 1.6). In many cases, co-benefits can be identified that help bring about health benefits while advancing sustainable development targets in other sectors *(76)*. A number of strategies for achieving intersectoral alignment are outlined in this section.

Linking public health policies and planning, and sustained provision of strategic health advice, to overarching national development plans and processes

Health plans that incorporate a clear orientation towards determinants, rather than an exclusively health care systems focus, will allow for greater intersectoral alignment. Intersectoral approaches to governance – such as the Health in All Policies approach *(77)* – create supportive systems for providing strategic advice to the range of different agencies implementing country development plans and for co-designing policies (Box 1.3). At the same time, the health sector becomes more open to other sectors' priorities.

Contributing to the development of population-based policies addressing socioeconomic problems

The WHO Commission on Social Determinants of Health referred to "structural determinants" related to discrimination, the labour market and the welfare state, and to policies addressing poverty, inequalities, social exclusion and early child development. Enhancing social protection yields enormous economic, security, health and equity co-benefit. Potential approaches here include: (a) cash transfers (Box 1.4); (b) maternal and paternal leave; (c) interventions on minimum wages and employment

Table 1.6
Examples of opportunities for leveraging intersectoral action to improve health and achieve multiple other SDG targets

Exposure	Key health outcomes	Intersectoral action: examples of key actions beyond the health sector	SDG targets
Inadequate water, sanitation and hygiene	Diarrhoeal diseases, protein-energy malnutrition, intestinal nematode infections, schistosomiasis, hepatitis A and E, typhoid and poliomyelitis	Actions by water, sanitation, and education sectors to improve management, affordability, and use of appropriate technologies, while empowering communities	1.4; 4.1; 6.1; 6.2; 16.7
Poverty and food insecurity	Under-five child deaths, stunting and wasting	Social welfare cash transfer programmes for better child nutrition and improved use of preventive health services	1.1; 1.2; 1.3; 2.1; 2.2; 10.4
Air pollution	Cardiovascular diseases (CVDs), chronic obstructive pulmonary disease (COPD), respiratory infections and lung cancer	Health-promoting urban design and transport systems resulting in multiple health and environmental co-benefits	7.1; 7.2; 9.1; 11.2; 11.6; 13.1
Substandard and unsafe housing, and unsafe communities	Asthma, CVDs, injuries and violence deaths	Implementation of housing standards and urban design that promote health	1.4; 5.2; 7.1; 7.2; 9.1; 11.1; 11.6; 12.6; 16.1
Hazardous, unsafe and unhealthy work environments	COPD, CVDs, lung cancer, leukaemia, hearing loss, back pain, injuries, depression	Labour sector promotion of occupational standards and workers' rights to protect worker health and safety across different industries (including the informal economy)	8.5; 8.8; 12.6; 13.1; 16.10
Exposure to carcinogens through unsafe chemicals and foods	Cancers, neurological disorders	Sound management of chemicals and food across the food industry, agriculture sector, and different areas of industrial production	6.3; 12.3; 12.4
Unhealthy food consumption and lack of physical activity	Obesity, CVDs, diabetes, cancers and dental caries	Improving product standards, public spaces, and using information and financial incentives, involving the education, agriculture, trade, transport, and urban planning sectors	2.2; 2.3; 4.1; 9.1; 12.6
Inadequate child care and learning environments	Suboptimal cognitive, social and physical development	Specific early child development programmes designed by the health and other sectors, with supportive social policies (for example, paid parental leave, free pre-primary schooling and improvements in female education)	1.3; 4.1; 4.2; 4.5; 5.1; 8.6; 8.7

Box 1.3
Instruments of overarching intersectoral work and governance for health and health equity *(80–83)*

Finnish developments for equity and well-being 2015

To take into account health, well-being and equity in all sectors in Finland, the Ministry of Social Affairs and Health, with help from the National Institute for Health and Welfare, is leading a process of voluntary inter-ministerial collaboration around health equity and well-being. The collaboration initially targets a limited number of key government programmes being implemented by different ministries (including the digitalization of public services; energy and climate strategies; reform of vocational upper secondary education; and the "youth guarantee" to tackle unemployment among young people). Equity is seen by many as an intersectoral goal, rather than being the domain of the health sector alone.

Starting South Australia's Health in All Policies 2007–2017

The South Australian Health in All Policies approach uses a model specific to the government's organizational structure to address the government's overarching strategic objectives. By incorporating a focus on population health into the policy development process of different agencies, the government is able to better address the social determinants of health in a systematic manner. The successful adoption and implementation of Health in All Policies in South Australia has been influenced by the following four factors: a high-level mandate from central government, an overarching policy framework which can accommodate health lens application to diverse areas, a commitment to work collaboratively across agencies, and a strong evaluation process.

Estonian National Health Plan 2009–2020 Core Action Areas

• Social cohesion and equal opportunities
• Safe and healthy development of children and adolescents
• Living, working and learning environment
• Healthy lifestyle
• Development of the health care system

Box 1.4
Socioeconomic policies *(84–87)*

Cash transfers in Zambia

The Kalomo cash transfer, launched in 2004 by the Ministry of Community Development originally covered 1000 households in Kalomo District. A monthly grant was provided to households considered destitute. Those benefiting were the most vulnerable (70% impacted by HIV/AIDS; orphanhood among children was 30% (national average 17%); 55% of households heads were aged 65 or over). By 2007, the population enrolled in the programme had increased their food consumption and reported reduced illness (Figure 1.18). Owing to the positive impacts recorded, by 2014, the number of beneficiaries had risen to 48 000 households.

Mexico Prospera (previously, Opportunidades)

This conditional cash transfer programme was implemented in 1997 to ameliorate extreme poverty. *Prospera* has systematically demonstrated direct beneficial effects on health and nutrition outcomes, and on important social determinants such as education. One of the main indicators used to monitor its performance is the percentage of people living in extreme poverty. There is evidence indicating that *Prospera* has contributed to the gradual reduction in extreme poverty.

Chile "grows with you"

Chile Crece Contigo (Chile Grows with You) is a social protection policy for children 0–4 years of age, based on a system of benefits, interventions and social services. It includes home visits, education groups on parenting skills and child development, child care, health care, counselling and referral services. The poorest households have free access to nurseries and pre-schools, as do vulnerable families and those with special needs.

Figure 1.18
Pre- and post-analysis of Kalomo cash transfer, Zambia, 2004–2007

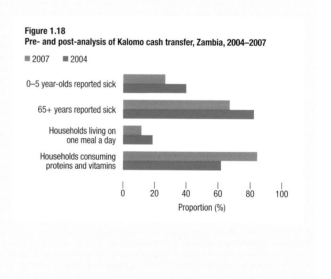

conditions for vulnerable groups (such as workers in the informal economy and children); and (d) affordable housing. Such policies address socioeconomic and health inequalities, thus contributing to SDG 1 on poverty, SDG 2 on hunger, SDG 4 on education, SDG 5 on gender equality and SDG 10 on inequality, while also contributing to the sustainability of health care systems, with direct relevance to SDG 3. For example, it has been estimated that each additional month of paid maternity leave in LMIC is associated with 7.9 fewer infant deaths per 1000 live births *(78)*, while integrated social and medical services, tailored to disadvantaged families and delivered by nurses in homes, result in significant developmental benefits *(79)*.

Leveraging world production, consumption and trade systems, and global phenomena such as migration and climate change

Economic and legal levers such as tax, regulation and laws have been used to change the production and trade of consumables such as tobacco, alcohol, fat and sugars to address associated health risks such as smoking, poor nutrition, interpersonal violence and obesity. Regulatory levers are also effective in regulating products used in construction (for example, asbestos or lead paint). A 2014 World Health Assembly resolution on public health impacts of exposure to mercury and mercury compounds *(88)*, aims to protect human health and the environment from the adverse effects of mercury, and encourages ministries of health to cooperate with related ministries including those for the environment, labour, industry and agriculture. In other areas, global health security can be improved through national intersectoral committees constituted in accordance with the International Health Regulations (2005), while the issue of global migration is being given an increasing public health focus, broadening from codes of practice on international health worker recruitment to encompass refugee and economic migrant populations *(89)*.

Creating health-promoting physical, economic and social environments

Placing a strong focus on creating healthy environments – as, for example, in the Healthy Cities initiative *(90)* – can bring enormous health gains across disease types, and can be achieved through intersectoral action and integrated policies involving national and local governments. Policies for environmental services (including safe water, sanitation facilities and waste removal), integrated safe and active transportation, adequate housing, clean air, space for exercise, healthy and safe schools and workplaces, affordable nutritious and healthy food, and control of tobacco, alcohol, fat and sugar consumption are all important in addressing communicable and noncommunicable diseases, and promoting maternal and child health.

Roles of the health sector

All health sector roles – whether lead agency, negotiator or partner – require strong public health leadership skills. Health authorities may: (a) initiate actions; (b) join up to initiatives developed by the head of government or new integrated government entities (such as initiatives on migration or equity); (c) partner with authorities outside health that are leading on an issue (such as the prevention of road deaths); or (d) ensure linkages between national authorities and local government to support community action *(91)*. Whole-of-government approaches – such as Health in All Policies – supported by tools such as the Framework for Country Action Across Sectors *(92)* and training resources *(93)* are practical means to strengthen all spheres of intersectoral work. Multidisciplinary technical knowledge in local settings is valuable and requires development through intersectoral partnerships. Practice-oriented evidence tools are increasingly available in a wide range of areas, including children's environmental health, NCDs, nutrition, climate change, WASH in health facilities, chemical risk assessments and food safety.[1] National policy-makers can capitalize on the range of international custodian and partner roles to be played by WHO in relation to 27 SDG targets across nine SDGs (SDGs 1–3, 5–7, 11, 13, 16 and 17).

Influencing the agendas, policies and laws of other sectors requires: (a) the sharing of health-based targets with the other sectors; (b) understanding their policy imperatives; (c) using prospective evaluation techniques (such as human-impact assessments) to design policies; (d) developing guidance on the health implications of non-health-sector policies; (e) assessing the costs of such policies and decisions, and integrating strategies; and (f) tracking the health impacts of such policies and ensuring joint accountability through routine national public health reports. At the core of such efforts, health-sector staff dedicated to, and valued for, their intersectoral work at the policy level will be essential, along with efforts to engage with the higher levels of central leadership *(77)*.

Other policy sectors as major health players

Central government at the highest level plays a key role in elevating population health as a key outcome of development. Building a whole-of-government commitment to population health can only be spearheaded if the head of government, cabinet and/or parliament, as well as the administrative leadership of different sectors, are all fully engaged. Such engagement can result in an incentivized environment for joint work – and the valuing of joint problem solving and integrated policy design. High-level policy processes can be facilitated and responsibilities embedded into government strategies, goals and targets across policy sectors.

The health sector can be provided with the policy space needed to engage other sectors of the government, with the involvement of such sectors depending upon the signals given regarding national high-level priorities, and the understanding that considering health aspects in all policy offers significant co-benefits. Ultimately, creating strong alliances and partnerships that recognize mutual interests and share targets will be essential for success.

---

[1] For a range of available resources in these areas see: http://www.who.int/ceh/capacity/training_modules/en/; http://www.who.int/nmh/action-plan-tools/en/; http://www.who.int/elena/en/; http://www.who.int/globalchange/mediacentre/news/country-profiles/en/; https://www.washinhcf.org/home/; http://www.who.int/ipcs/methods/en/

References

1. Transforming our world: the 2030 Agenda for Sustainable Development. Resolution adopted by the General Assembly on 25 September 2015 [without reference to a Main Committee (A/70/L.1)]. A/RES/70/1. United Nations General Assembly, Seventieth session, agenda items 15 and 116 (https://sustainabledevelopment.un.org/post2015/transformingourworld/publication, accessed 13 March 2017).

2. Our common future. Report of the United Nations World Commission on Environment and Development. Geneva: United Nations World Commission on Environment and Development (www.un-documents.net/our-common-future.pdf, accessed 13 March 2017).

3. Measurement of healthy life expectancy and wellbeing. Report of a technical meeting, Geneva, Switzerland, 10–11 December 2012. Geneva: World Health Organization (http://www.who.int/healthinfo/SAGE_MeetingReport_Dec2012.pdf?ua=1, accessed 13 March 2017).

4. WHO Framework Convention on Tobacco Control. Geneva: World Health Organization; 2003, updated reprint 2004, 2005 (http://apps.who.int/iris/bitstream/10665/42811/1/9241591013.pdf?ua=1, accessed 13 March 2017).

5. Addis Ababa Action Agenda of the Third International Conference on Financing for Development. Addis Ababa, Ethiopia, 13–16 July 2015. New York: United Nations; 2015 (http://www.un.org/esa/ffd/wp-content/uploads/2015/08/AAAA_Outcome.pdf, accessed 13 March 2017).

6. Transforming our world: the 2030 Agenda for Sustainable Development. Resolution adopted by the General Assembly on 25 September 2015 [without reference to a Main Committee (A/70/L.1)]. A/RES/70/1. United Nations General Assembly, Seventieth session, agenda items 15 and 116; paragraphs 72–91 (http://www.un.org/ga/search/view_doc.asp?symbol=A/RES/70/1&Lang=E, accessed 3 April 2017).

7. Based on data reported to the WHO Mortality Database (http://www.who.int/healthinfo/mortality_data/en/) as of 12 October 2016.

8. Global Health Estimates 2015: Deaths by cause, age, sex, by country and by region, 2000–2015. Geneva: World Health Organization; 2016 (http://www.who.int/healthinfo/global_burden_disease/estimates/en/index1.html, accessed 22 March 2017).

9. WHO methods and data sources for global causes of death 2000–2011. Global Health Estimates Technical Paper WHO/HIS/HSI/GHE/2013.3. Geneva: World Health Organization; 2013 (http://www.who.int/healthinfo/statistics/GHE_TR2013-3_COD_MethodsFinal.pdf , accessed 3 April 2017).

10. Adapted from: Kieny MP, Bekedam H, Dovlo D, Fitzgerald J, Habicht J, Harrison G, et al. Strengthening health systems for universal health coverage and sustainable development. Bull World Health Organ. 2017 [forthcoming].

11. International Health Partnership for UHC 2030 [website]. See: https://www.internationalhealthpartnership.net/en/

12. Global strategy on human resources for health: Workforce 2030. Geneva: World Health Organization; 2016 (see: http://www.who.int/hrh/resources/pub_globstrathrh-2030/en/).

13. The global strategy for women's, children's and adolescents' health (2016–2030). Survive, thrive, transform. Every Woman Every Child; 2015 (see: http://www.who.int/life-course/partners/global-strategy/en/).

14. Global health sector strategies for HIV, viral hepatitis, STIs, 2016-2021. Geneva: World Health Organization (see: http://www.who.int/hiv/strategy2016-2021/en/).

15. Global action plan for the prevention and control of noncommunicable diseases 2013-2020. Geneva: World Health Organization; 2013 (see: http://www.who.int/nmh/events/ncd_action_plan/en/).

16. Health Data Collaborative. Data for health and sustainable development [website]. See: https://www.healthdatacollaborative.org/

17. Universal Health Coverage Data Portal [online database]. Geneva: World Health Organization (http://apps.who.int/gho/cabinet/uhc.jsp).

18. Universal health coverage: financial protection [website]. Copenhagen: WHO Regional Office for Europe (http://www.euro.who.int/en/health-topics/Health-systems/health-systems-financing/publications/clusters/universal-health-coverage-financial-protection).

19. Toward universal health coverage and equity in Latin America and the Caribbean. Evidence from selected countries. Dmytraczenko T, Almeida G, editors. Washington (DC): World Bank; 2015 (see: http://www.paho.org/hq/index.php?option=com_content&view=article&id=11065%3A2015-universal-health-coverage-latin-america-caribbean&catid=3316%3Apublications&Itemid=3562&lang=en).

20. WHO Eastern Mediterranean Region Framework for health information systems and core indicators for monitoring the health situation and health system performance. Cairo: WHO Regional Office for the Eastern Mediterranean; 2016 (WHO-EM/HST/242/E; http://applications.emro.who.int/dsaf/EMROPUB_2016_EN_19169.pdf?ua=1, accessed 7 April 2017).

21. Universal health coverage. Moving towards better health [website]. New Delhi: WHO Regional Office for South-East Asia (http://apps.searo.who.int/uhc).

22. Millennium Development Goal 8. Taking stock of the Global Partnership for Development. MDG Gap Task Force Report 2015. New York (NY): United Nations; 2015 (www.un.org/en/development/desa/policy/mdg_gap/mdg_gap2015/2015GAP_FULLREPORT_EN.pdf, accessed 7 April 2017).

23. WHO Global Health Workforce Statistics [online database]. Health workforce. Geneva: World Health Organization (http://who.int/hrh/statistics/hwfstats/en/).

24. Health Equity Monitor [online database]. Global Health Observatory (GHO) data. Geneva: World Health Organization (http://www.who.int/gho/health_equity/en/).

25. Sustainable health financing, universal coverage and social health insurance. Resolution WHA58.33. In: Fifty-eighth World Health Assembly, Geneva, 16-25 May 2005. Resolutions and decisions, annex. Geneva: World Health Organization; 2005 (WHA58/2005/REC/1; http://apps.who.int/medicinedocs/documents/s21475en/s21475en.pdf, accessed 7 April 2017).

26. OECD/WHO/Eurostat. A System of Health Accounts: 2011 Edition, Paris: OECD Publishing; 2011 (http://www.oecd-ilibrary.org/social-issues-migration-health/a-system-of-health-accounts/classification-of-health-care-financing-schemes-icha-hf_9789264116016-9-en, accessed 7 April 2017).

27. WHO Global Health Expenditure Database [online database]. Geneva: World Health Organization (http://apps.who.int/nha/database/Select/Indicators/en, accessed 20 March 2017). Global and regional aggregates are unweighted averages. Income classification is based on the World Bank analytical income of economies (July 2016), based on the 2015 Atlas gross national income per capita estimates.

28. World Development Indicators [online database]. Washington (DC): World Bank (http://data.worldbank.org/data-catalog/world-development-indicators, accessed 20 March 2017).

29. State of inequality: reproductive, maternal, newborn and child health. Geneva: World Health Organization; 2015 (http://apps.who.int/iris/bitstream/10665/164590/1/9789241564908_eng.pdf?ua=1, accessed 8 April 2017).

30. State of inequality: childhood immunization. Geneva: World Health Organization; 2016 (http://apps.who.int/iris/bitstream/10665/252541/1/9789241511735-eng.pdf?ua=1, accessed 8 April 2017).

31. Are efforts to meet the MDGs reducing health gaps between countries? In: World Health Statistics 2013. Part II. Highlighted topics. Geneva: World Health Organization; 2013 (see: http://www.who.int/gho/publications/world_health_statistics/2013/en/, accessed 8 April 2017).

32. Humanity divided: Confronting inequality in developing countries. New York: UNDP; 2014 (see: http://www.undp.org/content/undp/en/home/librarypage/poverty-reduction/humanity-divided--confronting-inequality-in-developing-countries.html, accessed 8 April 2017); and: Income inequality. The gap between rich and poor. Paris: OECD; 2015 (see: http://www.oecd.org/social/income-inequality-9789264246010-en.htm, accessed 8 April 2017).

33. Gwatkin DR. Trends in health inequalities in developing countries. Lancet Glob Health. 2017;5(4):e371-2 (http://thelancet.com/journals/langlo/article/PIIS2214-109X(17)30080-3/fulltext#back-bib8, accessed 8 April 2017).

34. Victora CG, Barros AJD, França GVA, da Silva ICM, Carvajal-Velez L, Amouzou A. The contribution of poor and rural populations to national trends in reproductive, maternal, newborn, and child health coverage: analyses of cross-sectional surveys from 64 countries. Lancet Glob Health. 2017;5(4):e402-7 (http://www.thelancet.com/pdfs/journals/langlo/PIIS2214-109X(17)30077-3.pdf, accessed 8 April 2017).

35. Paciorek CJ, Stevens GA, Finucane MM, Ezzati M and on behalf of the Nutrition Impact Model Study Group (Child Growth). Children's height and weight in rural and urban populations in low-income and middle-income countries: a systematic analysis of population-representative data. Lancet Glob Health. 2013;1(5):e300-9 (https://www.ncbi.nlm.nih.gov/pmc/articles/PMC4547325/, accessed 8 April 2017).

36. Case A, Deaton A. Rising morbidity and mortality in midlife among white non-Hispanic Americans in the 21st century. Proc Natl Acad Sci USA, 2015;112(49):15078-83 (doi: 10.1073/pnas.1518393112).

37. Chetty R, Stepner M, Abraham S, Lin S, Scuderi B, Turner N et al. The association between income and life expectancy in the United States, 2001-2014. JAMA. 2016;315(16):1750-66 (doi:10.1001/jama.2016.4226).

38. Wang H, Schumacher AE, Levitz CE, Mokdad AH, Murray CJL. Left behind: widening disparities for males and females in US county life expectancy, 1985-2010. Popul Health Metr. 2013;11:8.

39. Newton JN, Briggs ADM, Murray CJL, Dicker D, Foreman KJ, Wang H et al. Changes in health in England, with analysis by English regions and areas of deprivation, 1990-2013: a systematic analysis for the Global Burden of Disease Study 2013. Lancet. 2015;386(10010):2257-74.

40. Di Cesare M, Khang Y-H, Asaria P, Blakely T, Cowan MJ, Farzadfar F et al. Inequalities in non-communicable diseases and effective responses. Lancet. 2013;381(9866):585-597 (http://www.thelancet.com/journals/lancet/article/PIIS0140-6736(12)61851-0/fulltext, accessed 8 April 2017); and: Sommer I, Griebler U, Mahlknecht P, Thaler K, Bouskill K, Gartlehner G et al. Socioeconomic inequalities in non-communicable diseases and

their risk factors: an overview of systematic reviews. BMC Public Health. 2015;15:914 (http://bmcpublichealth.biomedcentral.com/articles/10.1186/s12889-015-2227-y, accessed 8 April 2017); and: Allen L, Williams J, Townsend N, Mikkelsen B, Roberts N, Foster C et al. Socioeconomic status and non-communicable disease behavioural risk factors in low-income and lower-middle-income countries: a systematic review. Lancet Glob Health. 2017;5(3):e277-89 (http://www.thelancet.com/journals/langlo/article/PIIS2214-109X(17)30058-X/fulltext, accessed 8 April 2017).

41. Adapted from: Handbook on health inequality monitoring: with a special focus on low- and middle-income countries. Geneva: World Health Organization; 2013 (http://apps.who.int/iris/bitstream/10665/85345/1/9789241548632_eng.pdf?ua=1, accessed 5 April 2017).

42. The DHS Program [website]. Rockville (MD): United States Agency for International Development (http://dhsprogram.com).

43. Statistics and monitoring: Multiple Indicator Cluster Survey (MICS) [website]. New York (NY): United Nations Children's Fund (http://www.unicef.org/statistics/index_24302.html).

44. Human rights indicators: A guide to measurement and implementation. New York (NY) and Geneva: United Nations Office of the High Commissioner for Human Rights (see: http://www.ohchr.org/EN/Issues/Indicators/Pages/documents.aspx, accessed 8 April 2017).

45. Hosseinpoor AR, Bergen N, Schlotheuber A, Victora C, Boerma T, Barros AJD. Data Resource Profile: WHO Health Equity Monitor (HEM). International J Epidemiol. 2016;45(5):1404-5e (https://academic.oup.com/ije/article/45/5/1404/2450924/Data-Resource-Profile-WHO-Health-Equity-Monitor, accessed 8 April 2017).

46. Country Planning Cycle Database. A World Health Organization Resource [online database]. Geneva: World Health Organization (http://www.nationalplanningcycles.org/).

47. Strategizing national health in the 21st century: a handbook. Geneva: World Health Organization; 2016 (see: http://www.who.int/healthsystems/publications/nhpsp-handbook/en/, accessed 8 April 2017).

48. Gwatkin DR, Ergo A. Universal health coverage: friend or foe of health equity? Lancet. 2011;377(9784):2160-1 (http://www.thelancet.com/journals/lancet/article/PIIS0140-6736%2810%2962058-2/fulltext, accessed 8 April 2017).

49. The Innov8 approach for reviewing national health programmes to leave no one behind. Technical handbook. Geneva: World Health Organization; 2016 (see: http://www.who.int/life-course/partners/innov8/innov8-technical-handbook/en/, accessed 8 April 2017).

50. Thomson S, Foubister T, Figueras J, Kutzin J, Permanand G, Bryndová L. Addressing financial sustainability in health systems. Copenhagen: WHO Regional Office for Europe; 2009 (http://www.euro.who.int/__data/assets/pdf_file/0005/64949/E93058.pdf, accessed 15 March 2017).

51. Tandon A. Financial sustainability challenges in transitioning from external sources of financing [meeting presentation]. Washington (DC): World Bank. Presented at: UHC2030 Working Group meeting on sustainability, transition from aid, and health system strengthening. April, 2017 (https://www.internationalhealthpartnership.net/fileadmin/uploads/ihp/Documents/About_IHP_/working_groups/Transition_working_group_docs/ATandon_TransitionSustainability.pdf, accessed 23 April 2017).

52. Kutzin J, Sparkes SP. Health systems strengthening, universal health coverage, health security and resilience. Bull World Health Organ. 2016;94(1):2 (http://www.who.int/bulletin/volumes/94/1/15-165050.pdf, accessed 15 March 2017).

53. Kutzin J, Yip W, Cashin C. Alternative financing strategies for universal health coverage. World Scientific Handbook of Global Health Economics and Public Policy. World Scientific; 2016:267–309 (http://www.worldscientific.com/doi/pdf/10.1142/9789813140493_0005, accessed 15 March 2017).

54. Kutzin J. Anything goes on the path to universal health coverage? No. Bull World Health Organ. 2012;90(11):867–8 (http://www.who.int/bulletin/volumes/90/11/12-113654.pdf, accessed 15 March 2017).

55. Public financing for health in Africa: from Abuja to the SDGs. Geneva: World Health Organization; 2016 (http://apps.who.int/iris/bitstream/10665/249527/1/WHO-HIS-HGF-Tech.Report-16.2-eng.pdf?ua=1, accessed 15 March 2017).

56. Jowett M, Kutzin J. Raising revenues for health in support of UHC: strategic issues for policy makers. Geneva: World Health Organization; 2015 (http://apps.who.int/iris/bitstream/10665/192280/1/WHO_HIS_HGF_PolicyBrief_15.1_eng.pdf?ua=1, accessed 15 March 2017).

57. Fryatt R, Mills A. Taskforce on Innovative International Financing for Health Systems: showing the way forward. Bull World Health Organ. 2010;88(6):476–7 (http://www.who.int/bulletin/volumes/88/6/09-075507/en/, accessed 15 March 2017).

58. Buckley GJ, Lange JE, Peterson EA, editors. Investing in global health systems: sustaining gains, transforming lives. Washington (DC): National Academies Press; 2014.

59. Jowett M, Brunal MTP, Flores G, Cylus J. Spending targets for health: no magic number. Geneva: World Health Organization; 2016 (http://apps.who.int/iris/bitstream/10665/250048/1/WHO-HIS-HGF-HFWorkingPaper-16.1-eng.pdf?ua=1, accessed 15 March 2017).

60. Fuchs VR. What every philosopher should know about health economics. Proc Am Philos Soc. 1996; 140(2):186–96 (http://www.worldscientific.com/doi/suppl/10.1142/8167/suppl_file/8167_p155_free.pdf, accessed 15 March 2017).

61. Fragmentation in pooling arrangements. Technical Briefing Series – Brief No 5. Geneva: World Health Organization; 2010 (http://www.who.int/healthsystems/topics/financing/healthreport/FragmentationTBNo5.pdf?ua=1, accessed 15 March 2017).

62. Kutzin J, Shishkin S, Bryndová L, Schneider P, Hroboň P. Reforms in the pooling of funds. In: Kutzin J, Cashin C, Jakab M, editors. Implementing health financing reform. Lessons from countries in transition. Copenhagen: World Health Organization, on behalf of the European Observatory on Health Systems and Policies; 2010: 119–53 (http://www.euro.who.int/__data/assets/pdf_file/0014/120164/E94240.pdf, accessed 15 March 2017).

63. Londoño J-L, Frenk J. Structured pluralism: towards an innovative model for health system reform in Latin America. Health Policy. 1997;41(1):1–36.

64. Frenk J. Comprehensive policy analysis for health system reform. Health Policy. 1995;32(1–3):257–77.

65. Addis Ababa Action Agenda of the Third International Conference on Financing for Development. Addis Ababa, Ethiopia, 13–16 July 2015. New York: United Nations; 2015 (http://www.un.org/esa/ffd/wp-content/uploads/2015/08/AAAA_Outcome.pdf, accessed 13 March 2017).

66. Global Observatory on Health R&D [online database]. Geneva: World Health Organization (http://www.who.int/research-observatory/en/).

67. Røttingen J-A, Regmi S, Eide M, Young AJ, Viergever RF, Årdal C et al. Mapping of available health research and development data: what's there, what's missing, and what role is there for a global observatory. Lancet. 2013;382(9900):1286–307 (summary: http://www.thelancet.com/journals/lancet/article/PIIS0140-6736(13)61046-6/fulltext, accessed 8 April 2017).

68. Kieny MP, Viergever RF, Adam T, Boerma T, Røttingen J-A. Global platform to inform investments for health R&D. Lancet. 2016;387(10024):1157 (http://www.thelancet.com/journals/lancet/article/PIIS0140-6736(16)00705-4/fulltext, accessed 8 April 2017).

69. Organisation for Economic Co-operation and Development (OECD) database (http://stats.oecd.org/, accessed 15 December 2016).

70. Health GERD data are from the United Nations Educational, Scientific and Cultural Organization (UNESCO) as of 15 December 2016. Data on GDP are from the WHO Global Health Expenditure Database (see reference 27).

71. Solar O, Valentine N, Rice M, Albrecht D. Moving forward to equity in health. What kind of intersectoral action is needed? An approach to an intersectoral typology. Partnership and Intersectoral Action [Conference Working Document]. Geneva: World Health Organization. Presented at: 7th Global Conference on Health Promotion, Promoting Health and Development: Closing the Implementation Gap. Nairobi, Kenya, 26–30 October 2009. (http://pediatriesociale.fondationdrjulien.org/wp-content/uploads/2015/08/8-Solar-et-al.-2009.pdf, accessed 5 May 2017).

72. Prüss-Ustün et al. Preventing disease through healthy environments: a global assessment of the burden of disease from environmental risks. Geneva: World Health Organization; 2016 (http://apps.who.int/iris/bitstream/10665/204585/1/9789241565196_eng.pdf?ua=1, accessed 28 April 2016).

73. IHME Global Health Data Exchange [online database]. Seattle: Institute for Health Metrics and Evaluation (http://ghdx.healthdata.org/gbd-results-tool, accessed 21 April 2017).

74. Travis P, Egger D, Davies P, Mechbal A. Towards better stewardship: concepts and critical issues. Geneva: World Health Organization; 2002 (WHO/EIP/DP/02.48; www.who.int/healthinfo/paper48.pdf, accessed 9 April 2017); and: Jakubowski E, Donaldson L, Martin-Moreno JM. Developing public health leadership. In: Facets of public health in Europe. Rechel B, McKee M, editors. Brussels: European Observatory on Health Systems and Policies Series; 2014:267–83.

75. Intersectoral action on health. A path for policy-makers to implement effective and sustainable action on health. Kobe: World Health Organization, The WHO Centre for Health Development; 2011 (http://www.who.int/kobe_centre/publications/ISA-booklet_WKC-AUG2011.pdf, accessed 9 April 2017).

76. Shanghai Declaration on promoting health in the 2030 Agenda for Sustainable Development. Geneva: World Health Organization; 2016 (http://www.who.int/entity/healthpromotion/conferences/9gchp/shanghai-declaration.pdf?ua=1, accessed 21 April 2017).

77. Adelaide Statement II. Implementing the Sustainable Development Agenda through good governance for health and wellbeing: building on the experience of Health in All Policies. Outcome Statement from the 2017 International Conference on Health in All Policies: progressing the Sustainable Development Goals, Adelaide, Australia, 2017. Geneva and Adelaide: World Health Organization and Government of South Australia; 2017 (http://www.who.int/social_determinants/SDH-adelaide-statement-2017.pdf?ua=1, accessed 27 April 2017).

78. Nandi A, Hajizadeh M, Harper S, Koski A, Strumpf EC, Heymann J. Increased duration of paid maternity leave lowers infant mortality in low- and middle-income countries: a quasi-experimental study. PLoS Med. 2016;13(3):e1001985 (doi:10.1371/journal.pmed.1001985).

79. Howard KS, Brooks-Gunn J. The role of home-visiting programs in preventing child abuse and neglect. The Future of Children; 2009:19(2):119–46.

80. Rotko T, et al. How to take into account health, wellbeing and equity in all sectors in Finland. In: Progressing the Sustainable Development Goals through Health in All Policies: Case studies from around the world, editors: Vivian Lin, Ilona Kickbusch. Geneva and Adelaide: World Health Organization and Government of South Australia; 2017 (forthcoming).

81. Williams C, et al. Health in All Policies in South Australia: lessons from 10 years of practice. In: Progressing the Sustainable Development Goals through Health in All Policies: Case studies from around the world, editors: Vivian Lin, Ilona Kickbusch. Geneva and Adelaide: World Health Organization and Government of South Australia; 2017 (forthcoming).

82. National Health Plan 2009–2020. Tallinn: Government of Estonia; 2008 (amended 2012) (https://www.sm.ee/sites/default/files/content-editors/eesmargid_ja_tegevused/Tervis/Aruanded/rta_2009-2020_2012_eng.pdf, accessed 27 April 2017).

83. National Health Plan: better life for longer. Tallinn: Government of Estonia (http://www.nationalplanningcycles.org/sites/default/files/country_docs/Estonia/nhp_estonia.pdf, accessed 27 April 2017).

84. Social protection: shared interests in vulnerability reduction and development. Social Determinants of Health Sectoral Briefing Series. Geneva: World Health Organization; 2012 (http://apps.who.int/iris/bitstream/10665/44876/1/9789241503655_eng.pdf, accessed 9 April 2017).

85. Innovative practices for intersectoral action on health: a case study of four programmes for social equity. Las Condes, Santiago: Chile: Social Determinants of Health Initiative. From: The Database on Intersectoral Action for Health Equity (ISACS) [online database]. Geneva: World Health Organization (https://extranet.who.int/isacs/case/1087, accessed 9 April 2017); and: Richter LM, Daelmans B, Lombardi J, Heymann J, Lopez Boo F, Behrman JR et al. Investing in the foundation of sustainable development: pathways to scale up for early childhood development. Lancet; 2017;389(10064):103–18.

86. A decade towards better health in Chile. Bull World Health Organ. Special theme: Social determinants of health. 2011;89(10):701–76.

87. Martinez Valle, A. The Mexican experience in monitoring and evaluation of public policies addressing social determinants of health. Glob Health Action. Special issue: Monitoring health determinants with an equity focus. 2016;9 (Doi: 10.3402/gha.v9.29030).

88. Public health impacts of exposure to mercury and mercury compounds: the role of WHO and ministries of public health in the implementation of the Minamata Convention. WHA67.11. In: Sixty-seventh World Health Assembly, Geneva, 19–24 May 2014. Resolutions and decisions, annexes. Geneva: World Health Organization; 2014:21–23 (WHA67/2014/REC/1; http://apps.who.int/gb/ebwha/pdf_files/WHA67-REC1/A67_2014_REC1-en.pdf#page=1, accessed 9 April 2017).

89. The 2nd Global Consultation on Migrant Health: Resetting the agenda. Geneva: World Health Organization; 2017 (see: http://www.who.int/migrants/news-events/en/#global-consultationMH, accessed 9 April 2017).

90. Shanghai Consensus on Healthy Cities 2016. Geneva: World Health Organization; 2016 (see: http://www.who.int/healthpromotion/conferences/9gchp/healthy-city-pledge/en/, accessed 9 April 2017).

91. Practising a health in all policies approach – lessons for universal health coverage and health equity: a policy briefing for ministries of health based on experiences from Africa, South-East Asia and the Western Pacific. Geneva: World Health Organization; 2013 (http://apps.who.int/iris/bitstream/10665/105529/1/9789241506632_eng.pdf, accessed 9 April 2017).

92. First draft of the framework for country action across sectors for health and health equity. Geneva: World Health Organization; 2015 (http://www.who.int/nmh/events/WHO-discussion-paper2.pdf?ua=1, accessed 9 April 2017).

93. Health in all policies training manual. Geneva: World Health Organization; 2015 (see: http://www.who.int/social_determinants/publications/health-policies-manual/en/, accessed 9 April 2017).

2 STATUS OF THE HEALTH-RELATED SDGs

Overview

More than 50 SDG indicators, across more than 10 goals, have been selected to measure health outcomes, direct determinants of health or health-service provision. These health-related indicators may be grouped into the following seven thematic areas:

- reproductive, maternal, newborn and child health
- infectious diseases
- noncommunicable diseases and mental health
- injuries and violence
- universal health coverage and health systems
- environmental risks
- health risks and disease outbreaks.

Available data indicate that despite the progress made during the MDG era major challenges remain in terms of reducing maternal and child mortality, improving nutrition, and making further progress in the battle against communicable diseases such as HIV/AIDS, tuberculosis (TB), malaria, neglected tropical diseases and hepatitis. Furthermore, the results of situation analyses provide clear evidence of the crucial importance of addressing NCDs and their risk factors – such as tobacco use, mental health problems, road traffic injuries and environmental conditions – within the sustainable development agenda. In

many countries, weak health systems remain an obstacle to progress and result in deficiencies in coverage for even the most basic health services, as well as poor preparedness for health emergencies. Based on the latest available data, the global and regional situation in relation to the above seven thematic areas is summarized below. Country-specific findings by indicator, where available, are presented graphically in Annex A and in tabular form in Annex B.

2.1 Reproductive, maternal, newborn and child health

Worldwide, approximately 830 women died every single day due to complications during pregnancy or childbirth in 2015 (1). Reducing the global maternal mortality ratio (MMR) from 216 per 100 000 live births in 2015 to less than 70 per 100 000 live births by 2030 (SDG Target 3.1) will require a global annual rate of reduction of at least 7.5% – which is more than triple the annual rate of reduction that was achieved between 1990 and 2015 (2). Most maternal deaths are preventable as the necessary medical interventions are well known. It is therefore crucially important to increase women's access to quality care before, during and after childbirth. In 2016, millions of births globally were not assisted by a trained midwife, doctor or nurse, with only 78% of births were in the presence of a skilled birth attendant (3).

In 2016, 77% of women of reproductive age who were married or in-union had their family planning need met with a modern contraceptive method. While nine out of 10 women in the WHO Western Pacific Region had their family planning need satisfied, only half of women in the WHO African Region did (4). Globally, the adolescent birth rate in 2015 was 44.1 per 1000 adolescent girls aged 15–19 years (5).

The global under-five mortality rate in 2015 was 43 per 1000 live births, while the neonatal mortality rate was 19 per 1000 live births – representing declines of 44% and 37% respectively compared to the rates in 2000. Newborn deaths represented half or more of all deaths among children under 5 years of age in all WHO regions in 2015 with the exception of the WHO African Region where one third of under-five deaths occurred after the first month of life (Figure 2.1). The WHO African Region also had the highest under-five mortality rate (81.3 per 1000 live births) that year – almost double the global rate (6).

Figure 2.1
Under-five mortality rates by age at death, by WHO region, 2015

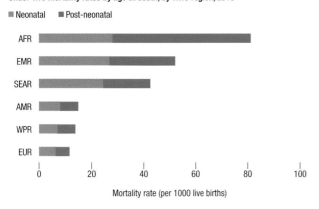

Mortality rate (per 1000 live births)

Globally in 2016, there were 155 million children under the age of five who were stunted (too short for their age), 52 million wasted (too light for their height) and 41 million overweight (too heavy for their height). Stunting prevalence was highest (34%) in the WHO African Region and the WHO South-East Asia Region. Both the highest prevalence of wasting (15.3%) and number of wasted children (27 million) were found in the WHO South-East Asia Region. Between 2000 and 2016, the number of overweight children under the age of five increased globally by 33% (7).

2.2 Infectious diseases

Globally, 2.1 million people were estimated to have become newly infected with HIV in 2015, representing a rate of 0.3 new infections per 1000 uninfected people. In the same year, an estimated 1.1 million people died of HIV-related illnesses. At the end of 2015, an estimated 36.7 million people were living with HIV. The WHO African Region

remains the most severely affected, with 4.4% of adults aged 15–49 years living with HIV. Globally, 18.2 million people living with HIV were on antiretroviral therapy by mid 2016 (8).

In 2015, there were an estimated 212 million malaria cases globally, translating into an incidence rate of 94 per 1000 persons at risk – a 41% decrease from the rate in 2000. The greatest decrease was achieved in the WHO European Region, with the number of indigenous cases being reduced to zero in 2015. There were an estimated 429 000 malaria deaths globally, with the heaviest burden borne by the WHO African Region – where an estimated 92% of all deaths occurred – and by children under 5 years of age, who accounted for more than 70% of all deaths (9).

Tuberculosis (TB) remains a major global health problem, despite being a treatable and curable disease. In 2015, there were an estimated 10.4 million new TB cases and 1.4 million TB deaths, with an additional 0.4 million deaths resulting from TB among HIV-positive people. In 2015, the TB case fatality rate (calculated as mortality divided by incidence) varied widely – from under 5% in some countries to more than 20% in most countries in the WHO African Region. This finding highlights the persistence of large inequities in access to high-quality diagnostic and treatment services. The WHO European Region had the highest incidence rate of multidrug- or rifampicin-resistant TB (MDR/RR-TB) at 14 per 100 000 population (10).

The number of global deaths in 2015 attributable to hepatitis is estimated to be in the order of 1.3 million (11). This figure includes deaths from acute hepatitis, liver cancer due to hepatitis and cirrhosis due to hepatitis. In the same year, an estimated 257 million people were living with hepatitis B virus infection, and 71 million people were living with hepatitis C virus infection (12). Global coverage with three doses of hepatitis B vaccine (a priority intervention) reached 84% among infants in 2015. However, in 36 countries the estimated coverage was less than 80% (Figure 2.2) (13).

In 2015, a reported 1.6 billion people required mass or individual treatment and care for neglected tropical diseases (NTDs) – down from 2.0 billion people in 2010. Most of these people required mass treatment for lymphatic filariasis, soil-transmitted helminthiases, schistosomiasis, trachoma and/or onchocerciasis. The progress made in reducing the number of people requiring mass treatment has been driven in large part by the fact that lymphatic filariasis and trachoma have either been eliminated or are under surveillance for verification of elimination in 18 and eight countries respectively. In 2015, fewer people required individual treatment and care for dracunculiasis, human African trypanosomiasis and visceral leishmaniasis than ever before (14).

Figure 2.2
Hepatitis B third-dose (HepB3) immunization coverage among one-year olds (%), 2015

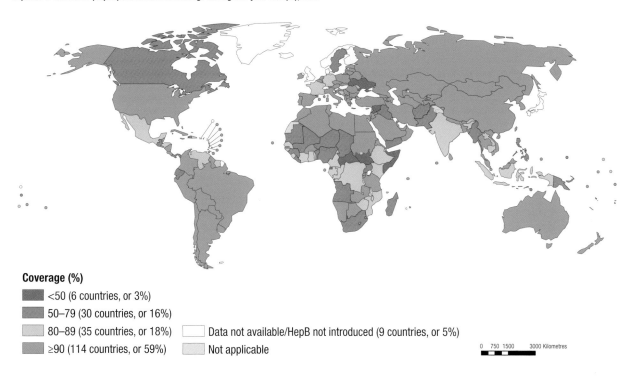

Coverage (%)

■ <50 (6 countries, or 3%)
■ 50–79 (30 countries, or 16%)
■ 80–89 (35 countries, or 18%)   □ Data not available/HepB not introduced (9 countries, or 5%)
■ ≥90 (114 countries, or 59%)   ▨ Not applicable

0   750 1500   3000 Kilometres

2.3 Noncommunicable diseases and mental health

In 2015, an estimated 40 million deaths occurred due to NCDs, accounting for 70% of the overall total of 56 million deaths. The majority of such deaths were caused by the four main NCDs, namely: cardiovascular disease, 17.7 million deaths (accounting for 45% of all NCD deaths); cancer, 8.8 million deaths (22%); chronic respiratory disease, 3.9 million deaths (10%); and diabetes, 1.6 million deaths (4%). The risk of dying from any one of the four main NCDs between ages 30 and 70 decreased from 23% in 2000 to 19% in 2015. In high-income countries, age-standardized cardiovascular mortality rates have declined rapidly in recent years, while mortality rates from the other main NCDs have fallen at a slower pace. Although age-standardized cardiovascular mortality rates and chronic respiratory mortality rates have improved substantially in low- and middle-income countries (LMIC), they remain far higher than rates in high-income countries (Figure 2.3) *(11)*.

The worldwide level of alcohol consumption in 2016 was 6.4 litres of pure alcohol per person aged 15 years or older, with considerable variation between WHO regions *(15)*. Available data indicate that treatment coverage for alcohol and drug-use disorders is inadequate, though further work is needed to improve the measurement of such coverage.

In 2015, more than 1.1 billion people smoked tobacco, with far more males than females currently engaging in this behaviour *(16)*. The WHO Framework Convention on

Figure 2.3
Global trends in age-standardized mortality rate by NCD cause, by country income groups, 2000–2015

■ Cardiovascular diseases   ■ Diabetes mellitus
■ Cancers   ■ Chronic respiratory diseases

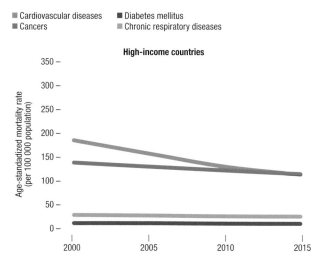

High-income countries

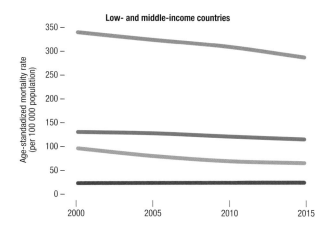

Low- and middle-income countries

Tobacco Control has now been ratified by 180 Parties representing 90% of the global population. More than 80% of Parties have either strengthened their existing tobacco control laws and regulations or have adopted new ones.

Almost 800 000 deaths by suicide occurred in 2015, making it the second leading cause of death by injury after road traffic injuries. Men are almost twice as likely as women to die as a result of suicide. Suicide mortality rates are highest in the WHO European Region (14.1 per 100 000 population) and lowest in the WHO Eastern Mediterranean Region (3.8 per 100 000 population) *(11)*.

2.4 Injuries and violence

Around 1.25 million people died from road traffic injuries in 2013, with up to 50 million people sustaining non-fatal injuries as a result of road traffic collisions or crashes. Road traffic injuries are the main cause of death among people aged 15–29 years and disproportionately affect vulnerable road users, namely pedestrians, cyclists and motorcyclists. Between 2000 and 2013 the number of road traffic deaths globally increased by approximately 13% *(17)*.

Latest estimates indicate that globally almost one quarter of adults (23%) suffered physical abuse as a child *(18)* and about one third (35%) of women experienced either physical and/or sexual intimate partner violence or non-partner sexual violence at some point in their life *(19)*.

During the period 2011–2015, the global annual average death rate due to natural disasters was 0.3 deaths per 100 000 population. The WHO Western Pacific Region had the highest rate at 0.5 deaths per 100 000 population *(11)*.

In 2015, there were an estimated 468 000 murders, with four fifths of all homicide victims being male. Men in the WHO Region of the Americas suffered the highest rate of homicide deaths at 32.9 per 100 000 population, 12 times the rate among men in the WHO Western Pacific Region (Figure 2.4). Globally, during the period 2000–2015 there was a marked decline (19%) in homicide rates *(11)*.

Figure 2.4
Homicide rates by sex, by WHO region and globally, 2015

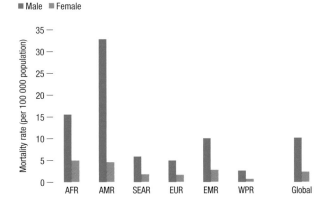

It is estimated that in 2015, 152 000 people were killed in wars and conflicts, corresponding to around 0.3% of all global deaths that year. This estimate does not include deaths due to the indirect effects of war and conflict on the spread of diseases, poor nutrition and collapse of health services *(11)*.

2.5 Universal health coverage and health systems

The average national percentage of total government expenditure devoted to health was 11.7% in 2014. Regionally, such average ranged from 8.8% in the WHO Eastern Mediterranean Region to 13.6% in the WHO Region of the Americas *(20)*. This measure indicates the level of government spending on health within the total expenditure for public sector operations in a country, and is part of SDG indicator 1.a.2 on the proportion of total government spending on essential services (education, health and social protection).

Consultations with WHO Member States on estimating the SDG indicators needed to monitor SDG Target 3.8 on UHC began in February 2017. Once completed, estimates of the SDG indicators 3.8.1 and 3.8.2 – coverage of essential health services; and the proportion of population with large household expenditures on health as a share of total household expenditure or income, respectively – will provide the first comparable set of SDG monitoring figures for developing an index for use as a measure of financial protection. On average, countries have data since 2010 for around 70% of tracer indicators within SDG indicator 3.8.1,[1] with 50% of countries having at least one data source for SDG indicator 3.8.2 since 2005.

In 2015, global coverage of three doses of diphtheria-tetanus-pertussis (DTP3) vaccine, as a proxy for full immunization among children, was 86% *(13)*. Data from 2007–2014 show that the median availability of selected essential medicines in the public sector was only 60% in selected low-income countries and 56% in selected lower-middle-income countries *(21)*. Access to medicines for chronic conditions and NCDs is even worse than that for acute conditions. Despite improvements in recent decades, the development of innovative new products remains focused away from the health needs of those living in developing countries. As a result, the current landscape of health research and development (see section 1.5) is insufficiently aligned with global health demands and needs. Health workforce densities are also distributed unevenly across the globe. As shown in Figure 2.5, WHO regions with the highest burden of disease expressed in disability-

---

[1] SDG indicator 3.8.1 – Coverage of essential health services – is defined as the average coverage of essential services based on tracer interventions that include reproductive, maternal, newborn and child health, infectious diseases, noncommunicable diseases and service capacity and access, among the general and the most disadvantaged populations.

Figure 2.5
Figure 2.5
Regional health workforce density, 2005–2015, and estimated total burden of disease, 2010

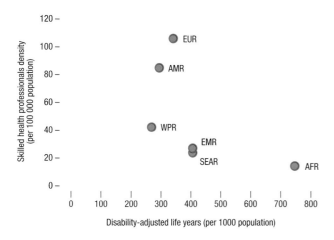

adjusted life years *(22)* also have the lowest densities of health workforce required to deliver much-needed health services. Data from 2005–2015 show that around 40% of countries have less than one physician per 1000 population and around half of all countries have less than three nursing and midwifery personnel per 1000 population *(23)*. Even in countries with higher national health worker densities, the workforce is often inequitably distributed, with rural and hard-to-reach areas tending to be understaffed compared to capital cities and other urban areas.

In the area of monitoring and evaluation (see section 1.1 above), WHO estimates that only half of its 194 Member States register at least 80% of deaths, with associated information provided on cause of death *(11, 24)*. In addition, data-quality problems further limit the use of such information.

2.6 Environmental risks

Around 3 billion people still heat their homes and cook using solid fuels (that is, using wood, crop wastes, charcoal, coal or dung) in open fires and leaky stoves. The use of such inefficient fuels and technologies leads to high levels of household air pollution. In 2012, such household air pollution caused 4.3 million deaths globally. Women and children are at particularly high risk of disease caused by exposure to household air pollution, accounting for 60% of all deaths attributed to such pollution *(25)*.

In 2014, 92% of the world population was living in places where WHO air quality guideline standards were not met. Outdoor air pollution in both cities and rural areas was estimated to have caused 3 million deaths worldwide in 2012. Some 87% of these deaths occurred in LMIC *(26)*. Jointly, indoor and outdoor air pollution caused an estimated 6.5 million deaths (11.6% of all global deaths) in 2012 *(27)*.

Unsafe water, unsafe sanitation and lack of hygiene also remain important causes of death, with an estimated 871 000 associated deaths occurring in 2012.[1] Such deaths disproportionately occur in low-income communities and among children under 5 years of age *(28, 29)*. Although 6.6 billion people used an improved drinking-water source in 2015 the coverage of safely managed drinking-water services remains low, with preliminary estimates of 68% coverage in urban areas and only 20% in rural areas *(30, 31)*. Around one third of the world population (32%) did not have access to improved sanitation facilities in 2015, including 946 million people who practised open defecation *(30)*.

An estimated 108 000 deaths were caused by unintentional poisonings in 2015. In LMIC, pesticides, kerosene, household chemicals and carbon monoxide are all common causes of such poisoning. In high-income countries, the substances involved primarily include carbon monoxide, drugs, and cleaning and personal-care products in the home. The number deaths attributed to this cause are highest among children under 5 years of age and among adults aged 60 years or older. Mortality rates are also higher among men than among women across all age groups (Figure 2.6) *(11)*.

Figure 2.6
Global mortality rate due to unintentional poisonings, by age and sex, 2015

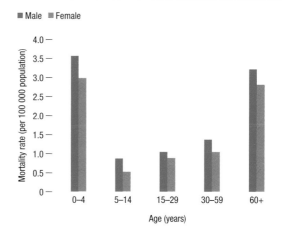

2.7 Health risks and disease outbreaks

The International Health Regulations (IHR) monitoring process involved the use of a self-assessment questionnaire sent to States Parties to assess the implementation status of 13 core capacities. In 2016, 129 States Parties (66% of all States Parties) responded to the monitoring questionnaire. The average core capacity scores of all reporting countries in 2016 was 76% *(32, 33)*.

---

[1] Includes deaths from diarrhoea, intestinal nematode infections and protein-energy malnutrition attributable to lack of access to WASH services.

References

1. Trends in maternal mortality: 1990 to 2015. Estimates by WHO, UNICEF, UNFPA, World Bank Group and the United Nations Population Division. Geneva: World Health Organization; 2015 (http://www.who.int/reproductivehealth/publications/monitoring/maternal-mortality-2015/en/, accessed 23 March 2017).

2. Alkema L, Chou D, Hogan D, Zhang S, Moller A-B, Gemmill et al. Global, regional, and national levels and trends in maternal mortality between 1990 and 2015, with scenario-based projections to 2030: a systematic analysis by the UN Maternal Mortality Estimation Inter-Agency Group. Lancet. 2016;387(10017):462-74 (http://www.thelancet.com/pb/assets/raw/Lancet/pdfs/S0140673615008387.pdf, accessed 23 March 2017).

3. WHO global database on maternal health indicators, 2017 update [online database]. Geneva: World Health Organization (http://www.who.int/gho/maternal_health/en/).

4. Estimates and projections of family planning indicators 2016. New York (NY): United Nations, Department of Economic and Social Affairs, Population Division; 2015 (see: http://www.un.org/en/development/desa/population/theme/family-planning/cp_model.shtml, accessed 23 March 2017). Special tabulations were prepared for estimates by WHO region.

5. World Population Prospects, the 2015 Revision (DVD edition). New York (NY): United Nations, Department of Economic and Social Affairs, Population Division; 2015 (http://esa.un.org/unpd/wpp/Download/Standard/Fertility/, accessed 13 April 2016).

6. Levels & Trends in Child Mortality. Report 2015. Estimates developed by the UN Inter-agency Group for Child Mortality Estimation. United Nations Children's Fund, World Health Organization, World Bank and United Nations. New York (NY): United Nations Children's Fund; 2015 (http://www.unicef.org/publications/files/Child_Mortality_Report_2015_Web_9_Sept_15.pdf, accessed 22 March 2017).

7. Global database on child growth and malnutrition [online database]. Geneva: World Health Organization; 2017 (http://www.who.int/nutgrowthdb/database/en).

8. AIDS by the numbers: AIDS is not over, but it can be. Geneva: UNAIDS; 2015 (http://www.unaids.org/sites/default/files/media_asset/AIDS-by-the-numbers-2016_en.pdf , accessed 18 April 2016). Estimates by WHO region were calculated by WHO.

9. World Malaria Report 2016. Geneva: World Health Organization; 2016 (http://www.who.int/malaria/publications/world-malaria-report-2016/report/en/, accessed 22 March 2017).

10. Global tuberculosis report 2016. Geneva: World Health Organization; 2016 (http://apps.who.int/iris/bitstream/10665/250441/1/9789241565394-eng.pdf?ua=1, accessed 22 March 2017).

11. Global Health Estimates 2015: Deaths by cause, age, sex, by country and by region, 2000–2015. Geneva: World Health Organization; 2016 (http://www.who.int/healthinfo/global_burden_disease/estimates/en/index1.html, accessed 22 March 2017).

12. Global hepatitis report, 2017. Geneva: World Health Organization; 2017 (http://www.who.int/hepatitis/publications/global-hepatitis-report2017/en/, accessed 17 April 2017).

13. WHO/UNICEF estimates of national immunization coverage. July 2016 revision (http://www.who.int/immunization/monitoring_surveillance/routine/coverage/en/index4.html, accessed 22 March 2017).

14. Neglected tropical diseases [online database]. Global Health Observatory (GHO) data. Geneva: World Health Organization (http://www.who.int/gho/neglected_diseases/en/); and the Preventive chemotherapy and transmission control (PCT) databank. Geneva: World Health Organization (http://www.who.int/neglected_diseases/preventive_chemotherapy/databank/en/).

15. WHO Global Information System on Alcohol and Health (GISAH) [online database]. Global Health Observatory (GHO) data. Geneva: World Health Organization (http://www.who.int/gho/alcohol/en/).

16. WHO global report on trends in prevalence of tobacco smoking 2015. Geneva: World Health Organization; 2015 (http://apps.who.int/iris/bitstream/10665/156262/1/9789241564922_eng.pdf, accessed 22 March 2017).

17. Global status report on road safety 2015. Geneva: World Health Organization; 2015 (http://www.who.int/violence_injury_prevention/road_safety_status/2015/en/, accessed 22 March 2017).

18. World Health Organization, United Nations Office on Drugs and Crime and United Nations Development Programme. Global status report on violence prevention 2014. Geneva: World Health Organization; 2014 (see: http://www.who.int/violence_injury_prevention/violence/status_report/2014/en/, accessed 23 March 2017).

19. World Health Organization, London School of Hygiene & Tropical Medicine and South African Medical Research Council. Global and regional estimates of violence against women: prevalence and health effects of intimate partner violence and non-partner sexual violence. Geneva: World Health Organization; 2013 (http://www.who.int/reproductivehealth/publications/violence/9789241564625/en/, accessed 23 March 2017).

20. Unweighted averages of country-specific data from WHO Global Health Expenditure Database [online database]. Geneva: World Health Organization (http://apps.who.int/nha/database/Select/Indicators/en, accessed 22 March 2017).

21. Millennium Development Goal 8: taking stock of the global partnership for development. MDG Gap Task Force Report 2015. New York (NY): United Nations; 2015 (www.un.org/en/development/desa/policy/mdg_gap/mdg_gap2015/2015GAP_FULLREPORT_EN.pdf, accessed 23 March 2017).

22. Global Health Estimates 2015: DALYs by cause, age, sex, by country and by region, 2000–2015. Geneva: World Health Organization; 2016 (http://www.who.int/healthinfo/global_burden_disease/estimates/en/index2.html, accessed 23 March 2017).

23. WHO Global Health Workforce Statistics. 2014 update [online database]. Geneva: World Health Organization (http://who.int/hrh/statistics/hwfstats/en/).

24. Based on data reported to the WHO Mortality Database (http://www.who.int/healthinfo/mortality_data/en/) as of 12 October 2016.

25. Burning opportunity: clean household energy for health, sustainable development, and wellbeing of women and children. Geneva: World Health Organization; 2016 (http://apps.who.int/iris/bitstream/10665/204717/1/9789241565233_eng.pdf, accessed 23 March 2017).

26. Ambient air pollution: a global assessment of exposure and burden of disease. Geneva: World Health Organization; 2016 (see: http://who.int/phe/publications/air-pollution-global-assessment/en/, accessed 23 March 2017).

27. Public health and environment [online database]. Global Health Observatory (GHO) data. Geneva: World Health Organization (http://www.who.int/gho/phe/en/ and http://apps.who.int/gho/data/view.main.SDGAIRBODREGv?lang=en, accessed 10 Aprié 2017)

28. Preventing disease through healthy environments. A global assessment of the burden of disease from environmental risks. Geneva: World Health Organization; 2016 (http://apps.who.int/iris/bitstream/10665/204585/1/9789241565196_eng.pdf?ua=1, accessed 23 March 2017).

29. Preventing diarrhoea through better water, sanitation and hygiene. Exposures and impacts in low- and middle-income countries. Geneva: World Health Organization; 2014 (http://apps.who.int/iris/bitstream/10665/150112/1/9789241564823_eng.pdf?ua=1&ua=1, accessed 23 March 2017).

30. Progress on sanitation and drinking water – 2015 update and MDG assessment. New York (NY): UNICEF; and Geneva: World Health Organization; 2015 (http://apps.who.int/iris/bitstream/10665/177752/1/9789241509145_eng.pdf?ua=1, accessed 23 March 2017).

31. Hutton, G, Varughese M. The costs of meeting the 2030 Sustainable Development Goals targets on drinking water, sanitation and hygiene. Washington (DC): World Bank; 2016 (http://documents.worldbank.org/curated/en/415441467988938343/pdf/103171-PUB-Box394556B-PUBLIC-EPI-K8543-ADD-SERIES.pdf, accessed 10 April 2017).

32. International Health Regulations (2005) Monitoring Framework [online database]. Global Health Observatory (GHO) data. Geneva: World Health Organization (http://www.who.int/gho/ihr/en/).

33. States Parties to the International Health Regulations (2005) [website]. Geneva: World Health Organization (http://www.who.int/ihr/legal_issues/states_parties/en/, accessed 24 April 2017).

3

COUNTRY SUCCESS STORIES

Overview

The 2030 Agenda for Sustainable Development lays out an ambitious array of goals and targets, including one SDG on health and many health-related SDG targets. Faced with this potentially daunting challenge, countries have maintained and accelerated actions to improve the health of their populations. In Part 3, a selection of stories are presented which illustrate the wide range of actions that countries have taken to achieve documented progress. These stories demonstrate that the health-related SDG targets can be reached through the six lines of action outlined in Part 1 of this report.

One central theme in this part has been the diverse range of intersectoral actions taken by Ghana, Ireland, the Republic of Korea, the Russian Federation, and Uruguay in bringing about significant improvements in strengthening IHR capacity, and reducing mortality due to noncommunicable diseases, suicide, harmful use of alcohol, and tobacco use, respectively. These actions have variously involved collaborations with the agricultural, financial, transportation, customs and immigration, and housing sectors, among others. Many of these intersectoral actions involved innovative strategies and interventions, such as the trailblazing nationwide ban on smoking in all

enclosed public places and workplaces in Ireland, and the largest-in-the-world warning labels placed on cigarette packs in Uruguay.

Another prominent strand in these country success stories is the vital importance of health system strengthening. The importance of relentless efforts to implement known health system interventions using validated strategies should not be underestimated. This was demonstrated by the experiences of Cambodia, Papua New Guinea and the Russian Federation in their efforts to improve coverage of hepatitis B vaccination, reduce malaria incidence and treat alcohol-use disorders, respectively. These stories show that reaching all populations, as well as being an important goal in itself, is a necessary step in ensuring high levels of population coverage by interventions. In Papua New Guinea, the challenge of ensuring sustainable financing was also highlighted – where funding sources for an activity are not maintained, any progress made will be put at risk.

The importance of monitoring in raising awareness, identifying areas for improvement and identifying successful policy actions cannot be overstated. The existence of monitoring data demonstrating an improvement in a health-related SDG indicator was a prerequisite for the selection of country stories. In Kazakhstan and the Islamic Republic of Iran a specific focus was placed on improving monitoring systems for capturing maternal deaths and on building up the national CRVS system for monitoring mortality by cause, respectively.

The evidence presented here of successful efforts to enhance country capacities to achieve the health-related SDG targets and ultimately to improve population health is encouraging. The stories selected range across different countries, WHO regions and income levels, and across the broad spectrum of health-related SDG targets and indicators. All share the common message that efforts made in accordance with the six lines of action described in this report can be the catalyst for bringing about profound change in the lives of so many.

3.1 Ending preventable maternal deaths in Kazakhstan

SDG Target 3.1
By 2030, reduce the global maternal mortality ratio to less than 70 per 100 000 live births

Indicator 3.1.1: Maternal mortality ratio

Country: **Kazakhstan**
WHO region: **European Region**
World Bank income category, 2015: **Upper middle income**
Life expectancy at birth, 2015: **70.2 years**
Maternal mortality ratio, 2015: **12 per 100 000 live births**

Despite global progress in reducing the maternal mortality ratio (MMR) (1) immediate action is needed to meet SDG Target 3.1 – and ultimately eliminate preventable maternal mortality. Although the rates of reduction that are needed to achieve country-specific SDG targets may be ambitious for most high-mortality countries, some countries have already made remarkable progress in reducing their MMR. Such countries can provide inspiration and guidance on how to accomplish the acceleration of efforts needed to reduce the number of preventable maternal deaths.

Measuring maternal mortality is challenging because of limited data availability, and even countries with well-functioning civil registration and vital statistics (CRVS) systems have difficulties, due to misclassification, in ascertaining the causes of maternal deaths. The United Nations Maternal Mortality Estimation Inter-Agency Group (UN-MMEIG), of which WHO is a member, has published a succession of MMR estimates used for global reporting and comparison (2–7). Before each release of new MMR estimates, WHO conducts a country consultation process during which countries have the opportunity to review and discuss the estimates made, and the data and methodology used to generate them. A particular focus is placed on the strengths and limitations of data inputs and on problems related to the misclassification of maternal deaths.

In acknowledging the problem of misclassification, Kazakhstan is one of a number of countries that have implemented specialized surveillance systems and conducted "confidential enquiries" into maternal deaths. This has allowed for the strengthening of CRVS systems, and for the reviewing and correction of mistakes in cause-of-death assignment. Such confidential enquiries are designed to improve maternal health and health care by collecting data, identifying any shortfalls in the care provided and devising recommendations to improve future care. The approach involves identifying and investigating the cause of all deaths of women of reproductive age using multiple sources of data – including interviews with family members and community health workers, and reviews of CRVS data, household surveys, health-care facility records and burial records.

Kazakhstan initiated its confidential enquiry system in 2011, when the Central Confidential Audit Commission (CCAC) audited the officially reported maternal deaths for 2009–2010 to determine why these deaths occurred (8). This audit resulted in recommendations to revise clinical guidelines. In 2014, the CCAC audit was expanded to cover deaths in women of reproductive age that were not officially assigned to maternal causes. The CCAC then reviewed pregnancy-related deaths[1] that had occurred between 2011 and 2013. These included 166 deaths that had officially been registered as maternal deaths[2] and 18 deaths that had been registered as accidents or deaths due to other causes. Following CCAC review, 10 of the original 166 deaths were found not to have been due to maternal causes, while eight of the 18 pregnancy-related deaths were re-categorized as maternal deaths (Table 3.1) (9).

This example shows how the proactive reviewing and reclassification of maternal deaths can improve the classification of cases and quantify the accuracy of the data systems used to monitor the MMR. Such efforts are recognized by the UN-MMEIG – for countries conducting and describing this type of high-quality study, UN estimates of maternal mortality can be computed directly from the country data without global adjustment factors. As a result, in countries with primarily high-quality CRVS data, national level data and global estimates are harmonized. Furthermore, the results of confidential enquiries can be used to revise and strengthen clinical guidelines, and to support activities aimed at ending preventable maternal deaths.

Table 3.1
Results of the 2014 CCAC confidential enquiry, Kazakhstan

Categorization	Number of deaths			
	2011	2012	2013	Total
Officially registered as maternal deaths (a)	65	52	49	166
Re-categorized as non-maternal deaths (b)	4	1	5	10
Confirmed maternal deaths (a - b = c)	61	51	44	156
Additional pregnancy-related deaths identified in the enquiry (d)	8	3	7	18
Re-categorized as maternal deaths (e)	4	2	2	8
Total maternal deaths (c + e)	**65**	**53**	**46**	**164**

---

[1] Defined as: ...*the death of a woman while pregnant or within 42 days of termination of pregnancy, irrespective of the cause of death* (International statistical classification of diseases and related health problems, 10th revision. Volume 2: Instruction manual. Geneva: World Health Organization; 2011).

[2] Defined as: ...*the death of a woman while pregnant or within 42 days of termination of pregnancy, irrespective of the duration and the site of the pregnancy, from any cause related to or aggravated by the pregnancy or its management, but not from accidental or incidental causes* (International statistical classification of diseases and related health problems, 10th revision. Volume 2: Instruction manual. Geneva: World Health Organization; 2011).

3.2 Reducing the level of malaria in Papua New Guinea

SDG Target 3.3
By 2030, end the epidemics of AIDS, tuberculosis, malaria and neglected tropical diseases and combat hepatitis, water-borne diseases and other communicable diseases

Indicator 3.3.3: Malaria incidence per 1000 population

Country:	**Papua New Guinea**
WHO region:	**Western Pacific Region**
World Bank income category, 2015:	**Lower middle income**
Life expectancy at birth, 2015:	**62.9 years**
Malaria incidence, 2015:	**122 per 1000 population at risk**

Papua New Guinea is largely mountainous but has a diverse geography which also includes coastal plains, swamps, plantations and offshore atolls. Malaria is highly endemic in coastal areas, where two thirds of the population live. People in these areas are continuously exposed to malaria, with both cases and deaths being concentrated in younger age groups. Patterns of malaria are less stable in the Highlands Region, which is prone to epidemics that cause a significant number of fatalities. In 2005, an estimated 1.4 million cases occurred leading to an estimated 2800 deaths, representing one of the highest malaria morbidity and mortality rates outside Africa *(10)*.

The WHO-recommended package of core interventions to prevent infection and reduce morbidity and mortality comprises vector control, chemoprevention, diagnostic testing and treatment. Two forms of vector control – insecticide-treated nets (ITNs) and indoor residual spraying – are effective in a wide range of circumstances. WHO recommends that all cases of suspected malaria be confirmed using parasite-based diagnostic testing – using either microscopy or a rapid diagnostic test (RDT) – before any treatment is administered. All episodes of malaria should be treated with at least two effective antimalarial medicines with different mechanisms of action (combination therapy).

The reduction of malaria-related morbidity and mortality is a key objective of Papua New Guinea's National Health Plan, with the mass distribution of ITNs viewed as an essential component of the malaria-control strategy. In 2009, the country received US$ 102 million from the Global Fund and more than 7.5 million ITNs were distributed in three mass distribution rounds between 2009 and 2015. In addition, RDTs for improving diagnosis and guiding the use of combination therapy (artemether–lumefantrine) were introduced in 2011. Substantial investments, including investments in activities of nongovernmental organizations, were made to reach some of the most remote population groups in the world.

The numbers of malaria cases, admissions and deaths at health facilities is tracked through the national health information system. In addition, progress has been monitored through three nationally representative household surveys undertaken in 2009, 2011 and 2014 *(11–13)* and through health-facility surveys in 2010, 2011, 2012, 2014 and 2016 *(14)*. The household surveys showed that the proportion of the population that had access to long-lasting insecticidal nets (LLINs) increased, with a corresponding increase observed in the proportion of the population sleeping under such nets (Figure 3.1). The health-facility surveys showed that the proportion of suspected malaria cases receiving a diagnostic test rose from 17.5% in 2010 to 73.5% in 2016. Antimalarial prescriptions for febrile patients who were not tested declined over the same period.

Figure 3.1
Trends in LLIN access and use in Papua New Guinea, 2009–2014

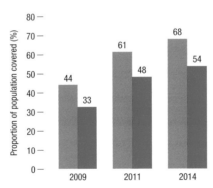

Household surveys *(11, 12)* also revealed a drop in parasite prevalence among the population living below an altitude of 1600 metres (Figure 3.2). In total, WHO estimated that in 2015 the number of malaria cases in Papua New Guinea had been reduced to 900 000, with 1200 deaths *(10)*.

Figure 3.2
Trend in prevalence of *Plasmodium falciparum* or P. *vivax* malaria parasites in Papua New Guinea, 2009–2014

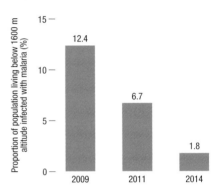

Despite the impressive progress made, gaps in programme coverage remain and continued efforts are needed to ensure the continuity of ITN distribution between mass campaigns, and to extend diagnostic testing and treatment to the most remote populations. However, the large reduction in malaria cases and deaths may result in the disease no longer being seen as a priority for funding. Approximately 80% of the financing for malaria programme expansion in Papua New Guinea stems from the Global Fund, and more diverse sources of funding will be needed to ensure programme stability. According to data reported to WHO *(10)* governmental funding for the country's malaria programme increased more than ten-fold between 2010 and 2015. However, Papua New Guinea's recent GDP growth, which allowed for this investment, is largely attributed to an expansion of natural resource projects and international demand for such resources can be volatile.

3.3 Combating viral hepatitis in Cambodia

SDG Target 3.3
By 2030, end the epidemics of AIDS, tuberculosis, malaria and neglected tropical diseases and combat hepatitis, water-borne diseases and other communicable diseases

Indicator 3.3.4: Hepatitis B incidence per 100 000 population

Country:	**Cambodia**
WHO region:	**Western Pacific Region**
World Bank income category, 2015:	**Lower middle income**
Life expectancy at birth, 2015:	**68.7 years**
Infants receiving three doses of hepatitis B vaccine, 2015:	**89%**

In 2015, infection with the hepatitis B virus (HBV) contributed to an estimated 887 000 deaths worldwide. Most of these deaths result from the chronic sequelae of HBV infection such as cirrhosis (52%) and liver cancer (38%) *(15)*. These chronic sequelae in adulthood are most often the result of HBV infections acquired at birth or during childhood. The prevalence of hepatitis B surface antigen (HBsAg) among children 5 years of age may be used as a surrogate indicator of the cumulated incidence of chronic HBV infections from birth to age five. Such early HBV infection can be prevented by timely vaccination.

Several studies had indicated that the prevalence of chronic HBV infection as measured by the prevalence of HBsAg was high in Cambodia, with prevalence in specific adult populations such as blood donors and emigrants ranging from 8% to 14% *(16)*. In 2001, Cambodia began to phase-in the universal immunization of infants against HBV, based upon a first dose administered as soon as possible after birth and two subsequent doses. HBV vaccination was implemented nationwide in 2005. Biomarker surveys conducted in 2006 and 2011 documented the improvement in immunization rates that had occurred since 2000.

The 2006 national biomarker survey was conducted specifically to provide a formal initial assessment prior to large-scale vaccine introduction *(16)*. The prevalence of HBsAg was measured among children 5 years of age – all of whom had been born prior to the introduction of routine hepatitis immunization in their geographical area. At the national level, it was found that 55 out of 1558 children were HBsAg positive, corresponding to a prevalence of 3.5%. Prevalence was higher in males than in females (4.8% versus 2.2% respectively) and in the least-developed areas compared with the most developed region (8.6% versus 3.2% respectively).

In 2011, a second biomarker survey was conducted in three provinces among children who had been born in 2006–2007 following the national roll-out of HBV vaccination *(17)*. In all three provinces, the prevalence of HBsAg had decreased compared with the estimates obtained for children born in similar settings in 2000. In Phnom Penh, where third-dose coverage and timely birth-dose coverage were 91% and 55% respectively, 0.33% of 1196 children were HBsAg positive. In Kratie (third-dose and timely birth-dose coverage 82% and 36% respectively) 1.41% of 569 children were HBsAg positive. In Ratanakiri (third-dose and timely birth-dose coverage 64% and 22% respectively) 3.45% of 637 children were HBsAg positive. Children born at home without a skilled birth attendant were 1.94 times less likely to have received a timely birth-dose compared with those born in a health facilities with a skilled birth attendant. Children who had received a first dose of vaccine after 7 days of life or who had never received the vaccine were found to have the highest prevalence of HBsAg (Figure 3.3).

Despite the absence of nationally representative data following the implementation of HBV vaccination, the intermediate biomarker-based assessment conducted in 2011 had suggested that Cambodia was on course to meet the goal set by the Regional Committee for the Western Pacific of reducing the seroprevalence of HBsAg to < 2% among children 5 years of age by 2012 *(18)*. The lessons learnt from this intermediate evaluation also led to successful national efforts to increase both third-dose coverage and timely birth-dose coverage (Figure 3.4). Such increases, if maintained, would allow the country to meet the new control goals of the global health sector strategy on viral hepatitis 2016–2021 of reducing HBsAg seroprevalence in children 5 years of age to 1% by 2020, and to 0.1% by 2030 *(19)*. In 2017, a new biomarker survey will further document the progress made towards these goals. The incorporation of robust monitoring and evaluation activities as part of HBV vaccine roll-out in Cambodia will allow for the efficient targeting of resources to ensure that all children are covered by the vaccination programme.

Figure 3.3
Prevalence of HBV infection (HBsAg) by first-dose vaccination timing among four- and five-year olds in Phnom Penh, Kratie, and Ratanakiri, Cambodia, 2011

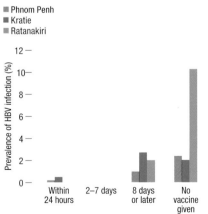

Figure 3.4
WHO and UNICEF estimates[a] of hepatitis B timely birth-dose and hepatitis B third-dose vaccination coverage, Cambodia, 2006–2015

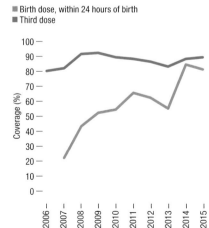

a Based on national immunization coverage data reported to WHO and UNICEF.

3.4 Improving health by clearing the air in Ireland

SDG Target 3.4
—⋀⋁◆ By 2030, reduce by one third premature mortality from noncommunicable diseases through prevention and treatment and promote mental health and well-being

Indicator 3.4.1: Mortality rate attributed to cardiovascular disease, cancer, diabetes or chronic respiratory disease

Country: **Ireland**

WHO region: **European Region**

World Bank income category, 2015: **High income**

Life expectancy at birth, 2015: **81.4 years**

Probability of dying from any of cardiovascular disease, cancer, diabetes or chronic respiratory disease, between age 30 and exact age 70, 2015: **10.3%**

SDG Target 3.4 on reducing premature mortality from noncommunicable diseases (NCDs) will require multifaceted action. Such action will include improving primary health care to treat heart disease, diabetes and hypertension; promoting healthy diets and physical activity; and building healthy environments. Between 2000 and 2015, the rate of mortality due to the four main NCDs[1] declined globally by 17% (15). Such recent improvements are estimated to be mainly due to reductions in cardiovascular and chronic respiratory disease mortality. Because of the myriad of ways in which deaths from cardiovascular disease can be prevented, modelling studies are typically used to estimate which particular factors have led to the observed reductions in mortality. These studies have shown that previous improvements in high-income countries were the result of reductions in risk factors and improvements in medical care in approximately equal measure (20, 21). In the case of chronic respiratory diseases, the main risk factors are tobacco smoking, outdoor air pollution and indoor use of solid fuels (22).

Ireland has achieved exemplary reductions in mortality from NCDs – having achieved the second largest reduction in mortality from the four main NCDs between 2000 and 2015. During this period, the probability of dying from any of the four main NCDs between the ages of 30 and 70 fell from 17.8% to 10.3% (Figure 3.5), corresponding to a reduction of 42%. Of the four main NCDs, the largest reductions were observed in the level of cardiovascular mortality (Figure 3.6). Among the factors contributing to these reductions were declining prevalence of both cigarette smoking (23, 24) and raised blood pressure (25), and improvements in medical treatment. A further contributing factor was a reduction in exposure to harmful particles in the air.

Breathing fine particles is known to cause cardiovascular disease, respiratory disease and cancers (26). These dangerous particles may come from tobacco smoke, smoke from fires for home energy needs, or from transportation and industrial sources. Depending on the source,

exposure may occur indoors or outdoors. Policies implemented in Ireland to reduce exposure to dangerous particles have resulted in documented reductions in mortality from chronic respiratory diseases. In September 1990, a ban on the sale

Figure 3.5
Probability of dying from any of the four main NCDs between age 30 and exact age 70, Ireland (by sex), WHO European Region and the world

■ Ireland (all)
■ Ireland (males)
□ Ireland (females)
■ World
■ EUR

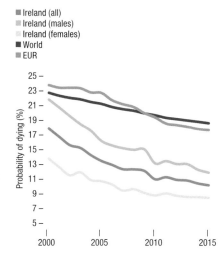

Figure 3.6
Age-standardized mortality rate by cause, four main NCDs, Ireland

■ Cancers
■ Cardiovascular diseases
■ Chronic respiratory diseases
■ Diabetes

of bituminous (smoky) coal abruptly improved air quality in Dublin and reduced chronic respiratory disease mortality (27). The ban was subsequently extended to other cities and large towns in the following decades, contributing to declines in measured black smoke concentrations and to the reductions in NCD-associated mortality observed from 2000 onwards.

Although the Dublin coal ban was implemented more than 25 years ago, bituminous coal is still used for home energy needs in small towns and rural areas in Ireland. Currently, smoke from solid fuel use continues to be the main source of particulate matter (PM) in rural areas – where PM_{10} concentrations[2] are similar to those seen in cities and large towns (28). These exposures are expected to reduce following the scheduled nationwide implementation of the coal ban by the end of 2018 (29).

In 2004, Ireland became the first country in the world to ban smoking in all enclosed public places and workplaces. The ban is strictly enforced and includes bars, restaurants, clubs, offices, public buildings, company cars, trucks, taxis and vans. A private residence is considered a workplace when trades people, such as plumbers or electricians, are working there. Premises must display a sign informing patrons of the ban and providing the details of the person to be contacted in the event of any complaints. A workplace can be given a fine of €3000 for each person found smoking (resulting, for example, in a €15 000 for five people in violation). In addition, a compliance line has been set up by the Office of Tobacco Control that people can call to report incidences of smoking in an enclosed public place. Studies have found that the ban has resulted in significant reductions in hospital admissions for pulmonary disease and acute coronary syndromes (30) and in mortality from ischaemic heart disease, stroke and chronic obstructive pulmonary disease (31). These findings are consistent with international reviews of the health effects of smoking bans (32, 33). Together with other anti-tobacco initiatives, the ban on smoking may also have contributed to an observed decline in the rate of cigarette smoking.

---

[1] Refers to the probability of dying between age 30 and exact age 70 from any of cardiovascular disease, cancer, diabetes, or chronic respiratory disease.

[2] Concentrations of particulate matter with an aerodynamic diameter of 10 μm or less.

3.5 Preventing suicide in the Republic of Korea

SDG Target 3.4
By 2030, reduce by one third premature mortality from noncommunicable diseases through prevention and treatment and promote mental health and well-being

Indicator 3.4.2: Suicide mortality rate

Country: **Republic of Korea**

WHO region: **Western Pacific Region**

World Bank income category, 2015: **High income**

Life expectancy at birth, 2015: **82.3 years**

Suicide mortality rate, 2015: **28.3 per 100 000 population**[1]

In 2015, there were almost 800 000 suicide deaths, making suicide the second leading cause of injury death after road traffic injuries, and one of the leading causes of death overall *(15)*. Some suicides are linked to depression – a mental health disorder estimated to affect 311 million people worldwide *(34)*. Because of this link, suicide mortality was selected as one of the two indicators for SDG Target 3.4.

The importance of limiting access to means of suicide as an effective way of reducing suicide mortality was highlighted in the first-ever WHO report on suicide prevention in 2014 *(35)*. A leading means of suicide in many parts of the world is self-poisoning with pesticides *(36)*. The impact of access to pesticides on suicide rates was first identified in a 1995 study *(37)* that demonstrated both an increase in suicide mortality following the introduction of paraquat (a highly toxic herbicide) in Samoa in 1972, and a subsequent reduction in such mortality after its banning in 1981. Since then, further studies demonstrating the link between pesticide availability and suicide rates have emerged *(38–40)*. A recent study of a proposed ban on pesticides in India concluded that such a policy would reduce health inequities by providing "higher protection to the poor relative to the rich" given the greater availability of pesticides in rural areas *(41)*.

For many years, suicide mortality in the Republic of Korea has been high compared to other high-income countries and to the WHO Western Pacific Region in general (Figure 3.7) *(15)*. According to WHO estimates the suicide rate in the Republic of Korea was 14.8 per 100 000 population in 2000, 34.1 per 100 000 in 2010 and 28.3 per 100 000 in 2015[1] – with the suicide rate among males in 2015 being 2.5 times higher than that among females.

Figure 3.7
Estimated suicide mortality rates in the Republic of Korea,[1] high-income countries, and the WHO Western Pacific Region, 2000–2015

- Republic of Korea
- High-income countries
- WHO Western Pacific Region

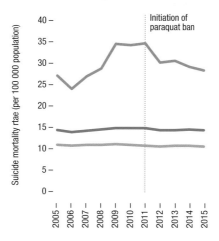

Suicides by pesticides accounted for about one fifth of all suicides in the Republic of Korea during 2006–2010 *(42)*. Efforts to control and minimize the harmful impact of pesticides in the Republic of Korea prior to 2011 had not had any meaningful impact as the pesticides that accounted for the majority of deaths were not adequately controlled. In 2011, the Republic of Korea cancelled the re-registration of paraquat and banned its sale in 2012. These actions resulted in an immediate and clear decline in pesticide-poisoning suicides, and contributed to a decline in overall suicide rates (Fig 3.8) *(15, 42–44)*. The intervention appeared to reduce suicide rates among all population groups, including men, women, all age groups, and those living in urban and rural areas *(42)*. More than

half of the overall reduction in the suicide rate between 2011 and 2013 could be attributed to the paraquat ban. Notably, this was achieved without any impact on crop yield.

Given the magnitude of suicide by pesticide self-poisoning around the world, tens of thousands of lives could be saved every year should effective regulation of pesticides be enforced worldwide. Ensuring safer access to pesticides will require an intersectoral approach, including pesticide bans and other related policies, community interventions *(45)*, improved health care *(46)*, and training and surveillance activities. The successful approach taken by the Republic of Korea provides an encouraging model for other countries aiming to reduce suicide deaths.

Figure 3.8
Total number of suicides and the proportion of suicides by pesticide in the Republic of Korea, 2009–2015[1]

- Total suicides
- % suicide by pesticide

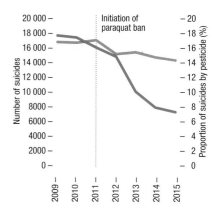

[1] The estimate of total suicide mortality for the Republic of Korea for the years 2014 and 2015 have been updated using data published in the WHO Mortality Database after the closure date for the Global Health Estimates 2015 *(15)*.

3.6 Preventing early deaths due to alcohol in the Russian Federation

SDG Target 3.5
Strengthen the prevention and treatment of substance abuse, including narcotic drug abuse and harmful use of alcohol

Indicator 3.5.2: Harmful use of alcohol, defined according to the national context as alcohol per capita consumption (aged 15 years and older) within a calendar year in litres of pure alcohol

Country: **Russian Federation**
WHO region: **European Region**
World Bank income category, 2015: **Upper middle income**
Life expectancy at birth, 2015: **70.5 years**
Total per capita (≥ 15 years of age) alcohol consumption, 2016: **13.9 litres of pure alcohol**

Following the dissolution of the Soviet Union in 1991, the Russian Federation experienced a major demographic and health crisis characterized by premature mortality, ill health and disability among young adults (47). Research on the underlying determinants of the increased mortality suggested that it was caused by the collapse of the social, economic and health systems; a high prevalence of unhealthy behaviours; and lack of concerted efforts to prevent and control NCDs. The privatization and deregulation of the alcohol market in the 1990s may have contributed to the escalation of alcohol-related problems (48, 49), with alcohol consumption contributing substantially to the increased morbidity and mortality levels (48–51).

The seriousness of the situation called for a major reframing of health policy to control the alcohol market and reduce the harmful use of alcohol. In 2004, the government began a process of strengthening alcohol-control policies (49, 51, 52). In 2005, the President of the Russian Federation explicitly acknowledged the urgency of this problem, linking the shorter life expectancy of the population compared to western European countries to the prevalence of NCDs and to alcohol use (47). Later the same year a series of amendments to the law governing regulation of the production and trading volume of alcohol products was passed. This was then followed by amendments to other laws and regulations related to alcohol (Box 3.1).

Between 2007 and 2016, total (recorded and unrecorded) alcohol consumption was reduced by 3.5 litres of pure alcohol per capita (Figure 3.9) (53). During the period 2005–2015, the number of new cases of alcoholic psychoses decreased from 52.3 to 20.5 per 100 000 population (54), with the death rate from alcohol use also declining, especially in males (Figure 3.10) (15). Similar patterns were also observed among patients diagnosed with alcohol dependence and other alcohol-related diseases, along with an important reduction in total adult mortality – all of which are likely to be a result of the downward trends in general alcohol consumption (55). Consumption of homemade alcohol seems not to have increased in response to limitations on the formal market for alcohol (56). The new policies seem to have made an important contribution to reducing alcohol consumption in the Russian Federation with beneficial effects on morbidity and mortality (57).

Many of the policies implemented in the period 2005–2016 have been evidence based, in line with the WHO *Global strategy to reduce the harmful use of alcohol* (58) and the *WHO Global action plan for the prevention and control of noncommunicable diseases 2013–2020* (59) and were introduced in a step-wise manner. The country's experience clearly demonstrates that comprehensive government initiatives that utilize evidence-based interventions and intersectoral approaches can produce notable results.

Figure 3.9
Total alcohol consumption per capita (adults 15 years and over) in the Russian Federation, WHO European Region and the European Union (EU), 2000–2016

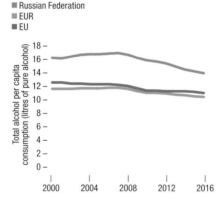

■ Russian Federation
■ EUR
■ EU

Figure 3.10
Death rate from alcohol use per 100 000 population in the Russian Federation,[a] WHO European Region, and upper middle-income countries (UMIC), 2000–2015

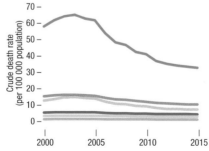

■ UMIC, males   ■ UMIC, females
■ EUR, males   ■ EUR, females
■ Russian Federation, males   ■ Russian Federation, females

[a] Latest year of data from the Russian Federation is 2011. Estimates for 2012–2015 are projections based on trends in prior years.

Box 3.1
Alcohol policy in the Russian Federation (2005–2016): timeline of selected key policy changes (52, 53, 57, 60)

— 2005 —
- Strengthening of the control system for production, distribution, and sales (wholesale and retail) of alcohol, and no sales at selected public spaces.
- Mandatory excise stamp on all alcoholic beverages for sale in the domestic market.
- Ban on sales of alcoholic beverages containing more than 15% ethanol alcohol by volume (ABV) in selected public places, by individuals, and other places not properly licensed.

— 2008 —
- Advertising ban for alcohol on all types of public transportation infrastructure.
- Alcohol excise duties increase 10% per year as part of an amendment to the tax code.

— 2010 —
- Adoption of a national programme of actions to reduce alcohol-related harm and prevent alcoholism among the Russian population for the period 2010–2020.
- Establishment of a minimum retail price for beverages stronger than 28% ABV.
- Zero tolerance for use of alcohol by drivers and 0.0% blood alcohol concentration for driving.

— 2011 —
- Strict enforcement and increased severity of administrative liability for the sale of alcohol products to minors.
- Prohibition of alcohol sales at gas stations.
- Implementation of an initiative to improve the treatment system for alcohol and drug use disorders.

— 2012 —
- Prohibition of sales of beer in selected places.
- Ban on alcohol advertising on the internet and in electronic media.

— 2013 —
- Ban on alcohol advertising in any printed media.
- Further increase in minimum retail prices of spirits.
- A limit of 0.16 mg/l (as a maximum measurement error) for a breathalyzer test introduced while maintaining a "zero tolerance" policy; increased severity of punishment for drink-driving.

— 2014 —
- A "Development of Health" programme initiated to prevent harmful use of alcohol.
- Further increase in fines for alcohol sales to minors, and criminal responsibility for repeated violation.
- Increase of alcohol excise duties by 33% and further increase of minimum prices for spirits.
- Relaxed advertising laws to accommodate domestic wine-making and the removal of some restrictions on advertising beer and beverages until 2019, in connection with the FIFA World Cup to be held in the Russian Federation in 2018.

— 2015 —
- Decrease in the minimum price of vodka.
- Initiation of the social communication project "Health Factory", aimed at addressing risk factors (including alcohol-use disorders) and targeted towards active people of working age.

— 2016 —
- Increase in the minimum price of vodka.
- Introduction of an alcohol-registration system at retail level.

3.7 Fighting the tobacco industry in Uruguay

SDG Target 3.a
Strengthen the implementation of the World Health Organization Framework Convention on Tobacco Control in all countries, as appropriate

Indicator 3.a.1: Age-standardized prevalence of current tobacco use among persons aged 15 years and older

Country: **Uruguay**

WHO region: **Region of the Americas**

World Bank income category, 2015: **High income**

Life expectancy at birth, 2015: **77.0 years**

Age-standardized prevalence of current tobacco smoking among persons aged 15 years and older, 2015: **26.7% (males), 19.4% (females)**

In September 2004, Uruguay became a Party to the WHO Framework Convention on Tobacco Control (WHO FCTC). Since then, the country has become a global leader in this area through its step-wise and comprehensive approach to the implementation of the Convention (Figure 3.10). In March 2005, the Health Ministry established a formal national tobacco control programme. Within months, pictures were added to health-warning labels and misleading terms such as "light", "ultra-light" and "mild" were prohibited. In 2006, Uruguay became the first country in Latin America to ban smoking in enclosed public places. In 2009, Uruguay implemented an ordinance permitting only one variant of a given tobacco brand to be on the market at any one time. This aim of this ordinance was to ensure that tobacco product packaging and labelling did not promote a tobacco product through any means that were false or misleading, including through packaging designs, colours, or any other feature that could create the false impression that one tobacco product was less harmful than another. In the same year, the size of warning labels was further increased to 80% of the primary pack surface area – the world's largest at that time. In order to monitor the impact of these and other interventions, national surveys were conducted in 2003, 2006, 2009 and 2013 to actively monitor the scale of tobacco use among adults.

In response to the actions taken by Uruguay, the international tobacco company Philip Morris International challenged the packaging and labelling laws through the unprecedented initiation of international arbitration in early 2010. At the World Bank International Centre for Settlement of Investment Disputes, the company claimed that Uruguay had violated its bilateral investment treaty with Switzerland. However, Uruguay was able to stand up against the tobacco industry and actively defend its national laws. Support for Uruguay was provided by WHO, the WHO FCTC Secretariat and the Pan American Health Organization, which filed amicus briefs, and by international and national NGOs and Michael Bloomberg, who provided financial support. In July 2016, the tobacco industry finally lost the six-year landmark battle to block Uruguay's strong tobacco packaging and labelling measures. This decision represented a major victory for the people of Uruguay and it showed countries everywhere that they can stand up to tobacco companies and win. Uruguay's experience sets an important precedent for other countries considering implementing similar legislation, and will strengthen the resolve of governments to not be intimidated by tobacco industry threats of litigation.

Based on the monitoring data collected by Uruguay, WHO has estimated that the proportion of adults who smoke tobacco in Uruguay almost halved during 2000–2015, from 40% to 22%, representing approximately twice the global rate of reduction during the same period (Fig 3.11) *(61)*. The approximate number of smokers aged 15 and over in Uruguay fell from one million in 2000 to less than 600 000 in 2015. By progressively strengthening its tobacco control measures and winning the fight against the tobacco industry, Uruguay has led the way in accelerating the implementation of the WHO FCTC.

Figure 3.11
Trends in prevalence of current smokers ≥ 15 years of age, globally and in Uruguay, and introduction of tobacco-control measures in Uruguay, 2000–2015

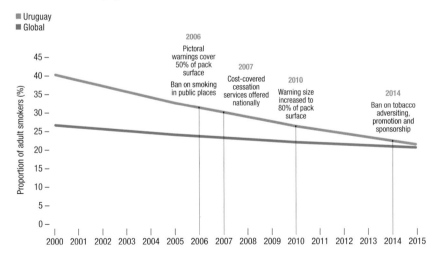

3.8 Strengthening health emergency preparedness in Ghana

SDG Target 3.d
Strengthen the capacity of all countries, in particular developing countries, for early warning, risk reduction and management of national and global health risks

Indicator 3.d.1: International Health Regulations (IHR) capacity and health emergency preparedness

Country: **Ghana**
WHO region: **African Region**
World Bank income category, 2015: **Lower middle income**
Life expectancy at birth, 2015: **62.4 years**
Average of 13 International Health Regulations core capacity scores, 2016: **74**

The International Health Regulations (2005) (IHR) *(62)* – a legal instrument that is binding on 196 countries including all WHO Member States – aim to help countries prevent and respond to acute public health risks that have the potential to cross borders and threaten people worldwide. In order to be able to notify the international community of events and respond to public health risks and emergencies, countries must have the capacity to detect such events through a well-established national surveillance and response infrastructure.

The IHR Monitoring and Evaluation Framework outlines an approach for reviewing the implementation of the core public health capacities required in this area. The Framework consists of four components: (a) States Parties annual reporting; (b) after-action review; (c) simulation exercises; and (d) joint external evaluation (JEE). This approach provides a comprehensive picture of a country's ability to respond to risks by identifying strengths, gaps and priorities. The implementation status of 13 IHR core capacities has therefore been selected as the indicator to monitor progress toward SDG Target 3.d.

The Ebola outbreak of 2014 in West Africa highlighted the need for African countries to strengthen their national capacities. During the outbreak, Ghana served as a vital coordination and operational base for response activities, and was thus well positioned to participate in and learn from the wide range of programme activities launched. Ghana was among the first countries in Africa to roll out the activities outlined in the Ebola virus disease (EVD) consolidated preparedness checklist *(63)* developed by WHO and its partners to guide preparedness activities in high-risk countries. In accordance with IHR requirements, these activities aimed to strengthen country capacities for early warning, risk reduction and the management of national and global health risks.

A well-functioning surveillance system plays a crucial role in guaranteeing the public health security of the community, and ensuring that public health events are promptly detected and addressed through coordinated response mechanisms. Surveillance-strengthening activities were conducted by the Ministry of Health of Ghana with the support of WHO. These activities included the orientation of 239 community health volunteers in five border districts on the Integrated Disease Surveillance and Response (IDSR) guidelines, and community outreach covering over 276 communities with public health messages. To enhance disease detection, WHO and Ministry of Health teams trained over 40 clinicians on the principles of IDSR. As part of promoting community engagement, Ghana rolled out the unique strategy of training over 200 representatives of the Traditional Medicine Practitioners Association and community radio operators on their roles in public health emergencies.

The lack of diagnostics reagents, materials and equipment has also been a persistent gap. Consumables and reagents for sample collection, packaging, transportation and diagnosis were therefore procured and distributed to national public health laboratories and research organizations as part of building diagnostic capacity. The procurement of such materials, along with the training of over 200 people on sample management and biosafety and biosecurity requirements, has enhanced Ghana's capacity to accurately and rapidly detect emerging and dangerous pathogens such as the Ebola virus. Some of these laboratory materials were later used during cholera and meningitis outbreaks reported in 2016.

Another key aspect of disease surveillance is monitoring points of entry. WHO trained 28 point-of-entry staff on ship inspection and ship sanitation, following updated IHR certification procedures.

To encourage cross-border communication and cooperation, a cross-border coordination meeting was also held at the Tatale border point involving over 30 representatives from Ghana and Togo.

All of these activities contributed towards strengthening Ghana's core capacities under the IHR – as highlighted by an assessment of the country's implementation of the EVD preparedness checklist during 2015 (Figure 3.12). In late 2015, as the threat of Ebola was decreasing in the region, preparedness activities were broadened to apply to all diseases. In 2016, Ghana carried out a tabletop exercise – in the form of a facilitated discussion of a simulated emergency situation – to test laboratory pre-diagnostic capacities (such as sample collection and transport) which helped to identify major gaps and key areas that required strengthening.

To complement the self-assessment undertaken as part of IHR annual reporting to the World Health Assembly, and to determine its level of preparedness after several months of intense preparation, Ghana volunteered for a JEE, which was carried out in February 2017. During the JEE process, an external team of experts conduct a series of multisectoral discussions based upon 19 technical areas defined in the JEE tool *(64)*. In Ghana, this consisted of a formal presentation of Ghana's national capacities with all national stakeholders in health security. During the conducting of the JEE process, best practices in all technical areas were identified and recommendations provided for further improvement. Although the outcome scores of the JEE process were lower than the results of the self-assessment carried out in 2016 (Figure 3.13), the JEE report allows the country to take stock of its findings and turn the recommendations made into actionable activities. This will result in further strengthening of Ghana's national IHR preparedness and response capacities.

Figure 3.12
Implementation of EVD preparedness checklist components, Ghana, 2015

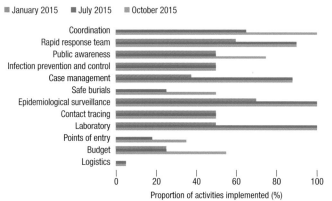

■ January 2015 ■ July 2015 ■ October 2015

Proportion of activities implemented (%)

Figure 3.13
Comparison of IHR self-assessment and JEE results, Ghana

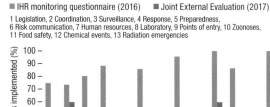

■ IHR monitoring questionnaire (2016) ■ Joint External Evaluation (2017)

1 Legislation, 2 Coordination, 3 Surveillance, 4 Response, 5 Preparedness, 6 Risk communication, 7 Human resources, 8 Laboratory, 9 Points of entry, 10 Zoonoses, 11 Food safety, 12 Chemical events, 13 Radiation emergencies

3.9 Monitoring mortality and cause of death in the Islamic Republic of Iran

Country: **Islamic Republic of Iran**

WHO region: **Eastern Mediterranean Region**

World Bank income category, 2015: **Upper middle income**

Life expectancy at birth, 2015: **75.5 years**

Completeness of cause-of-death registration, 2015: **90%**

A well-functioning civil registration and vital statistics (CRVS) system produces information on vital events such as births, marriages, deaths and causes of death. With 15 of the 17 SDGs requiring CRVS data to measure their indicators, investing in CRVS systems is a key step in SDG monitoring. It is only through the use of such systems that continuous and routine data can be generated on population, fertility and mortality by cause, disaggregated by socioeconomic status and geographic area.

In many countries, death registration lags behind birth registration. However, death registration is vitally important for a range of legal, administrative and statistical purposes, including monitoring the health of populations. In addition, more than a dozen SDG indicators require information on total or cause-specific mortality. Specific health-related SDG indicators generated from death registration data include those for maternal and infant mortality, and for cause-specific mortality such as deaths due to cancers, diabetes and cardiovascular conditions, as well as those due to external causes such as road traffic accidents, suicide and violence.

In the Islamic Republic of Iran there are two institutions that operate death registration systems: the National Organization for Civil Registration (NOCR) and the Ministry of Health and Medical Education (MOH&ME). The NOCR is legally responsible for the registration of four vital events: births, deaths, marriages and divorces. However, only limited information on cause of death is recorded in the NOCR system. In response to the demand for timely and accurate cause-of-death data, the MOH&ME developed the Deputy of Health (DH) programme, which aims to improve death registration data, including through improvements in the medical certification of cause of death (65). The DH programme operates in parallel with the NOCR system, with both systems receiving a copy of each death certificate issued.

First piloted in 1997, the DH programme in 1999 was still only capturing cause-of-death data in four provinces, with a coverage rate of 5% of all deaths in the entire country. In 2001, the system was expanded to cover 18 provinces, and by 2014 was covering 30 out of 31 provinces,

covering 65 million people and around 75% of all deaths (Figure 3.14). Tehran, the most populous province, was the only province not covered. In 2015 a programme was launched to collect all death certificates sent to Tehran cemeteries – thereby capturing cause-of-death information for all provinces nationwide. In addition to geographic expansion, the capturing of death and cause-of-death data has also been strengthened by the cross-checking of data using multiple sources at the district level, such as NOCR, cemetery and facility data, to identify omissions and duplication.

In addition to the substantial increase in the proportion of deaths with cause recorded, the level of detail on cause of death has also increased. During the period 2006–2012, cause-of-death data were coded to a condensed list of 318 cause categories using the ICD-10 classification system. Since then, major investments in system strengthening (including the training of certifiers

and coders) have resulted in data for the year 2013 onwards being coded to the ICD-10 detailed (four-digit) codes corresponding to over 1500 cause categories. Such detailed data enable epidemiological research to be conducted to support evidence-based policy decision-making in the country.

As clearly demonstrated by the Islamic Republic of Iran, a long-term, step-wise strategy of CRVS system development is crucial to the foundation of a solid evidence base with which to monitor the health of a nation. The use of multiple data sources by the MOH&ME to assess completeness and improve the capture of mortality data has allowed the country to build a system for monitoring mortality by cause, and hence for monitoring many of the health-related SDGs – all in less than two decades. Future MOH&ME plans to further improve the capture of mortality data include linking death registration in the DH programme and NCOR systems.

Figure 3.14
Coverage of NOCR death registration, coverage of DH programme total death registration, coverage of DH programme death registration with medical certification of cause of death, and number of provinces with the DH programme, Islamic Republic of Iran, 2001–2015[a]

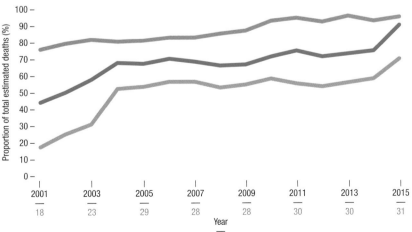

■ NOCR
■ DH (total)
■ DH (medically certified)

Number of provinces with DH programme coverage

[a] Data on numbers of deaths captured by the NOCR and DH programme, number of provinces covered, and numbers of deaths medically certified were provided to WHO by the Islamic Republic of Iran. Estimated coverage (%) was then calculated using WHO estimates of total mortality in the Islamic Republic of Iran (15).

References

1. Trends in maternal mortality: 1990 to 2015. Estimates by WHO, UNICEF, UNFPA, World Bank Group and the United Nations Population Division. Geneva: World Health Organization; 2015 (http://www.who.int/reproductivehealth/publications/monitoring/maternal-mortality-2015/en/, accessed 30 March 2017).

2. Maternal mortality in 1995: Estimates developed by WHO, UNICEF, UNFPA. Geneva: World Health Organization; 2001 (http://apps.who.int/iris/bitstream/10665/66837/1/WHO_RHR_01.9.pdf, accessed 30 March 2017).

3. Maternal mortality in 2000: Estimates developed by WHO, UNICEF, UNFPA. Geneva: World Health Organization; 2004 (http://apps.who.int/iris/bitstream/10665/42930/1/9241562706.pdf, accessed 30 March 2017).

4. Trends in maternal mortality: 1990 to 2008. Estimates by WHO, UNICEF, UNFPA, World Bank Group and the United Nations Population Division. Geneva: World Health Organization; 2010 (http://www.who.int/reproductivehealth/publications/monitoring/9789241500265/en/, accessed 30 March 2017).

5. Trends in maternal mortality: 1990 to 2010. Estimates by WHO, UNICEF, UNFPA, World Bank Group and the United Nations Population Division. Geneva: World Health Organization; 2012 (http://www.who.int/reproductivehealth/publications/monitoring/9789241503631/en/, accessed 30 March 2017).

6. Trends in maternal mortality: 1990 to 2013. Estimates by WHO, UNICEF, UNFPA, World Bank Group and the United Nations Population Division. Geneva: World Health Organization; 2014 (http://www.who.int/reproductivehealth/publications/monitoring/maternal-mortality-2013/en/, accessed 30 March 2017).

7. Alkema L, Chou D, Hogan D, Zhang S, Moller A-B, Gemmill et al. Global, regional, and national levels and trends in maternal mortality between 1990 and 2015, with scenario-based projections to 2030: a systematic analysis by the UN Maternal Mortality Estimation Inter-Agency Group. Lancet. 2016;387(10017):462–74 (http://www.thelancet.com/pb/assets/raw/Lancet/pdfs/S0140673615008387.pdf, accessed 30 March 2017).

8. Improvement of maternal and child health in Kazakhstan. Entre Nous, No. 74. 2011: pages16-7 (http://www.euro.who.int/__data/assets/pdf_file/0008/146978/313914_Entre_Nous_74_low.pdf, accessed 30 March 2017).

9. Commission CCA. Findings of a confidential audit of maternal mortality rates in the Republic of Kazakhstan 2011-2013. Astana: Ministry of Health; 2014.

10. World Malaria Report 2016. Geneva: World Health Organization; 2016 (http://www.who.int/malaria/publications/world-malaria-report-2016/en/, accessed 18 March 2017).

11. Hetzel MW, Pulford J, Ura Y, Robinson L, Morris H, Mueller I et al. Country-wide household survey 2010/11: malaria control intervention coverage and prevalence of parasitaemia. Goroka: Papua New Guinea Institute of Medical Research; 2012 (http://www.adi.org.au/wp-content/uploads/2016/11/Country-Wide-Household-Survey-Malaria-Control-Intervention-Coverage-and-Prevalence-of-Parasitaemia-2014.pdf, accessed 18 March 2017).

12. Hetzel MW, Pulford J, Gouda H, Hodge A, Siba PM, Mueller I. The Papua New Guinea National Malaria Control Program: primary outcome and impact indicators, 2009-2014. Goroka: Papua New Guinea Institute of Medical Research; 2014 (http://www.pngimr.org.pg/research%20publications/IMR%20-%20outcome%20and%20impact%202014.pdf, accessed 18 March 2017).

13. Hetzel MW, Choudhury AAK, Pulford J, Ura Y, Whittaker M, Siba PM et al. Progress in mosquito net coverage in Papua New Guinea. Malar J. 2014;13:242 (https://malariajournal.biomedcentral.com/articles/10.1186/1475-2875-13-242, accessed 18 March 2017).

14. Kurumop SF, Tandrapah A, Hetzel MW, Siba PM, Mueller I, Pulford J. The Papua New Guinea National Malaria Control Program: health facility surveys, 2010-2106. Goroka: Papua New Guinea Institute of Medical Research; 2016 (http://www.pngimr.org.pg/research%20publications/PNGIMR%202016%20-%20HFS%202010-2016.pdf, accessed 18 March 2017).

15. Global Health Estimates 2015: Deaths by cause, age, sex, by country and by region, 2000–2015. Geneva: World Health Organization; 2016 (http://www.who.int/healthinfo/global_burden_disease/estimates/en/index1.html, accessed 18 March 2017).

16. Soeung SC, Rani M, Huong V, Sarath S, Kimly C, Kohei T. Results from nationwide hepatitis B serosurvey in Cambodia using simple and rapid laboratory test: implications for National Immunization Program. Am J Trop Med Hyg. 2009;81(2):252-7 (http://www.ajtmh.org/content/journals/10.4269/ajtmh.2009.81.252#html_fulltext, accessed 18 March 2017).

17. Mao B, Patel MK, Hennessey K, Duncan RJW, Wannemuehler K, Soeung SC. Prevalence of chronic hepatitis B virus infection after implementation of a hepatitis B vaccination program among children in three provinces in Cambodia. Vaccine. 2013;31(40):4459–64 (https://www.ncbi.nlm.nih.gov/pmc/articles/PMC4663664/, accessed 18 March 2017).

18. Measles Elimination, Hepatitis B Control and Poliomyelitis Eradication. Resolution WPR/RC56.R8. In: Report of the Regional Committee for the Western Pacific fifty-sixth session, Noumea, 19–23 September 2005 (http://www2.wpro.who.int/rcm/en/archives/rc56/rc_resolutions/wpr_rc56_r08.htm, accessed 18 March 2017).

19. Global health sector strategy on viral hepatitis 2016–2021. Towards ending viral hepatitis. Geneva: World Health Organization; 2016 (http://apps.who.int/iris/bitstream/10665/246177/1/WHO-HIV-2016.06-eng.pdf?ua=1, accessed 18 March 2017).

20. Di Cesare M, Bennett JE, Best N, Stevens GA, Danaei G, Ezzati M. The contributions of risk factor trends to cardiometabolic mortality decline in 26 industrialized countries. Int J Epidemiol. 2013;42(3):838-48 (https://academic.oup.com/ije/article/42/3/838/912718/The-contributions-of-risk-factor-trends-to, accessed 32 March 2017).

21. Ezzati M, Obermeyer Z, Tzoulaki I, Mayosi BM, Elliott P, Leon DA. Contributions of risk factors and medical care to cardiovascular mortality trends. Nat. Rev. Cardiol. 2015;12(9):508–30 (abstract: http://www.ncbi.nlm.nih.gov/pubmed/26076950, accessed 31 March 2017).

22. Institute for Health Metrics and Evaluation. GBD Compare. Viz Hub [online tool]. Seattle (WA): University of Washington; 2017 (see: http://vizhub.healthdata.org/gbd-compare, accessed 22 February 2017).

23. Smoking in Ireland 2014: Synopsis of key patterns. Dublin: Health Service Executive; 2015 (http://www.hse.ie/eng/about/Who/TobaccoControl/Research/smokinginireland2014.pdf, accessed 31 March 2017).

24. Tobacco use. Data by country [online database]. Global Health Observatory data repository. Geneva: World Health Organization (http://apps.who.int/gho/data/node.main.65).

25. Mean systolic blood pressure trends, age-standardized (mmHg). Estimates by country [online database]. Global Health Observatory data repository. Geneva: World Health Organization (http://apps.who.int/gho/data/node.main.A882?lang=en).

26. Burnett RT, Pope III CA, Ezzati M, Olives C, Lim SS, Mehta S et al. An integrated risk function for estimating the global burden of disease attributable to ambient fine particulate matter exposure. Environ Health Perspect. 2014;122(4):397–403 (https://ehp.niehs.nih.gov/1307049/, accessed 31 March 2017).

27. Dockery DW, Rich DQ, Goodman PG, Clancy L, Ohman-Strickland P, George P et al. Effect of air pollution control on mortality and hospital admissions in Ireland. Research Report 176. Boston (MA): Health Effects Institute; 2013 (https://www.healtheffects.org/system/files/Dockery-176.pdf, accessed 31 March 2017).

28. Air quality in Ireland 2015: Key indicators of ambient air quality. County Wexford: Environmental Protection Agency; 2016 (http://www.epa.ie/pubs/reports/air/quality/Air%20Quality%20Report%202015.pdf, accessed 31 March 2017).

29. Smokeless zones. Brief outline of the "smoky coal" ban [website]. Greenheat (http://www.greenheat.ie/useful-information/smoky-coal-ban/, accessed 31 March 2017).

30. Kent BD, Sulaiman I, Nicholson TT, Lane SJ, Moloney ED. Acute pulmonary admissions following implementation of a national workplace smoking ban. Chest. 2012;142(3):673–9 (https://www.ncbi.nlm.nih.gov/pubmed/22383660, accessed 31 March 2017).

31. Stallings-Smith S, Zeka A, Goodman P, Kabir Z, Clancy L. Reductions in cardiovascular, cerebrovascular, and respiratory mortality following the national Irish smoking ban: Interrupted time-series analysis. PloS One. 2013;8(4)1–7 (http://journals.plos.org/plosone/article?id=10.1371/journal.pone.0062063, accessed 1 April 2017).

32. Frazer K, Callinan JE, McHugh J, van Baarsel S, Clarke A, Doherty K et al. Legislative smoking bans for reducing harms from secondhand smoke exposure, smoking prevalence and tobacco consumption (Review). Cochrane Database of Systematic Reviews 2016, Issue 2. Art. No.: CD005992 (abstract: http://onlinelibrary.wiley.com/doi/10.1002/14651858.CD005992.pub3/epdf/abstract, accessed 1 April 2017).

33. Tan CE, Glantz SA. Association between smoke-free legislation and hospitalizations for cardiac, cerebrovascular, and respiratory diseases: a meta-analysis. Circulation. 2012;126(18):2177–83 (https://www.ncbi.nlm.nih.gov/pubmed/23109514, accessed 1 April 2017).

34. Global, regional, and national incidence, prevalence, and years lived with disability for 310 diseases and injuries, 1990–2015: a systematic analysis for the Global Burden of Disease Study 2015. GBD 2015 Disease and Injury Incidence and Prevalence Collaborators. Lancet. 2016;388(10053):1545–1602 (http://www.thelancet.com/journals/lancet/article/PIIS0140-6736(16)31678-6/fulltext, accessed 1 April 2017).

35. Preventing suicide: a global imperative. Geneva: World Health Organization; 2014 (see: http://www.who.int/mental_health/suicide-prevention/world_report_2014/en/, accessed 1 April 2017).

36. Gunnell D, Eddleston M, Phillips MR, Konradsen F. The global distribution of fatal pesticide self-poisoning: systematic review. BMC Public Health. 2007;7:357 (http://bmcpublichealth.biomedcentral.com/articles/10.1186/1471-2458-7-357, accessed 1 April 2017).

37. Bowles JR. Suicide in Western Samoa: an example of a suicide prevention programme in a developing country. In: Diekstra, RFW, Gulbinat W, Kienhorst I, de Leo D, editors. Preventive strategies on suicide. Leiden: Brill Academic Publishers; 1995:173–206.

38. Kong Y, Zhang J. Access to farming pesticides and risk for suicide in Chinese rural young people. Psychiatry Res. 2010;179(2):217–21 (doi: 10.1016/j.psychres.2009.12.005).

39. Gunnell D, Fernando R, Hewagama M, Priyangika WDD, Konradsen F, Eddleston D. The impact of pesticide regulations on suicide in Sri Lanka. Int J Epidemiol. 2007;36(6):1235–42 (doi:10.1093/ije/dym164).

40. Knipe DW, Metcalfe C, Fernando R, Pearson M, Konradsen F, Eddleston M et al. Suicide in Sri Lanka 1975–2012: age, period and cohort analysis of police and hospital data. BMC Public Health. 2014;14:839 (http://bmcpublichealth.biomedcentral.com/articles/10.1186/1471-2458-14-839, accessed 1 April 2017).

41. Nigam A, Raykar R, Chisholm D. Self-harm in India: Cost-effectiveness analysis of a proposed pesticide ban. 2015. Unpublished Working Paper (available at: www.dcp-3.org, accessed 1 April 2017).

42. Cha ES, Chang SS, Gunnell D, Eddleston M, Khang YH, Lee WJ. Impact of paraquat regulation on suicide in South Korea. Int J Epidemiol. 2016;45(2):470–9 (https://academic.oup.com/ije/article/45/2/470/2572538/Impact-of-paraquat-regulation-on-suicide-in-South, accessed 1 April 2017).

43. Korea Statistical Information Service. Cause of Death. Daejeon: Statistics Korea; 2016. (https://mdis.kostat.go.kr/index.do, accessed 9 March 2017).

44. Myung W, Lee GH, Won HH, Fava M, Mishoulon D, Nyer M et al. Paraquat prohibition and change in the suicide rate and methods in South Korea. PLoS ONE. 2015;10(6):e0128980. doi:10.1371/journal.pone.0128980

45. Safer access to pesticides for suicide prevention: Experiences from community interventions. Geneva: World Health Organization; 2016 (http://apps.who.int/iris/bitstream/10665/246233/1/WHO-MSD-MER-16.3-eng.pdf?ua=1, accessed 1 April 2017).

46. Clinical management of acute pesticide intoxication: Prevention of suicidal behaviours. Geneva: World Health Organization; 2008 (http://www.who.int/mental_health/prevention/suicide/pesticides_intoxication.pdf, accessed 1 April 2017).

47. Dying too young: Addressing premature mortality and ill health due to non-communicable diseases and injuries in the Russian Federation. Washington (DC): World Bank; 2005 (http://siteresources.worldbank.org/INTECA/Resources/DTY-Final.pdf, accessed 13 April 2017).

48. Nemtsov AV. Alcohol-related human losses in Russia in the 1980s and 1990s. Addiction. 2002;97(11):1413–25.

49. Interpersonal violence and alcohol in the Russian Federation: Policy briefing. 2006, Copenhagen: WHO Regional Office for Europe; 2006 (http://www.euro.who.int/__data/assets/pdf_file/0011/98804/E88757.pdf, accessed 1 April 2017).

50. Leon, D.A., et al., Hazardous alcohol drinking and premature mortality in Russia: a population based case-control study. Lancet, 2007. 369(9578): p. 2001-9.

51. Levintova M. Russian alcohol policy in the making. Alcohol Alcohol. 2007;42(5):500–5.

52. Yashkin AP. The dynamics of alcohol consumption in the Russian Federation: Implications of using price related policies to control alcohol use. Doctoral dissertation. Department of Health Policy and Management, University of South Florida, Tampa, Florida, the USA; 2013:110.

53. WHO Global Information System on Alcohol and Health [online database]. Geneva: World Health Organization; 2017 (http://apps.who.int/gho/data/node.main.GISAH?showonly=GISAH).

54. Diseases of social importance in the population of Russia in 2015. Statistical materials. Moscow: Ministry of Health of the Russian Federation; 2016.

55. Shield KD, Rylett M, Rehm J. Public health successes and missed opportunities. Trends in alcohol consumption and attributable mortality in the WHO European Region, 1990–2014. Copenhagen: WHO Regional Office for Europe; 2016 (http://www.euro.who.int/__data/assets/pdf_file/0018/319122/Public-health-successes-and-missed-opportunities-alcohol-mortality-19902014.pdf, accessed 1 April 2017).

56. Radaev V. Impact of a new alcohol policy on homemade alcohol consumption and sales in Russia. Alcohol Alcohol. 2015;50(3):365–72 (https://academic.oup.com/alcalc/article-lookup/doi/10.1093/alcalc/agv008, accessed 13 April 2017).

57. Neufeld M, Rehm J. Alcohol consumption and mortality in Russia since 2000: are there any changes following the alcohol policy changes starting in 2006? Alcohol Alcohol. 2013;48(2):222–30 (https://academic.oup.com/alcalc/article-lookup/doi/10.1093/alcalc/ags134, accessed 13 April 2017).

58. Global strategy to reduce the harmful use of alcohol. Geneva: World Health Organization; 2010 (see: http://www.who.int/substance_abuse/activities/gsrhua/en/, accessed 1 April 2017).

59. Global action plan for the prevention and control of noncommunicable diseases 2013–2020. Geneva: World Health Organization; 2013 (see: http://www.who.int/nmh/events/ncd_action_plan/en/, accessed 1 April 2017).

60. Alcohol policy timeline database of countries in the WHO European Region [online database]. Global Health Observatory data repository. Geneva: World Health Organization (http://apps.who.int/gho/data/node.main.A1500?lang=en&showonly=GISAH).

61. WHO global report on trends in prevalence of tobacco smoking 2015. Geneva: World Health Organization; 2015 (http://apps.who.int/iris/bitstream/10665/156262/1/9789241564922_eng.pdf, accessed 22 March 2017).

62. International Health Regulations (2005). Third edition. Geneva: World Health Organization; 2016 (see: http://www.who.int/ihr/publications/9789241580496/en/, accessed 2 April 2017).

63. Ebola virus disease. Consolidated preparedness checklist. Geneva: World Health Organization; 2014: Revision 1; 15 January 2015 (WHO/EVD/Preparedness/14 Rev.1; see: http://www.who.int/csr/resources/publications/ebola/ebola-preparedness-checklist/en/, accessed 2 April 2017).

64. IHR (2005) Monitoring and Evaluation Framework. Joint external evaluation tool and process overview. Geneva: World Health Organization; 2016 (WHO/HSE/GCR/2016.18; http://www.who.int/ihr/publications/WHO-HSE-GCR-2016-18/en/, accessed 2 April 2017).

65. Khosravi A, Taylor R, Naghavi M, Lopez A. Mortality in the Islamic Republic of Iran, 1964–2004. Bull World Health Organ. 2007;85(8):607–14 (http://www.who.int/bulletin/volumes/85/8/06-038802/en/, accessed 2 April 2017).

ANNEX A
Summaries of selected health-related SDG indicators

Explanatory notes

The statistics shown below represent official WHO statistics for selected health-related SDG indicators based on evidence available in early 2017. They have been compiled primarily using publications and databases produced and maintained by WHO or United Nations groups of which WHO is a member. A number of statistics have been derived from data produced and maintained by other international organizations. In some cases, as indicator definitions are being refined and baseline data are being collected, proxy indicators are presented. All such proxy indicators appearing in this annex are clearly indicated as such through the use of accompanying footnotes.

For indicators with a reference period expressed as a range, country values refer to the latest available year in the range unless otherwise noted. Within each WHO region, countries are sorted in ascending order for mortality, incidence and risk-factor indicators, and in descending order for coverage and capacity indicators. Countries for which data are not available or applicable are sorted alphabetically at the bottom of each region, unless otherwise noted.

Wherever possible, estimates have been computed using standardized categories and methods in order to enhance cross-national comparability. This approach may result in some cases in differences between the estimates presented here and the official national statistics prepared and endorsed by individual WHO Member States. It is important to stress that these estimates are also subject to considerable uncertainty, especially for countries with weak statistical and health information systems where the quality of the underlying empirical data is limited.

More details on the indicators and estimates presented here are available at the WHO Global Health Observatory.[1]

---

[1] The Global Health Observatory (GHO) is WHO's portal providing access to data and analyses for monitoring the global health situation. See: http://www.who.int/gho/en/, accessed 18 March 2017.

MATERNAL MORTALITY

SDG Target 3.1
By 2030, reduce the global maternal mortality ratio to less than 70 per 100 000 live births

Indicator 3.1.1: Maternal mortality ratio

Maternal mortality ratio (per 100 000 live births), 2015[1]

AFR

Cabo Verde	42
Mauritius	53
Botswana	129
South Africa	138
Algeria	140
Sao Tome and Principe	156
Zambia	224
Namibia	265
Rwanda	290
Gabon	291
Senegal	315
Ghana	319
Comoros	335
Equatorial Guinea	342
Uganda	343
Ethiopia	353
Madagascar	353
Togo	368
Burkina Faso	371
Swaziland	389
United Republic of Tanzania	398
Benin	405
Congo	442
Zimbabwe	443
Angola	477
Lesotho	487
Mozambique	489
Eritrea	501
Kenya	510
Guinea-Bissau	549
Niger	553
Mali	587
Cameroon	596
Mauritania	602
Malawi	634
Côte d'Ivoire	645
Guinea	679
Democratic Republic of the Congo	693
Gambia	706
Burundi	712
Liberia	725
South Sudan	789
Nigeria	814
Chad	856
Central African Republic	882
Sierra Leone	1360

AMR

Canada	7
United States of America	14
Uruguay	15
Chile	22
Costa Rica	25
Barbados	27
Grenada	27
Belize	28
Mexico	38
Cuba	39
Brazil	44
Saint Vincent and the Grenadines	45
Saint Lucia	48
Argentina	52
El Salvador	54
Trinidad and Tobago	63
Colombia	64
Ecuador	64
Peru	68
Bahamas	80
Guatemala	88
Jamaica	89
Dominican Republic	92
Panama	94
Venezuela (Bolivarian Republic of)	95
Honduras	129
Paraguay	132
Nicaragua	150
Suriname	155
Bolivia (Plurinational State of)	206
Guyana	229
Haiti	359

SEAR

Thailand	20
Sri Lanka	30
Maldives	68
Democratic People's Republic of Korea	82
Indonesia	126
Bhutan	148
India	174
Bangladesh	176
Myanmar	178
Timor-Leste	215
Nepal	258

EUR

Finland	3
Greece	3
Iceland	3
Poland	3
Austria	4
Belarus	4
Czechia	4
Italy	4
Sweden	4
Israel	5
Norway	5
Spain	5
Switzerland	5
Denmark	6
Germany	6
Slovakia	6
Belgium	7
Cyprus	7
Montenegro	7
Netherlands	7
Croatia	8
France	8
Ireland	8
The Former Yugoslav Republic of Macedonia	8
Estonia	9
Malta	9
Slovenia	9
United Kingdom	9
Lithuania	10
Luxembourg	10
Portugal	10
Bosnia and Herzegovina	11
Bulgaria	11
Kazakhstan	12
Turkey	16
Hungary	17
Serbia	17
Latvia	18
Republic of Moldova	23
Ukraine	24
Armenia	25
Azerbaijan	25
Russian Federation	25
Albania	29
Romania	31
Tajikistan	32
Georgia	36
Uzbekistan	36
Turkmenistan	42
Kyrgyzstan	76

EMR

Kuwait	4
United Arab Emirates	6
Libya	9
Saudi Arabia	12
Qatar	13
Bahrain	15
Lebanon	15
Oman	17
Iran (Islamic Republic of)	25
Egypt	33
Iraq	50
Jordan	58
Tunisia	62
Syrian Arab Republic	68
Morocco	121
Pakistan	178
Djibouti	229
Sudan	311
Yemen	385
Afghanistan	396
Somalia	732

WPR

Japan	5
Australia	6
Singapore	10
New Zealand	11
Republic of Korea	11
Brunei Darussalam	23
China	27
Fiji	30
Malaysia	40
Mongolia	44
Samoa	51
Viet Nam	54
Vanuatu	78
Kiribati	90
Micronesia (Federated States of)	100
Philippines	114
Solomon Islands	114
Tonga	124
Cambodia	161
Lao People's Democratic Republic	197
Papua New Guinea	215

[1] Trends in maternal mortality: 1990 to 2015. Estimates by WHO, UNICEF, UNFPA, World Bank Group and the United Nations Population Division. Geneva: World Health Organization; 2015 (http://www.who.int/reproductivehealth/publications/monitoring/maternal-mortality-2015/en/, accessed 23 March 2017). WHO Member States with a population of less than 100 000 in 2015 were not included in the analysis.

SKILLED BIRTH ATTENDANCE

SDG Target 3.1
By 2030, reduce the global maternal mortality ratio to less than 70 per 100 000 live births

Indicator 3.1.2: Proportion of births attended by skilled health personnel

Proportion of births attended by skilled health personnel (%), 2005–2016[1]

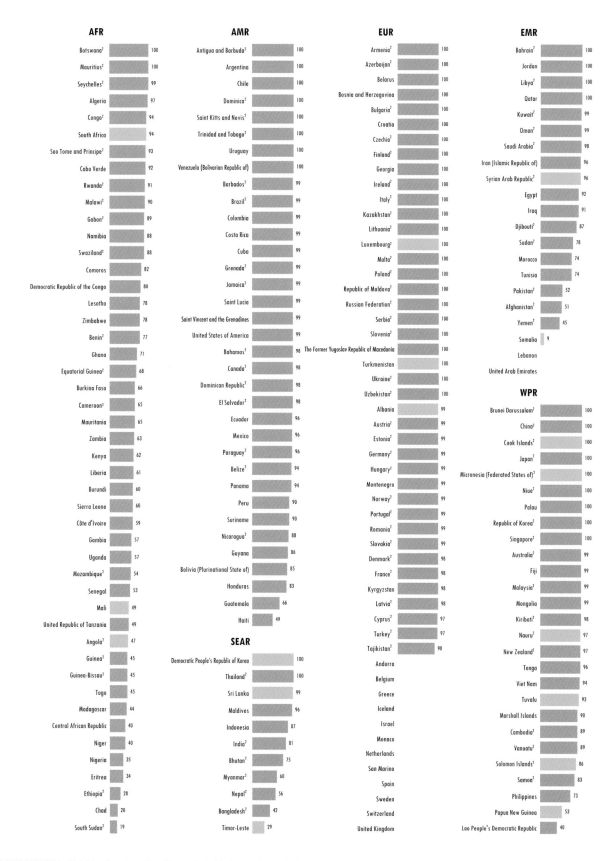

AFR

Country	%
Botswana[2]	100
Mauritius[2]	100
Seychelles[2]	99
Algeria	97
Congo[2]	94
South Africa	94
Sao Tome and Principe[2]	93
Cabo Verde	92
Rwanda[2]	91
Malawi[2]	90
Gabon[2]	89
Namibia	88
Swaziland[2]	88
Comoros	82
Democratic Republic of the Congo	80
Lesotho	78
Zimbabwe	78
Benin[2]	77
Ghana	71
Equatorial Guinea[2]	68
Burkina Faso	66
Cameroon[2]	65
Mauritania	65
Zambia	63
Kenya	62
Liberia	61
Burundi	60
Sierra Leone	60
Côte d'Ivoire	59
Gambia	57
Uganda	57
Mozambique[2]	54
Senegal	53
Mali	49
United Republic of Tanzania	49
Angola[2]	47
Guinea[2]	45
Guinea-Bissau[2]	45
Togo	45
Madagascar	44
Central African Republic	40
Niger	40
Nigeria	35
Eritrea	34
Ethiopia[2]	28
Chad	20
South Sudan[2]	19

AMR

Country	%
Antigua and Barbuda[2]	100
Argentina	100
Chile	100
Dominica[2]	100
Saint Kitts and Nevis[2]	100
Trinidad and Tobago[2]	100
Uruguay	100
Venezuela (Bolivarian Republic of)	100
Barbados[2]	99
Brazil[2]	99
Colombia	99
Costa Rica	99
Cuba	99
Grenada[2]	99
Jamaica[2]	99
Saint Lucia	99
Saint Vincent and the Grenadines	99
United States of America	99
Bahamas[2]	98
Canada[2]	98
Dominican Republic[2]	98
El Salvador[2]	98
Ecuador	96
Mexico	96
Paraguay[2]	96
Belize[2]	94
Panama	94
Peru	90
Suriname	90
Nicaragua[2]	88
Guyana	86
Bolivia (Plurinational State of)	85
Honduras	83
Guatemala	66
Haiti	49

SEAR

Country	%
Democratic People's Republic of Korea	100
Thailand[2]	100
Sri Lanka	99
Maldives	96
Indonesia	87
India[2]	81
Bhutan[2]	75
Myanmar[2]	60
Nepal[2]	56
Bangladesh[2]	42
Timor-Leste[2]	29

EUR

Country	%
Armenia[2]	100
Azerbaijan[2]	100
Belarus	100
Bosnia and Herzegovina	100
Bulgaria[2]	100
Croatia	100
Czechia[2]	100
Finland[2]	100
Georgia	100
Ireland[2]	100
Italy[2]	100
Kazakhstan[2]	100
Lithuania[2]	100
Luxembourg[2]	100
Malta[2]	100
Poland[2]	100
Republic of Moldova[2]	100
Russian Federation[2]	100
Serbia[2]	100
Slovenia[2]	100
The Former Yugoslav Republic of Macedonia	100
Turkmenistan	100
Ukraine[2]	100
Uzbekistan[2]	100
Albania	99
Austria[2]	99
Estonia[2]	99
Germany[2]	99
Hungary[2]	99
Montenegro	99
Norway[2]	99
Portugal[2]	99
Romania[2]	99
Slovakia[2]	99
Denmark[2]	98
France[2]	98
Kyrgyzstan	98
Latvia[2]	98
Cyprus[2]	97
Turkey[2]	97
Tajikistan[2]	90
Andorra	
Belgium	
Greece	
Iceland	
Israel	
Monaco	
Netherlands	
San Marino	
Spain	
Sweden	
Switzerland	
United Kingdom	

EMR

Country	%
Bahrain[2]	100
Jordan	100
Libya[2]	100
Qatar	100
Kuwait[2]	99
Oman[2]	99
Saudi Arabia[2]	98
Iran (Islamic Republic of)	96
Syrian Arab Republic[2]	96
Egypt	92
Iraq	91
Djibouti[2]	87
Sudan[2]	78
Morocco	74
Tunisia	74
Pakistan[2]	52
Afghanistan[2]	51
Yemen[2]	45
Somalia	9
Lebanon	
United Arab Emirates	

WPR

Country	%
Brunei Darussalam[2]	100
China[2]	100
Cook Islands[2]	100
Japan[2]	100
Micronesia (Federated States of)[2]	100
Niue[2]	100
Palau	100
Republic of Korea[2]	100
Singapore[2]	100
Australia[2]	99
Fiji	99
Malaysia[2]	99
Mongolia	99
Kiribati[2]	98
Nauru[2]	97
New Zealand[2]	97
Tonga	96
Viet Nam	94
Tuvalu	93
Marshall Islands	90
Cambodia[2]	89
Vanuatu[2]	89
Solomon Islands[2]	86
Samoa[2]	83
Philippines	73
Papua New Guinea	53
Lao People's Democratic Republic	40

[1] WHO/UNICEF joint Global Database 2017. (http://www.who.int/gho/maternal_health/en/ and https://data.unicef.org/topic/maternal-health/delivery-care). The data are extracted from public available sources and have not undergone country consultation. Data shown are the latest available for 2005–2016. Data from 2005–2009 are shown in pale orange.

[2] Non-standard definition. For more details see the WHO/UNICEF joint Global Database 2017.

SDG Target 3.2

By 2030, end preventable deaths of newborns and children under 5 years of age, with all countries aiming to reduce neonatal mortality to at least as low as 12 per 1000 live births and under-five mortality to at least as low as 25 per 1000 live births

Indicator 3.2.1: Under-five mortality rate
Indicator 3.2.2: Neonatal mortality rate

Under-five mortality and neonatal mortality rates (per 1000 live births), 2015[1]

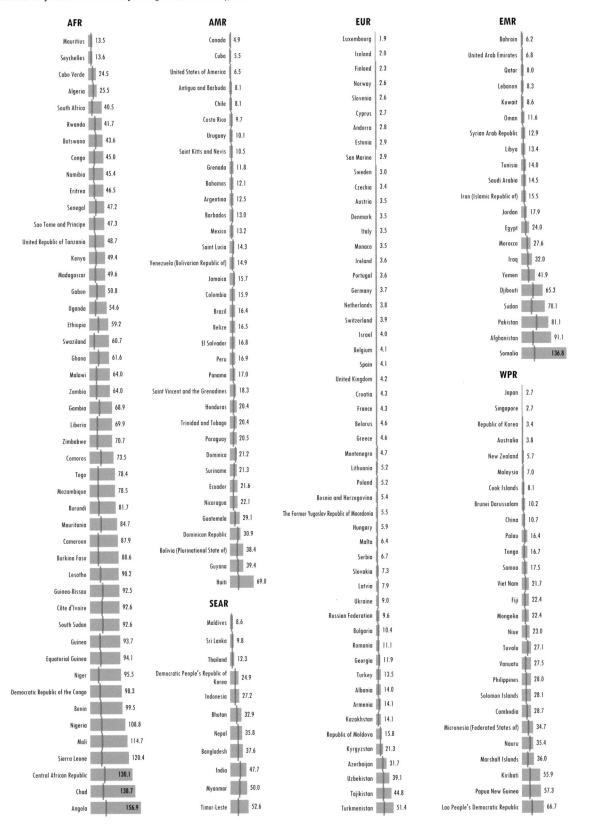

AFR

Country	Rate
Mauritius	13.5
Seychelles	13.6
Cabo Verde	24.5
Algeria	25.5
South Africa	40.5
Rwanda	41.7
Botswana	43.6
Congo	45.0
Namibia	45.4
Eritrea	46.5
Senegal	47.2
Sao Tome and Principe	47.3
United Republic of Tanzania	48.7
Kenya	49.4
Madagascar	49.6
Gabon	50.8
Uganda	54.6
Ethiopia	59.2
Swaziland	60.7
Ghana	61.6
Malawi	64.0
Zambia	64.0
Gambia	68.9
Liberia	69.9
Zimbabwe	70.7
Comoros	73.5
Togo	78.4
Mozambique	78.5
Burundi	81.7
Mauritania	84.7
Cameroon	87.9
Burkina Faso	88.6
Lesotho	90.2
Guinea-Bissau	92.5
Côte d'Ivoire	92.6
South Sudan	92.6
Guinea	93.7
Equatorial Guinea	94.1
Niger	95.5
Democratic Republic of the Congo	98.3
Benin	99.5
Nigeria	108.8
Mali	114.7
Sierra Leone	120.4
Central African Republic	130.1
Chad	138.7
Angola	156.9

AMR

Country	Rate
Canada	4.9
Cuba	5.5
United States of America	6.5
Antigua and Barbuda	8.1
Chile	8.1
Costa Rica	9.7
Uruguay	10.1
Saint Kitts and Nevis	10.5
Grenada	11.8
Bahamas	12.1
Argentina	12.5
Barbados	13.0
Mexico	13.2
Saint Lucia	14.3
Venezuela (Bolivarian Republic of)	14.9
Jamaica	15.7
Colombia	15.9
Brazil	16.4
Belize	16.5
El Salvador	16.8
Peru	16.9
Panama	17.0
Saint Vincent and the Grenadines	18.3
Honduras	20.4
Trinidad and Tobago	20.4
Paraguay	20.5
Dominica	21.2
Suriname	21.3
Ecuador	21.6
Nicaragua	22.1
Guatemala	29.1
Dominican Republic	30.9
Bolivia (Plurinational State of)	38.4
Guyana	39.4
Haiti	69.0

SEAR

Country	Rate
Maldives	8.6
Sri Lanka	9.8
Thailand	12.3
Democratic People's Republic of Korea	24.9
Indonesia	27.2
Bhutan	32.9
Nepal	35.8
Bangladesh	37.6
India	47.7
Myanmar	50.0
Timor-Leste	52.6

EUR

Country	Rate
Luxembourg	1.9
Iceland	2.0
Finland	2.3
Norway	2.6
Slovenia	2.6
Cyprus	2.7
Andorra	2.8
Estonia	2.9
San Marino	2.9
Sweden	3.0
Czechia	3.4
Austria	3.5
Denmark	3.5
Italy	3.5
Monaco	3.5
Ireland	3.6
Portugal	3.6
Germany	3.7
Netherlands	3.8
Switzerland	3.9
Israel	4.0
Belgium	4.1
Spain	4.1
United Kingdom	4.2
Croatia	4.3
France	4.3
Belarus	4.6
Greece	4.6
Montenegro	4.7
Lithuania	5.2
Poland	5.2
Bosnia and Herzegovina	5.4
The Former Yugoslav Republic of Macedonia	5.5
Hungary	5.9
Malta	6.4
Serbia	6.7
Slovakia	7.3
Latvia	7.9
Ukraine	9.0
Russian Federation	9.6
Bulgaria	10.4
Romania	11.1
Georgia	11.9
Turkey	13.5
Albania	14.0
Armenia	14.1
Kazakhstan	14.1
Republic of Moldova	15.8
Kyrgyzstan	21.3
Azerbaijan	31.7
Uzbekistan	39.1
Tajikistan	44.8
Turkmenistan	51.4

EMR

Country	Rate
Bahrain	6.2
United Arab Emirates	6.8
Qatar	8.0
Lebanon	8.3
Kuwait	8.6
Oman	11.6
Syrian Arab Republic	12.9
Libya	13.4
Tunisia	14.0
Saudi Arabia	14.5
Iran (Islamic Republic of)	15.5
Jordan	17.9
Egypt	24.0
Morocco	27.6
Iraq	32.0
Yemen	41.9
Djibouti	65.3
Sudan	70.1
Pakistan	81.1
Afghanistan	91.1
Somalia	136.8

WPR

Country	Rate
Japan	2.7
Singapore	2.7
Republic of Korea	3.4
Australia	3.8
New Zealand	5.7
Malaysia	7.0
Cook Islands	8.1
Brunei Darussalam	10.2
China	10.7
Palau	16.4
Tonga	16.7
Samoa	17.5
Viet Nam	21.7
Fiji	22.4
Mongolia	22.4
Niue	23.0
Tuvalu	27.1
Vanuatu	27.5
Philippines	28.0
Solomon Islands	28.1
Cambodia	28.7
Micronesia (Federated States of)	34.7
Nauru	35.4
Marshall Islands	36.0
Kiribati	55.9
Papua New Guinea	57.3
Lao People's Democratic Republic	66.7

[1] Under five mortality rates are shown as bar and in numbers. Neonatal mortality rates are shown as vertical grey lines. Levels & Trends in Child Mortality. Report 2015. Estimates developed by the UN Inter-agency Group for Child Mortality Estimation. United Nations Children's Fund, World Health Organization, World Bank and United Nations. New York (NY): United Nations Children's Fund; 2015 (http://www.unicef.org/publications/files/Child_Mortality_Report_2015_Web_9_Sept_15.pdf, accessed 22 March 2017).

HIV INCIDENCE

SDG Target 3.3
By 2030, end the epidemics of AIDS, tuberculosis, malaria and neglected tropical diseases and combat hepatitis, water-borne diseases and other communicable diseases

Indicator 3.3.1: Number of new HIV infections per 1000 uninfected population, by sex, age and key populations

New HIV infections among adults 15–49 years old (per 1000 uninfected population), 2015[1]

AFR

Algeria	0.02
Senegal	0.14
Burundi	0.18
Niger	0.19
Eritrea	0.21
Equatorial Guinea	0.24
Mauritania	0.28
Democratic Republic of the Congo	0.34
Mauritius	0.42
Burkina Faso	0.45
Madagascar	0.50
Liberia	0.56
Cabo Verde	0.60
Benin	0.69
Sierra Leone	0.69
Ghana	0.77
Chad	1.02
Mali	1.05
Guinea	1.18
Togo	1.21
Gambia	1.24
Gabon	1.39
Rwanda	1.41
Angola	1.86
Côte d'Ivoire	1.88
United Republic of Tanzania	2.11
Central African Republic	2.40
Kenya	3.52
Cameroon	3.57
Malawi	3.82
Uganda	5.12
Namibia	6.79
Mozambique	7.07
Zambia	8.55
Zimbabwe	8.84
Botswana	9.37
South Africa	14.40
Lesotho	18.80
Swaziland	23.60
Comoros	
Congo	
Ethiopia	
Guinea-Bissau	
Nigeria	
Sao Tome and Principe	
Seychelles	
South Sudan	

AMR

Honduras	0.10
Ecuador	0.15
El Salvador	0.15
Mexico	0.16
Peru	0.17
Chile	0.19
Haiti	0.21
Argentina	0.23
Nicaragua	0.23
Bolivia (Plurinational State of)	0.24
Costa Rica	0.24
Uruguay	0.27
Paraguay	0.30
Venezuela (Bolivarian Republic of)	0.33
Dominican Republic	0.36
Brazil	0.39
Colombia	0.39
Guatemala	0.41
Cuba	0.48
Panama	0.48
Trinidad and Tobago	0.52
Suriname	0.62
Belize	0.82
Guyana	0.88
Jamaica	1.07
Barbados	1.19
Bahamas	2.26
Antigua and Barbuda	
Canada	
Dominica	
Grenada	
Saint Kitts and Nevis	
Saint Lucia	
Saint Vincent and the Grenadines	
United States of America	

SEAR

Bangladesh	0.01
Sri Lanka	0.05
Nepal	0.08
India	0.11
Thailand	0.20
Myanmar	0.41
Indonesia	0.50
Bhutan	
Democratic People's Republic of Korea	
Maldives	
Timor-Leste	

EUR

Uzbekistan	0.02
Spain	0.14
Italy	0.16
Greece	0.19
Azerbaijan	0.20
Armenia	0.26
Kyrgyzstan	0.28
Tajikistan	0.33
Kazakhstan	0.36
Georgia	0.50
Latvia	0.53
Republic of Moldova	0.55
Ukraine	0.68
Belarus	1.05
Albania	
Andorra	
Austria	
Belgium	
Bosnia and Herzegovina	
Bulgaria	
Croatia	
Cyprus	
Czechia	
Denmark	
Estonia	
Finland	
France	
Germany	
Hungary	
Iceland	
Ireland	
Israel	
Lithuania	
Luxembourg	
Malta	
Monaco	
Montenegro	
Netherlands	
Norway	
Poland	
Portugal	
Romania	
Russian Federation	
San Marino	
Serbia	
Slovakia	
Slovenia	
Sweden	
Switzerland	
The Former Yugoslav Republic of Macedonia	
Turkey	
Turkmenistan	
United Kingdom	

EMR

Egypt	0.03
Tunisia	0.04
Lebanon	0.05
Afghanistan	0.06
Morocco	0.07
Yemen	0.07
Iran (Islamic Republic of)	0.14
Pakistan	0.16
Somalia	0.48
Djibouti	1.09
Bahrain	
Iraq	
Jordan	
Kuwait	
Libya	
Oman	
Qatar	
Saudi Arabia	
Sudan	
Syrian Arab Republic	
United Arab Emirates	

WPR

Mongolia	0.03
Cambodia	0.08
Australia	0.10
Philippines	0.12
Malaysia	0.27
Viet Nam	0.28
Papua New Guinea	0.54
Brunei Darussalam	
China	
Cook Islands	
Fiji	
Japan	
Kiribati	
Lao People's Democratic Republic	
Marshall Islands	
Micronesia (Federated States of)	
Nauru	
New Zealand	
Niue	
Palau	
Republic of Korea	
Samoa	
Singapore	
Solomon Islands	
Tonga	
Tuvalu	
Vanuatu	

---

[1] UNAIDS/WHO estimates; 2016 (http://www.who.int/gho/hiv/epidemic_status/incidence/en/).

TUBERCULOSIS INCIDENCE

SDG Target 3.3
By 2030, end the epidemics of AIDS, tuberculosis, malaria and neglected tropical diseases and combat hepatitis, water-borne diseases and other communicable diseases

Indicator 3.3.2: Tuberculosis incidence per 100 000 population

Tuberculosis incidence (per 100 000 population), 2015[1]

AFR		AMR		EUR		EMR	
Seychelles	9.5	Barbados	0.0	Monaco	0.0	United Arab Emirates	1.6
Mauritius	22	United States of America	3.2	Iceland	2.4	Jordan	7.0
Comoros	35	Jamaica	4.6	San Marino	2.5	Oman	8.4
Burkina Faso	52	Canada	5.1	Israel	4.0	Saudi Arabia	12
Togo	52	Saint Kitts and Nevis	5.1	Greece	4.5	Lebanon	13
Rwanda	56	Grenada	5.4	Czechia	5.2	Egypt	15
Mali	57	Cuba	7.0	Finland	5.6	Iran (Islamic Republic of)	16
Benin	60	Saint Vincent and the Grenadines	7.4	Italy	5.8	Bahrain	18
Eritrea	65	Antigua and Barbuda	7.5	Netherlands	5.8	Syrian Arab Republic	20
Algeria	75	Saint Lucia	8.8	Denmark	6.0	Kuwait	22
Niger	95	Costa Rica	11	Luxembourg	6.1	Qatar	34
Sao Tome and Principe	97	Dominica	11	Cyprus	6.2	Tunisia	37
Mauritania	107	Chile	16	Norway	6.3	Libya	40
Burundi	122	Trinidad and Tobago	17	Andorra	6.5	Iraq	43
Cabo Verde	139	Bahamas	18	Slovakia	6.5	Yemen	48
Senegal	139	Mexico	21	Ireland	7.2	Sudan	88
South Sudan	146	Argentina	25	Slovenia	7.2	Morocco	107
Chad	152	Belize	25	Switzerland	7.4	Afghanistan	189
Côte d'Ivoire	159	Guatemala	25	Austria	7.6	Pakistan	270
Ghana	160	Venezuela (Bolivarian Republic of)	29	Germany	8.1	Somalia	274
Equatorial Guinea	172	Uruguay	30	France	8.2	Djibouti	378
Gambia	174	Colombia	31	Malta	8.8		
Guinea	177	Suriname	33	Sweden	9.2	**WPR**	
Ethiopia	192	Brazil	41	Hungary	9.3	Australia	6.0
Malawi	193	Paraguay	41	Belgium	9.4	New Zealand	7.4
Uganda	202	El Salvador	43	United Kingdom	10	Cook Islands	7.8
Cameroon	212	Honduras	43	Spain	12	Niue	8.1
Kenya	233	Panama	50	Croatia	13	Samoa	11
Madagascar	236	Nicaragua	51	The Former Yugoslav Republic of Macedonia	13	Tonga	15
Zimbabwe	242	Ecuador	52	Estonia	18	Japan	17
United Republic of Tanzania	306	Dominican Republic	60	Turkey	18	Singapore	44
Sierra Leone	307	Guyana	93	Albania	19	Fiji	51
Liberia	308	Bolivia (Plurinational State of)	117	Poland	19	Brunei Darussalam	58
Nigeria	322	Peru	119	Montenegro	21	Vanuatu	63
Democratic Republic of the Congo	324	Haiti	194	Serbia	21	China	67
Botswana	356			Portugal	23	Palau	76
Angola	370	**SEAR**		Bulgaria	24	Republic of Korea	80
Guinea-Bissau	373	Maldives	53	Bosnia and Herzegovina	37	Malaysia	89
Congo	379	Sri Lanka	65	Armenia	41	Solomon Islands	89
Central African Republic	391	Bhutan	155	Latvia	41	Nauru	113
Zambia	391	Nepal	156	Belarus	55	Micronesia (Federated States of)	124
Gabon	465	Thailand	172	Lithuania	56	Viet Nam	137
Namibia	489	India	217	Azerbaijan	69	Lao People's Democratic Republic	182
Mozambique	551	Bangladesh	225	Turkmenistan	70	Tuvalu	232
Swaziland	565	Myanmar	365	Uzbekistan	79	Philippines	322
Lesotho	788	Indonesia	395	Russian Federation	80	Marshall Islands	344
South Africa	834	Timor-Leste	498	Romania	84	Cambodia	380
		Democratic People's Republic of Korea	561	Tajikistan	87	Mongolia	428
				Kazakhstan	89	Papua New Guinea	432
				Ukraine	91	Kiribati	551
				Georgia	99		
				Kyrgyzstan	144		
				Republic of Moldova	152		

[1] Global tuberculosis report 2016. Geneva: World Health Organization; 2016 (http://apps.who.int/iris/bitstream/10665/250441/1/9789241565394-eng.pdf?ua=1, accessed 22 March 2017).

SDG Target 3.3
By 2030, end the epidemics of AIDS, tuberculosis, malaria and neglected tropical diseases and combat hepatitis, water-borne diseases and other communicable diseases

Indicator 3.3.3: Malaria incidence per 1000 population

Malaria incidence (per 1000 population at risk), 2015[1]

AFR		AMR		EUR		EMR	
Algeria	<0.1	Argentina	0.0	Azerbaijan	0.0	Iraq	0.0
Cabo Verde	0.2	Costa Rica	0.0	Georgia	0.0	Saudi Arabia	0.1
Botswana	0.9	Paraguay	0.0	Kyrgyzstan	0.0	Iran (Islamic Republic of)	0.5
Swaziland	1.4	El Salvador	<0.1	Tajikistan	0.0	Pakistan	8.6
South Africa	3.1	Belize	0.1	Turkey	0.0	Yemen	22.2
Comoros	5.0	Ecuador	0.1	Uzbekistan	0.0	Afghanistan	23.6
Namibia	14.0	Mexico	0.2	Albania		Djibouti	25.4
Eritrea	14.5	Dominican Republic	0.3	Andorra		Sudan	36.6
Sao Tome and Principe	17.8	Guatemala	1.4	Armenia		Somalia	85.5
Ethiopia	58.6	Suriname	1.7	Austria		Bahrain	
Mauritania	74.2	Honduras	2.6	Belarus		Egypt	
Guinea-Bissau	89.3	Nicaragua	2.9	Belgium		Jordan	
Senegal	97.6	Panama	3.7	Bosnia and Herzegovina		Kuwait	
Madagascar	104.2	Bolivia (Plurinational State of)	3.9	Bulgaria		Lebanon	
United Republic of Tanzania	113.9	Brazil	7.9	Croatia		Libya	
Zimbabwe	114.2	Haiti	8.4	Cyprus		Morocco	
Angola	124.0	Colombia	12.3	Czechia		Oman	
Burundi	126.3	Peru	21.2	Denmark		Qatar	
South Sudan	156.0	Guyana	40.7	Estonia		Syrian Arab Republic	
Chad	163.2	Venezuela (Bolivarian Republic of)	68.4	Finland		Tunisia	
Kenya	166.0	Antigua and Barbuda		France		United Arab Emirates	
Congo	173.3	Bahamas		Germany			
Zambia	173.7	Barbados		Greece		**WPR**	
Malawi	188.8	Canada		Hungary		China	<0.1
Gambia	208.8	Chile		Iceland		Viet Nam	0.3
Equatorial Guinea	215.1	Cuba		Ireland		Philippines	0.4
Uganda	218.3	Dominica		Israel		Republic of Korea	0.8
Gabon	232.4	Grenada		Italy		Malaysia	1.9
Democratic Republic of the Congo	246.0	Jamaica		Kazakhstan		Vanuatu	3.3
Liberia	246.2	Saint Kitts and Nevis		Latvia		Cambodia	13.0
Cameroon	264.2	Saint Lucia		Lithuania		Lao People's Democratic Republic	20.9
Ghana	266.4	Saint Vincent and the Grenadines		Luxembourg		Solomon Islands	67.0
Central African Republic	289.5	Trinidad and Tobago		Malta		Papua New Guinea	122.2
Benin	293.7	United States of America		Monaco		Australia	
Mozambique	297.7	Uruguay		Montenegro		Brunei Darussalam	
Rwanda	301.3			Netherlands		Cook Islands	
Sierra Leone	302.8	**SEAR**		Norway		Fiji	
Togo	345.1	Sri Lanka	0.0	Poland		Japan	
Côte d'Ivoire	348.8	Bhutan	0.1	Portugal		Kiribati	
Niger	356.5	Timor-Leste	0.2	Republic of Moldova		Marshall Islands	
Guinea	367.8	Bangladesh	0.8	Romania		Micronesia (Federated States of)	
Nigeria	380.8	Democratic People's Republic of Korea	1.0	Russian Federation		Mongolia	
Burkina Faso	389.2	Thailand	2.7	San Marino		Nauru	
Mali	448.6	Nepal	3.3	Serbia		New Zealand	
Lesotho		Myanmar	11.8	Slovakia		Niue	
Mauritius		India	18.6	Slovenia		Palau	
Seychelles		Indonesia	26.1	Spain		Samoa	
		Maldives		Sweden		Singapore	
				Switzerland		Tonga	
				The Former Yugoslav Republic of Macedonia		Tuvalu	
				Turkmenistan			
				Ukraine			
				United Kingdom			

[1] World Malaria Report 2016. Geneva: World Health Organization; 2016 (http://www.who.int/malaria/publications/world-malaria-report-2016/report/en/, accessed 22 March 2017).

HEPATITIS B INCIDENCE

SDG Target 3.3
By 2030, end the epidemics of AIDS, tuberculosis, malaria and neglected tropical diseases and combat hepatitis, water-borne diseases and other communicable diseases

Indicator 3.3.4: Hepatitis B incidence per 100 000 population

Infants receiving three doses of hepatitis B vaccine (%), 2015[1]

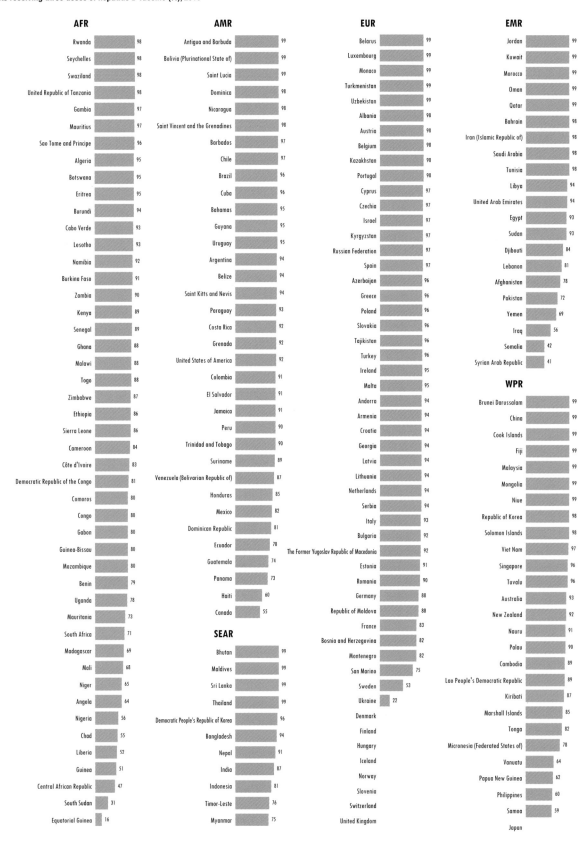

AFR		AMR		EUR		EMR	
Rwanda	98	Antigua and Barbuda	99	Belarus	99	Jordan	99
Seychelles	98	Bolivia (Plurinational State of)	99	Luxembourg	99	Kuwait	99
Swaziland	98	Saint Lucia	99	Monaco	99	Morocco	99
United Republic of Tanzania	98	Dominica	98	Turkmenistan	99	Oman	99
Gambia	97	Nicaragua	98	Uzbekistan	99	Qatar	99
Mauritius	97	Saint Vincent and the Grenadines	98	Albania	98	Bahrain	98
Sao Tome and Principe	96	Barbados	97	Austria	98	Iran (Islamic Republic of)	98
Algeria	95	Chile	97	Belgium	98	Saudi Arabia	98
Botswana	95	Brazil	96	Kazakhstan	98	Tunisia	98
Eritrea	95	Cuba	96	Portugal	98	Libya	94
Burundi	94	Bahamas	95	Cyprus	97	United Arab Emirates	94
Cabo Verde	93	Guyana	95	Czechia	97	Egypt	93
Lesotho	93	Uruguay	95	Israel	97	Sudan	93
Namibia	92	Argentina	94	Kyrgyzstan	97	Djibouti	84
Burkina Faso	91	Belize	94	Russian Federation	97	Lebanon	81
Zambia	90	Saint Kitts and Nevis	94	Spain	97	Afghanistan	78
Kenya	89	Paraguay	93	Azerbaijan	96	Pakistan	72
Senegal	89	Costa Rica	92	Greece	96	Yemen	69
Ghana	88	Grenada	92	Poland	96	Iraq	56
Malawi	88	United States of America	92	Slovakia	96	Somalia	42
Togo	88	Colombia	91	Tajikistan	96	Syrian Arab Republic	41
Zimbabwe	87	El Salvador	91	Turkey	96		
Ethiopia	86	Jamaica	91	Ireland	95	**WPR**	
Sierra Leone	86	Peru	90	Malta	95	Brunei Darussalam	99
Cameroon	84	Trinidad and Tobago	90	Andorra	94	China	99
Côte d'Ivoire	83	Suriname	89	Armenia	94	Cook Islands	99
Democratic Republic of the Congo	81	Venezuela (Bolivarian Republic of)	87	Croatia	94	Fiji	99
Comoros	80	Honduras	85	Georgia	94	Malaysia	99
Congo	80	Mexico	82	Latvia	94	Mongolia	99
Gabon	80	Dominican Republic	81	Lithuania	94	Niue	99
Guinea-Bissau	80	Ecuador	78	Netherlands	94	Republic of Korea	98
Mozambique	80	Guatemala	74	Serbia	94	Solomon Islands	98
Benin	79	Panama	73	Italy	93	Viet Nam	97
Uganda	78	Haiti	60	Bulgaria	92	Singapore	96
Mauritania	73	Canada	55	The Former Yugoslav Republic of Macedonia	92	Tuvalu	96
South Africa	71			Estonia	91	Australia	93
Madagascar	69	**SEAR**		Romania	90	New Zealand	92
Mali	68	Bhutan	99	Germany	88	Nauru	91
Niger	65	Maldives	99	Republic of Moldova	88	Palau	90
Angola	64	Sri Lanka	99	France	83	Cambodia	89
Nigeria	56	Thailand	99	Bosnia and Herzegovina	82	Lao People's Democratic Republic	89
Chad	55	Democratic People's Republic of Korea	96	Montenegro	82	Kiribati	87
Liberia	52	Bangladesh	94	San Marino	75	Marshall Islands	85
Guinea	51	Nepal	91	Sweden	53	Tonga	82
Central African Republic	47	India	87	Ukraine	22	Micronesia (Federated States of)	78
South Sudan	31	Indonesia	81	Denmark		Vanuatu	64
Equatorial Guinea	16	Timor-Leste	76	Finland		Papua New Guinea	62
		Myanmar	75	Hungary		Philippines	60
				Iceland		Samoa	59
				Norway		Japan	
				Slovenia			
				Switzerland			
				United Kingdom			

[1] This indicator is used here as a proxy for the SDG indicator. Data source: WHO/UNICEF estimates of national immunization coverage. July 2016 revision (http://www.who.int/immunization/monitoring_surveillance/routine/coverage/en/index4.html, accessed 22 March 2017).

SDG Target 3.3
By 2030, end the epidemics of AIDS, tuberculosis, malaria and neglected tropical diseases and combat hepatitis, water-borne diseases and other communicable diseases

Indicator 3.3.5: Number of people requiring interventions against neglected tropical diseases

Reported number of people requiring interventions against NTDs, 2015[1]

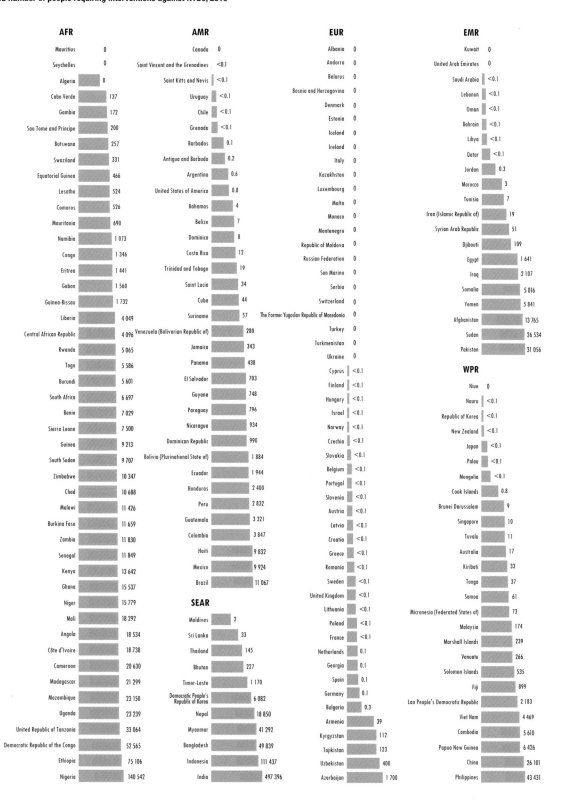

AFR

Mauritius	0
Seychelles	0
Algeria	8
Cabo Verde	137
Gambia	172
Sao Tome and Principe	200
Botswana	257
Swaziland	331
Equatorial Guinea	466
Lesotho	524
Comoros	526
Mauritania	690
Namibia	1 073
Congo	1 346
Eritrea	1 441
Gabon	1 560
Guinea-Bissau	1 732
Liberia	4 049
Central African Republic	4 096
Rwanda	5 065
Togo	5 586
Burundi	5 601
South Africa	6 697
Benin	7 029
Sierra Leone	7 500
Guinea	9 213
South Sudan	9 707
Zimbabwe	10 347
Chad	10 688
Malawi	11 426
Burkina Faso	11 659
Zambia	11 830
Senegal	11 849
Kenya	13 642
Ghana	15 537
Niger	15 779
Mali	18 292
Angola	18 534
Côte d'Ivoire	18 738
Cameroon	20 630
Madagascar	21 299
Mozambique	23 150
Uganda	23 239
United Republic of Tanzania	33 064
Democratic Republic of the Congo	52 565
Ethiopia	75 106
Nigeria	140 542

AMR

Canada	0
Saint Vincent and the Grenadines	<0.1
Saint Kitts and Nevis	<0.1
Uruguay	<0.1
Chile	<0.1
Grenada	<0.1
Barbados	0.1
Antigua and Barbuda	0.2
Argentina	0.6
United States of America	0.8
Bahamas	4
Belize	7
Dominica	8
Costa Rica	12
Trinidad and Tobago	19
Saint Lucia	34
Cuba	44
Suriname	57
Venezuela (Bolivarian Republic of)	280
Jamaica	343
Panama	438
El Salvador	703
Guyana	748
Paraguay	796
Nicaragua	934
Dominican Republic	990
Bolivia (Plurinational State of)	1 884
Ecuador	1 944
Honduras	2 400
Peru	2 832
Guatemala	3 321
Colombia	3 847
Haiti	9 832
Mexico	9 924
Brazil	11 067

SEAR

Maldives	2
Sri Lanka	33
Thailand	145
Bhutan	227
Timor-Leste	1 170
Democratic People's Republic of Korea	6 082
Nepal	18 850
Myanmar	41 292
Bangladesh	49 839
Indonesia	111 437
India	497 396

EUR

Albania	0
Andorra	0
Belarus	0
Bosnia and Herzegovina	0
Denmark	0
Estonia	0
Iceland	0
Ireland	0
Italy	0
Kazakhstan	0
Luxembourg	0
Malta	0
Monaco	0
Montenegro	0
Republic of Moldova	0
Russian Federation	0
San Marino	0
Serbia	0
Switzerland	0
The Former Yugoslav Republic of Macedonia	0
Turkey	0
Turkmenistan	0
Ukraine	0
Cyprus	<0.1
Finland	<0.1
Hungary	<0.1
Israel	<0.1
Norway	<0.1
Czechia	<0.1
Slovakia	<0.1
Belgium	<0.1
Portugal	<0.1
Slovenia	<0.1
Austria	<0.1
Latvia	<0.1
Croatia	<0.1
Greece	<0.1
Romania	<0.1
Sweden	<0.1
United Kingdom	<0.1
Lithuania	<0.1
Poland	<0.1
France	<0.1
Netherlands	0.1
Georgia	0.1
Spain	0.1
Germany	0.1
Bulgaria	0.3
Armenia	39
Kyrgyzstan	112
Tajikistan	123
Uzbekistan	400
Azerbaijan	1 700

EMR

Kuwait	0
United Arab Emirates	0
Saudi Arabia	<0.1
Lebanon	<0.1
Oman	<0.1
Bahrain	<0.1
Libya	<0.1
Qatar	<0.1
Jordan	0.3
Morocco	3
Tunisia	7
Iran (Islamic Republic of)	19
Syrian Arab Republic	51
Djibouti	109
Egypt	1 641
Iraq	2 107
Somalia	5 016
Yemen	5 841
Afghanistan	13 765
Sudan	26 534
Pakistan	31 056

WPR

Niue	0
Nauru	<0.1
Republic of Korea	<0.1
New Zealand	<0.1
Japan	<0.1
Palau	<0.1
Mongolia	<0.1
Cook Islands	0.8
Brunei Darussalam	9
Singapore	10
Tuvalu	11
Australia	17
Kiribati	33
Tonga	37
Samoa	61
Micronesia (Federated States of)	73
Malaysia	174
Marshall Islands	239
Vanuatu	266
Solomon Islands	535
Fiji	899
Lao People's Democratic Republic	2 183
Viet Nam	4 469
Cambodia	5 610
Papua New Guinea	6 426
China	26 101
Philippines	43 431

[1] Scale of bars is logarithmic. The value shown is the number of people requiring interventions against NTDs in thousands. Neglected tropical diseases [online database]. Global Health Observatory (GHO) data. Geneva: World Health Organization (http://www.who.int/gho/neglected_diseases/en/).

MORTALITY DUE TO NONCOMMUNICABLE DISEASES

SDG Target 3.4
By 2030, reduce by one third premature mortality from noncommunicable diseases through prevention and treatment and promote mental health and well-being

Indicator 3.4.1: Mortality rate attributed to cardiovascular disease, cancer, diabetes or chronic respiratory disease

Probability of dying from any of cardiovascular disease, cancer, diabetes, chronic respiratory disease between age 30 and exact age 70 (%), 2015[1]

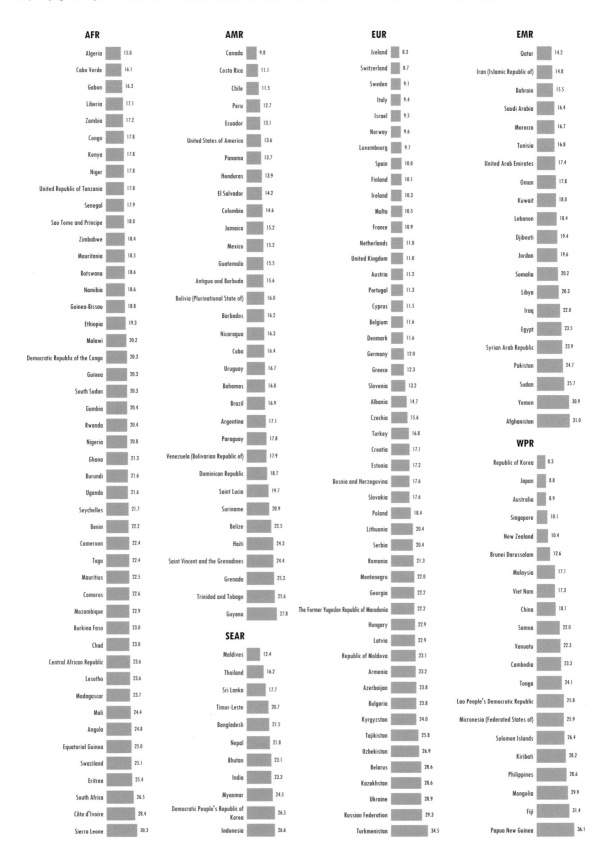

AFR

Algeria	15.0
Cabo Verde	16.1
Gabon	16.3
Liberia	17.1
Zambia	17.2
Congo	17.8
Kenya	17.8
Niger	17.8
United Republic of Tanzania	17.8
Senegal	17.9
Sao Tome and Principe	18.0
Zimbabwe	18.4
Mauritania	18.5
Botswana	18.6
Namibia	18.6
Guinea-Bissau	18.8
Ethiopia	19.3
Malawi	20.2
Democratic Republic of the Congo	20.3
Guinea	20.3
South Sudan	20.3
Gambia	20.4
Rwanda	20.4
Nigeria	20.8
Ghana	21.3
Burundi	21.6
Uganda	21.6
Seychelles	21.7
Benin	22.2
Cameroon	22.4
Togo	22.4
Mauritius	22.5
Comoros	22.6
Mozambique	22.9
Burkina Faso	23.0
Chad	23.0
Central African Republic	23.6
Lesotho	23.6
Madagascar	23.7
Mali	24.4
Angola	24.8
Equatorial Guinea	25.0
Swaziland	25.1
Eritrea	25.4
South Africa	26.5
Côte d'Ivoire	28.4
Sierra Leone	30.3

AMR

Canada	9.8
Costa Rica	11.1
Chile	11.5
Peru	12.7
Ecuador	13.1
United States of America	13.6
Panama	13.7
Honduras	13.9
El Salvador	14.2
Colombia	14.6
Jamaica	15.2
Mexico	15.2
Guatemala	15.5
Antigua and Barbuda	15.6
Bolivia (Plurinational State of)	16.0
Barbados	16.2
Nicaragua	16.3
Cuba	16.4
Uruguay	16.7
Bahamas	16.8
Brazil	16.9
Argentina	17.1
Paraguay	17.8
Venezuela (Bolivarian Republic of)	17.9
Dominican Republic	18.7
Saint Lucia	19.7
Suriname	20.9
Belize	22.5
Haiti	24.3
Saint Vincent and the Grenadines	24.4
Grenada	25.3
Trinidad and Tobago	25.6
Guyana	27.8

SEAR

Maldives	12.4
Thailand	16.2
Sri Lanka	17.7
Timor-Leste	20.7
Bangladesh	21.5
Nepal	21.8
Bhutan	23.1
India	23.3
Myanmar	24.5
Democratic People's Republic of Korea	26.5
Indonesia	26.6

EUR

Iceland	8.3
Switzerland	8.7
Sweden	9.1
Italy	9.4
Israel	9.5
Norway	9.6
Luxembourg	9.7
Spain	10.0
Finland	10.1
Ireland	10.3
Malta	10.5
France	10.9
Netherlands	11.0
United Kingdom	11.0
Austria	11.2
Portugal	11.3
Cyprus	11.5
Belgium	11.6
Denmark	11.6
Germany	12.0
Greece	12.3
Slovenia	13.2
Albania	14.7
Czechia	15.6
Turkey	16.8
Croatia	17.1
Estonia	17.2
Bosnia and Herzegovina	17.6
Slovakia	17.6
Poland	18.4
Lithuania	20.4
Serbia	20.4
Romania	21.3
Montenegro	22.0
Georgia	22.2
The Former Yugoslav Republic of Macedonia	22.2
Hungary	22.9
Latvia	22.9
Republic of Moldova	23.1
Armenia	23.2
Azerbaijan	23.8
Bulgaria	23.8
Kyrgyzstan	24.0
Tajikistan	25.8
Uzbekistan	26.9
Belarus	28.6
Kazakhstan	28.6
Ukraine	28.9
Russian Federation	29.3
Turkmenistan	34.5

EMR

Qatar	14.2
Iran (Islamic Republic of)	14.8
Bahrain	15.5
Saudi Arabia	16.4
Morocco	16.7
Tunisia	16.8
United Arab Emirates	17.4
Oman	17.8
Kuwait	18.0
Lebanon	18.4
Djibouti	19.4
Jordan	19.6
Somalia	20.2
Libya	20.3
Iraq	22.0
Egypt	23.5
Syrian Arab Republic	23.9
Pakistan	24.7
Sudan	25.7
Yemen	30.9
Afghanistan	31.0

WPR

Republic of Korea	8.3
Japan	8.8
Australia	8.9
Singapore	10.1
New Zealand	10.4
Brunei Darussalam	12.6
Malaysia	17.1
Viet Nam	17.3
China	18.1
Samoa	22.0
Vanuatu	22.3
Cambodia	23.3
Tonga	24.1
Lao People's Democratic Republic	25.8
Micronesia (Federated States of)	25.9
Solomon Islands	26.4
Kiribati	28.2
Philippines	28.6
Mongolia	29.9
Fiji	31.4
Papua New Guinea	36.1

[1] Global Health Estimates 2015: Deaths by cause, age, sex, by country and by region, 2000–2015. Geneva: World Health Organization; 2016 (http://www.who.int/healthinfo/global_burden_disease/estimates/en/index1.html, accessed 22 March 2017). WHO Member States with a population of less than 90 000 in 2015 were not included in this analysis.

SUICIDE MORTALITY RATE

SDG Target 3.4
By 2030, reduce by one third premature mortality from noncommunicable diseases through prevention and treatment and promote mental health and well-being

Indicator 3.4.2: Suicide mortality rate

Suicide mortality rate (per 100 000 population), 2015[1]

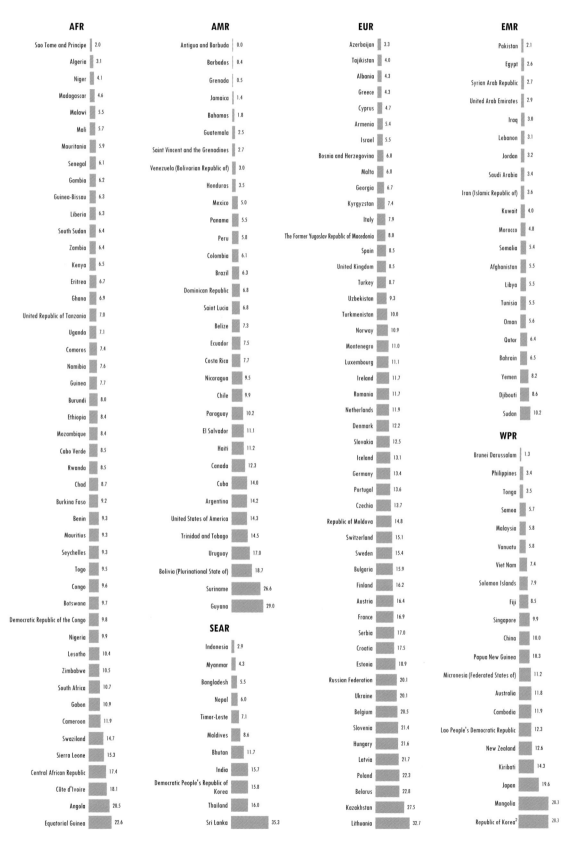

AFR

Sao Tome and Principe	2.0
Algeria	3.1
Niger	4.1
Madagascar	4.6
Malawi	5.5
Mali	5.7
Mauritania	5.9
Senegal	6.1
Gambia	6.2
Guinea-Bissau	6.3
Liberia	6.3
South Sudan	6.4
Zambia	6.4
Kenya	6.5
Eritrea	6.7
Ghana	6.9
United Republic of Tanzania	7.0
Uganda	7.1
Comoros	7.4
Namibia	7.6
Guinea	7.7
Burundi	8.0
Ethiopia	8.4
Mozambique	8.4
Cabo Verde	8.5
Rwanda	8.5
Chad	8.7
Burkina Faso	9.2
Benin	9.3
Mauritius	9.3
Seychelles	9.3
Togo	9.5
Congo	9.6
Botswana	9.7
Democratic Republic of the Congo	9.8
Nigeria	9.9
Lesotho	10.4
Zimbabwe	10.5
South Africa	10.7
Gabon	10.9
Cameroon	11.9
Swaziland	14.7
Sierra Leone	15.3
Central African Republic	17.4
Côte d'Ivoire	18.1
Angola	20.5
Equatorial Guinea	22.6

AMR

Antigua and Barbuda	0.0
Barbados	0.4
Grenada	0.5
Jamaica	1.4
Bahamas	1.8
Guatemala	2.5
Saint Vincent and the Grenadines	2.7
Venezuela (Bolivarian Republic of)	3.0
Honduras	3.5
Mexico	5.0
Panama	5.5
Peru	5.8
Colombia	6.1
Brazil	6.3
Dominican Republic	6.8
Saint Lucia	6.8
Belize	7.3
Ecuador	7.5
Costa Rica	7.7
Nicaragua	9.5
Chile	9.9
Paraguay	10.2
El Salvador	11.1
Haiti	11.2
Canada	12.3
Cuba	14.0
Argentina	14.2
United States of America	14.3
Trinidad and Tobago	14.5
Uruguay	17.0
Bolivia (Plurinational State of)	18.7
Suriname	26.6
Guyana	29.0

SEAR

Indonesia	2.9
Myanmar	4.3
Bangladesh	5.5
Nepal	6.0
Timor-Leste	7.1
Maldives	8.6
Bhutan	11.7
India	15.7
Democratic People's Republic of Korea	15.8
Thailand	16.0
Sri Lanka	35.3

EUR

Azerbaijan	3.3
Tajikistan	4.0
Albania	4.3
Greece	4.3
Cyprus	4.7
Armenia	5.4
Israel	5.5
Bosnia and Herzegovina	6.0
Malta	6.0
Georgia	6.7
Kyrgyzstan	7.4
Italy	7.9
The Former Yugoslav Republic of Macedonia	8.0
Spain	8.5
United Kingdom	8.5
Turkey	8.7
Uzbekistan	9.3
Turkmenistan	10.0
Norway	10.9
Montenegro	11.0
Luxembourg	11.1
Ireland	11.7
Romania	11.7
Netherlands	11.9
Denmark	12.2
Slovakia	12.5
Iceland	13.1
Germany	13.4
Portugal	13.6
Czechia	13.7
Republic of Moldova	14.8
Switzerland	15.1
Sweden	15.4
Bulgaria	15.9
Finland	16.2
Austria	16.4
France	16.9
Serbia	17.0
Croatia	17.5
Estonia	18.9
Russian Federation	20.1
Ukraine	20.1
Belgium	20.5
Slovenia	21.4
Hungary	21.6
Latvia	21.7
Poland	22.3
Belarus	22.8
Kazakhstan	27.5
Lithuania	32.7

EMR

Pakistan	2.1
Egypt	2.6
Syrian Arab Republic	2.7
United Arab Emirates	2.9
Iraq	3.0
Lebanon	3.1
Jordan	3.2
Saudi Arabia	3.4
Iran (Islamic Republic of)	3.6
Kuwait	4.0
Morocco	4.8
Somalia	5.4
Afghanistan	5.5
Libya	5.5
Tunisia	5.5
Oman	5.6
Qatar	6.4
Bahrain	6.5
Yemen	8.2
Djibouti	8.6
Sudan	10.2

WPR

Brunei Darussalam	1.3
Philippines	3.4
Tonga	3.5
Samoa	5.7
Malaysia	5.8
Vanuatu	5.8
Viet Nam	7.4
Solomon Islands	7.9
Fiji	8.5
Singapore	9.9
China	10.0
Papua New Guinea	10.3
Micronesia (Federated States of)	11.2
Australia	11.8
Cambodia	11.9
Lao People's Democratic Republic	12.3
New Zealand	12.6
Kiribati	14.3
Japan	19.6
Mongolia	28.3
Republic of Korea[2]	28.3

[1] Global Health Estimates 2015: Deaths by cause, age, sex, by country and by region, 2000–2015. Geneva: World Health Organization; 2016 (http://www.who.int/healthinfo/global_burden_disease/estimates/en/index1.html, accessed 22 March 2017). WHO Member States with a population of less than 90 000 in 2015 were not included in this analysis.

[2] The estimate of total suicide mortality for the Republic of Korea has been updated using data published in the WHO Mortality Database after the closure date for the Global Health Estimates 2015.

ALCOHOL USE

SDG Target 3.5
Strengthen the prevention and treatment of substance abuse, including narcotic drug abuse and harmful use of alcohol

Indicator 3.5.2: Harmful use of alcohol, defined according to the national context as alcohol per capita consumption (aged 15 years and older) within a calendar year in litres of pure alcohol

Total alcohol per capita (≥ 15 years of age) consumption (litres of pure alcohol), projected estimates, 2016[1]

AFR

Mauritania	0.1
Comoros	0.2
Niger	0.5
Senegal	0.5
Guinea	0.8
Algeria	1.0
Eritrea	1.2
Mali	1.2
Madagascar	1.8
Mozambique	2.3
Malawi	2.4
Benin	2.6
Togo	2.6
Democratic Republic of the Congo	3.0
Central African Republic	3.8
Zambia	3.9
Mauritius	4.0
Ghana	4.4
Kenya	4.4
Ethiopia	4.6
Gambia	5.0
Chad	5.2
Côte d'Ivoire	5.2
Guinea-Bissau	5.4
Liberia	5.4
Lesotho	5.7
Sierra Leone	5.7
Swaziland	6.0
United Republic of Tanzania	6.3
Burundi	6.9
Burkina Faso	7.6
Congo	7.9
Botswana	8.2
Cabo Verde	8.2
Zimbabwe	8.5
Sao Tome and Principe	8.8
Nigeria	9.1
Cameroon	9.9
Angola	10.8
Gabon	10.8
Seychelles	10.8
South Africa	11.2
Rwanda	11.5
Equatorial Guinea	11.6
Namibia	11.8
Uganda	11.8
South Sudan	

AMR

Guatemala	3.1
El Salvador	3.4
Honduras	3.8
Costa Rica	4.1
Dominica	5.0
Ecuador	5.1
Nicaragua	5.1
Colombia	5.2
Antigua and Barbuda	5.4
Bahamas	5.4
Cuba	5.4
Jamaica	5.5
Bolivia (Plurinational State of)	5.9
Haiti	6.3
Paraguay	6.3
Dominican Republic	6.6
Uruguay	6.8
Saint Kitts and Nevis	6.9
Mexico	7.1
Venezuela (Bolivarian Republic of)	7.1
Saint Lucia	7.6
Saint Vincent and the Grenadines	7.6
Barbados	7.8
Panama	7.9
Trinidad and Tobago	7.9
Suriname	8.0
Grenada	8.1
Belize	8.2
Guyana	8.7
Brazil	8.9
Peru	8.9
Chile	9.0
Argentina	9.1
United States of America	9.3
Canada	10.0

SEAR

Bangladesh	0.2
Bhutan	0.5
Indonesia	0.6
Timor-Leste	1.0
Maldives	1.7
Myanmar	2.2
Nepal	2.5
Democratic People's Republic of Korea	3.9
Sri Lanka	4.1
India	5.0
Thailand	7.2

EUR

Turkey	1.9
The Former Yugoslav Republic of Macedonia	2.8
Tajikistan	2.9
Israel	3.0
Azerbaijan	4.0
Uzbekistan	5.1
Armenia	5.4
Kyrgyzstan	5.5
Turkmenistan	5.5
Albania	5.7
Bosnia and Herzegovina	5.9
Iceland	7.5
Malta	7.5
Italy	7.6
Norway	7.8
Georgia	8.1
Greece	8.5
Kazakhstan	8.7
Netherlands	8.7
Sweden	8.8
Spain	9.2
Cyprus	9.3
Montenegro	9.6
Switzerland	10.0
Denmark	10.1
Andorra	10.5
Austria	10.6
Portugal	10.6
Finland	10.9
Ireland	10.9
Luxembourg	11.1
Slovenia	11.3
Germany	11.4
France	11.7
Serbia	11.8
Hungary	12.3
Latvia	12.3
Poland	12.3
Slovakia	12.3
United Kingdom	12.3
Estonia	12.8
Ukraine	12.8
Belgium	13.2
Bulgaria	13.6
Croatia	13.6
Czechia	13.7
Romania	13.7
Russian Federation	13.9
Republic of Moldova	15.9
Belarus	16.4
Lithuania	18.2
Monaco	
San Marino	

EMR

Libya	0.1
Kuwait	0.2
Pakistan	0.2
Saudi Arabia	0.2
Yemen	0.2
Djibouti	0.4
Egypt	0.4
Iraq	0.4
Afghanistan	0.5
Jordan	0.5
Oman	0.5
Somalia	0.5
Morocco	0.8
Syrian Arab Republic	0.8
Bahrain	0.9
Iran (Islamic Republic of)	1.0
Qatar	1.0
Lebanon	1.6
Tunisia	1.6
United Arab Emirates	3.0
Sudan	3.3

WPR

Brunei Darussalam	1.3
Vanuatu	1.3
Solomon Islands	1.4
Tonga	1.4
Malaysia	1.5
Singapore	1.9
Tuvalu	1.9
Micronesia (Federated States of)	2.4
Papua New Guinea	2.4
Kiribati	2.7
Samoa	2.8
Fiji	3.3
Nauru	3.6
Cook Islands	5.1
Cambodia	5.3
Philippines	5.6
Niue	7.1
Lao People's Democratic Republic	7.3
China	7.8
Japan	7.8
Mongolia	7.8
Viet Nam	8.6
New Zealand	10.1
Australia	11.2
Republic of Korea	11.9
Marshall Islands	
Palau	

[1] WHO Global Information System on Alcohol and Health (GISAH) [online database]. Geneva: World Health Organization (http://www.who.int/gho/alcohol/en/).

DEATHS FROM ROAD TRAFFIC INJURIES

SDG Target 3.6
By 2020, halve the number of global deaths and injuries from road traffic accidents

Indicator 3.6.1: Death rate due to road traffic injuries

Road traffic mortality rate (per 100 000 population), 2013[1]

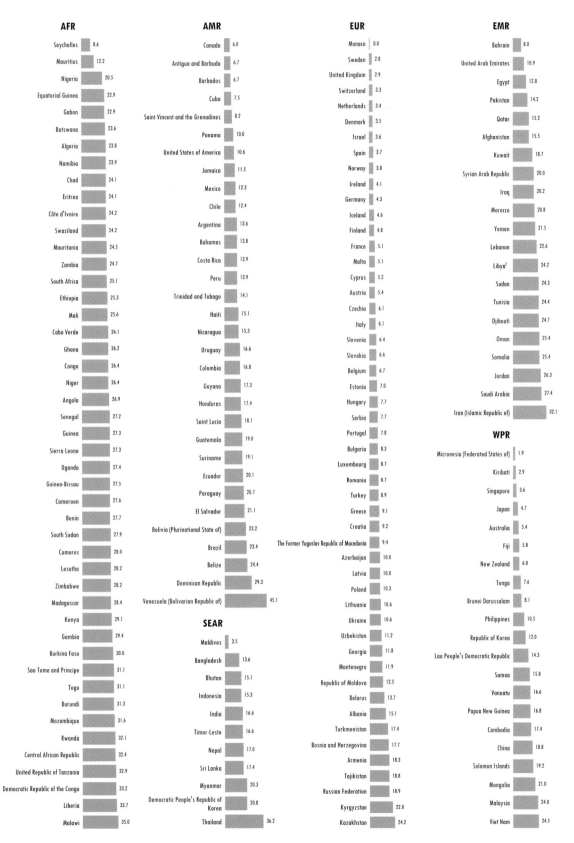

AFR

Country	Rate
Seychelles	8.6
Mauritius	12.2
Nigeria	20.5
Equatorial Guinea	22.9
Gabon	22.9
Botswana	23.6
Algeria	23.8
Namibia	23.9
Chad	24.1
Eritrea	24.1
Côte d'Ivoire	24.2
Swaziland	24.2
Mauritania	24.5
Zambia	24.7
South Africa	25.1
Ethiopia	25.3
Mali	25.6
Cabo Verde	26.1
Ghana	26.2
Congo	26.4
Niger	26.4
Angola	26.9
Senegal	27.2
Guinea	27.3
Sierra Leone	27.3
Uganda	27.4
Guinea-Bissau	27.5
Cameroon	27.6
Benin	27.7
South Sudan	27.9
Comoros	28.0
Lesotho	28.2
Zimbabwe	28.2
Madagascar	28.4
Kenya	29.1
Gambia	29.4
Burkina Faso	30.0
Sao Tome and Principe	31.1
Togo	31.1
Burundi	31.3
Mozambique	31.6
Rwanda	32.1
Central African Republic	32.4
United Republic of Tanzania	32.9
Democratic Republic of the Congo	33.2
Liberia	33.7
Malawi	35.0

AMR

Country	Rate
Canada	6.0
Antigua and Barbuda	6.7
Barbados	6.7
Cuba	7.5
Saint Vincent and the Grenadines	8.2
Panama	10.0
United States of America	10.6
Jamaica	11.5
Mexico	12.3
Chile	12.4
Argentina	13.6
Bahamas	13.8
Costa Rica	13.9
Peru	13.9
Trinidad and Tobago	14.1
Haiti	15.1
Nicaragua	15.3
Uruguay	16.6
Colombia	16.8
Guyana	17.3
Honduras	17.4
Saint Lucia	18.1
Guatemala	19.0
Suriname	19.1
Ecuador	20.1
Paraguay	20.7
El Salvador	21.1
Bolivia (Plurinational State of)	23.2
Brazil	23.4
Belize	24.4
Dominican Republic	29.3
Venezuela (Bolivarian Republic of)	45.1

SEAR

Country	Rate
Maldives	3.5
Bangladesh	13.6
Bhutan	15.1
Indonesia	15.3
India	16.6
Timor-Leste	16.6
Nepal	17.0
Sri Lanka	17.4
Myanmar	20.3
Democratic People's Republic of Korea	20.8
Thailand	36.2

EUR

Country	Rate
Monaco	0.0
Sweden	2.8
United Kingdom	2.9
Switzerland	3.3
Netherlands	3.4
Denmark	3.5
Israel	3.6
Spain	3.7
Norway	3.8
Ireland	4.1
Germany	4.3
Iceland	4.6
Finland	4.8
France	5.1
Malta	5.1
Cyprus	5.2
Austria	5.4
Czechia	6.1
Italy	6.1
Slovenia	6.4
Slovakia	6.6
Belgium	6.7
Estonia	7.0
Hungary	7.7
Serbia	7.7
Portugal	7.8
Bulgaria	8.3
Luxembourg	8.7
Romania	8.7
Turkey	8.9
Greece	9.1
Croatia	9.2
The Former Yugoslav Republic of Macedonia	9.4
Azerbaijan	10.0
Latvia	10.0
Poland	10.3
Lithuania	10.6
Ukraine	10.6
Uzbekistan	11.2
Georgia	11.8
Montenegro	11.9
Republic of Moldova	12.5
Belarus	13.7
Albania	15.1
Turkmenistan	17.4
Bosnia and Herzegovina	17.7
Armenia	18.3
Tajikistan	18.8
Russian Federation	18.9
Kyrgyzstan	22.0
Kazakhstan	24.2

EMR

Country	Rate
Bahrain	8.0
United Arab Emirates	10.9
Egypt	12.8
Pakistan	14.2
Qatar	15.2
Afghanistan	15.5
Kuwait	18.7
Syrian Arab Republic	20.0
Iraq	20.2
Morocco	20.8
Yemen	21.5
Lebanon	22.6
Libya[2]	24.2
Sudan	24.3
Tunisia	24.4
Djibouti	24.7
Oman	25.4
Somalia	25.4
Jordan	26.3
Saudi Arabia	27.4
Iran (Islamic Republic of)	32.1

WPR

Country	Rate
Micronesia (Federated States of)	1.9
Kiribati	2.9
Singapore	3.6
Japan	4.7
Australia	5.4
Fiji	5.8
New Zealand	6.0
Tonga	7.6
Brunei Darussalam	8.1
Philippines	10.5
Republic of Korea	12.0
Lao People's Democratic Republic	14.3
Samoa	15.8
Vanuatu	16.6
Papua New Guinea	16.8
Cambodia	17.4
China	18.8
Solomon Islands	19.2
Mongolia	21.0
Malaysia	24.0
Viet Nam	24.5

[1] Global status report on road safety 2015. Geneva: World Health Organization; 2015 (http://www.who.int/violence_injury_prevention/road_safety_status/2015/en/, accessed 22 March 2017). WHO Member States with a population of less than 90 000 in 2015 who did not participate in the survey used to produce the report were not included in the analysis.

[2] Estimate from Global Health Estimates 2015: Deaths by cause, age, sex, by country and by region, 2000–2015. Geneva: World Health Organization; 2016 (http://www.who.int/healthinfo/global_burden_disease/estimates/en/index1.html, accessed 22 March 2017).

SDG Target 3.7
By 2030, ensure universal access to sexual and reproductive health-care services, including for family planning, information and education, and the integration of reproductive health into national strategies and programmes

Indicator 3.7.1: Proportion of women of reproductive age (aged 15–49 years) who have their need for family planning satisfied with modern methods

Proportion of married or in-union women of reproductive age who have their need for family planning satisfied with modern methods (%), 2005–2015[1]

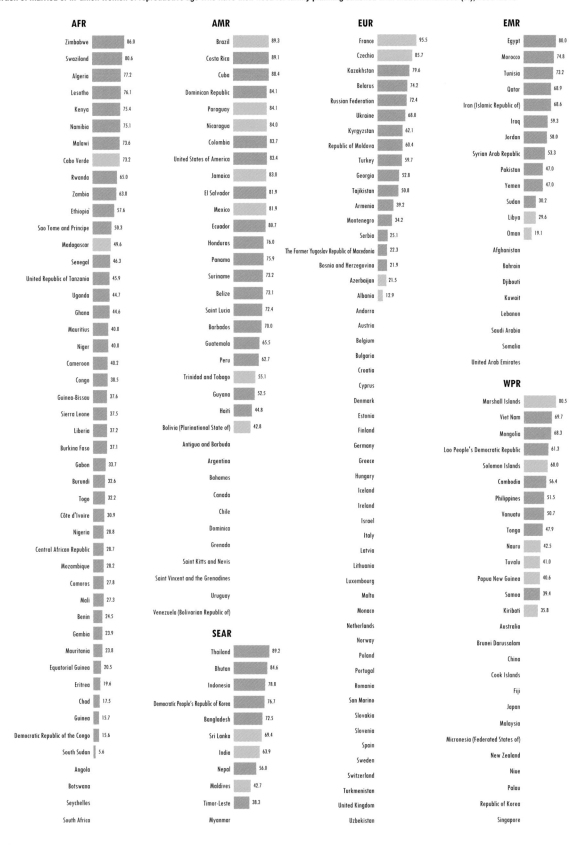

AFR

Zimbabwe	86.0
Swaziland	80.6
Algeria	77.2
Lesotho	76.1
Kenya	75.4
Namibia	75.1
Malawi	73.6
Cabo Verde	73.2
Rwanda	65.0
Zambia	63.8
Ethiopia	57.6
Sao Tome and Principe	50.3
Madagascar	49.6
Senegal	46.3
United Republic of Tanzania	45.9
Uganda	44.7
Ghana	44.6
Mauritius	40.8
Niger	40.8
Cameroon	40.2
Congo	38.5
Guinea-Bissau	37.6
Sierra Leone	37.5
Liberia	37.2
Burkina Faso	37.1
Gabon	33.7
Burundi	32.6
Togo	32.2
Côte d'Ivoire	30.9
Nigeria	28.8
Central African Republic	28.7
Mozambique	28.2
Comoros	27.8
Mali	27.3
Benin	24.5
Gambia	23.9
Mauritania	23.8
Equatorial Guinea	20.5
Eritrea	19.6
Chad	17.5
Guinea	15.7
Democratic Republic of the Congo	15.6
South Sudan	5.6
Angola	
Botswana	
Seychelles	
South Africa	

AMR

Brazil	89.3
Costa Rica	89.1
Cuba	88.4
Dominican Republic	84.1
Paraguay	84.1
Nicaragua	84.0
Colombia	83.7
United States of America	83.4
Jamaica	83.0
El Salvador	81.9
Mexico	81.9
Ecuador	80.7
Honduras	76.0
Panama	75.9
Suriname	73.2
Belize	73.1
Saint Lucia	72.4
Barbados	70.0
Guatemala	65.5
Peru	62.7
Trinidad and Tobago	55.1
Guyana	52.5
Haiti	44.8
Bolivia (Plurinational State of)	42.8
Antigua and Barbuda	
Argentina	
Bahamas	
Canada	
Chile	
Dominica	
Grenada	
Saint Kitts and Nevis	
Saint Vincent and the Grenadines	
Uruguay	
Venezuela (Bolivarian Republic of)	

SEAR

Thailand	89.2
Bhutan	84.6
Indonesia	78.8
Democratic People's Republic of Korea	76.7
Bangladesh	72.5
Sri Lanka	69.4
India	63.9
Nepal	56.0
Maldives	42.7
Timor-Leste	38.3
Myanmar	

EUR

France	95.5
Czechia	85.7
Kazakhstan	79.6
Belarus	74.2
Russian Federation	72.4
Ukraine	68.0
Kyrgyzstan	62.1
Republic of Moldova	60.4
Turkey	59.7
Georgia	52.8
Tajikistan	50.8
Armenia	39.2
Montenegro	34.2
Serbia	25.1
The Former Yugoslav Republic of Macedonia	22.3
Bosnia and Herzegovina	21.9
Azerbaijan	21.5
Albania	12.9
Andorra	
Austria	
Belgium	
Bulgaria	
Croatia	
Cyprus	
Denmark	
Estonia	
Finland	
Germany	
Greece	
Hungary	
Iceland	
Ireland	
Israel	
Italy	
Latvia	
Lithuania	
Luxembourg	
Malta	
Monaco	
Netherlands	
Norway	
Poland	
Portugal	
Romania	
San Marino	
Slovakia	
Slovenia	
Spain	
Sweden	
Switzerland	
Turkmenistan	
United Kingdom	
Uzbekistan	

EMR

Egypt	80.0
Morocco	74.8
Tunisia	73.2
Qatar	68.9
Iran (Islamic Republic of)	68.6
Iraq	59.3
Jordan	58.0
Syrian Arab Republic	53.3
Pakistan	47.0
Yemen	47.0
Sudan	30.2
Libya	29.6
Oman	19.1
Afghanistan	
Bahrain	
Djibouti	
Kuwait	
Lebanon	
Saudi Arabia	
Somalia	
United Arab Emirates	

WPR

Marshall Islands	80.5
Viet Nam	69.7
Mongolia	68.3
Lao People's Democratic Republic	61.3
Solomon Islands	60.0
Cambodia	56.4
Philippines	51.5
Vanuatu	50.7
Tonga	47.9
Nauru	42.5
Tuvalu	41.0
Papua New Guinea	40.6
Samoa	39.4
Kiribati	35.8
Australia	
Brunei Darussalam	
China	
Cook Islands	
Fiji	
Japan	
Malaysia	
Micronesia (Federated States of)	
New Zealand	
Niue	
Palau	
Republic of Korea	
Singapore	

[1] World Contraceptive Use 2016 [online database]. New York (NY): United Nations, Department of Economic and Social Affairs, Population Division; 2016. Data shown are the latest available for 2005–2015. Data from 2005–2009 are shown in pale orange.

ADOLESCENT BIRTH RATE

SDG Target 3.7
By 2030, ensure universal access to sexual and reproductive health-care services, including for family planning, information and education, and the integration of reproductive health into national strategies and programmes

Indicator 3.7.2: Adolescent birth rate (aged 10–14 years; aged 15–19 years) per 1000 women in that age group

Adolescent birth rate (per 1000 women aged 15–19 years), 2005–2014[1]

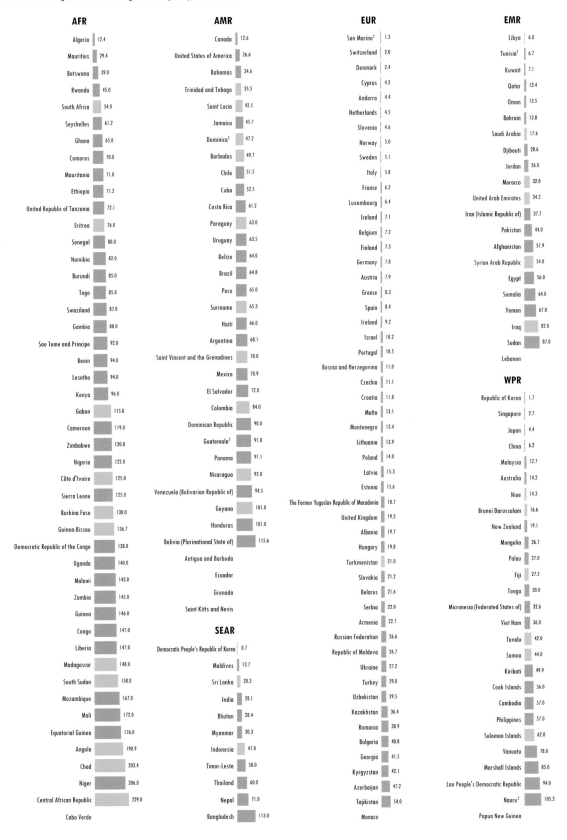

AFR

Country	Rate
Algeria	12.4
Mauritius	29.4
Botswana	39.0
Rwanda	45.0
South Africa	54.0
Seychelles	61.2
Ghana	65.0
Comoros	70.0
Mauritania	71.0
Ethiopia	71.2
United Republic of Tanzania	72.1
Eritrea	76.0
Senegal	80.0
Namibia	82.0
Burundi	85.0
Togo	85.0
Swaziland	87.0
Gambia	88.0
Sao Tome and Principe	92.0
Benin	94.0
Lesotho	94.0
Kenya	96.0
Gabon	115.0
Cameroon	119.0
Zimbabwe	120.0
Nigeria	122.0
Côte d'Ivoire	125.0
Sierra Leone	125.0
Burkina Faso	130.0
Guinea-Bissau	136.7
Democratic Republic of the Congo	138.0
Uganda	140.0
Malawi	143.0
Zambia	145.0
Guinea	146.0
Congo	147.0
Liberia	147.0
Madagascar	148.0
South Sudan	158.0
Mozambique	167.0
Mali	172.0
Equatorial Guinea	176.0
Angola	190.9
Chad	203.4
Niger	206.0
Central African Republic	229.0
Cabo Verde	

AMR

Country	Rate
Canada	12.6
United States of America	26.6
Bahamas	34.6
Trinidad and Tobago	35.5
Saint Lucia	42.5
Jamaica	45.7
Dominica[2]	47.2
Barbados	49.7
Chile	51.5
Cuba	52.5
Costa Rica	61.2
Paraguay	63.0
Uruguay	63.5
Belize	64.0
Brazil	64.8
Peru	65.0
Suriname	65.3
Haiti	66.0
Argentina	68.1
Saint Vincent and the Grenadines	70.0
Mexico	70.9
El Salvador	72.0
Colombia	84.0
Dominican Republic	90.0
Guatemala[2]	91.0
Panama	91.1
Nicaragua	92.0
Venezuela (Bolivarian Republic of)	94.5
Guyana	101.0
Honduras	101.0
Bolivia (Plurinational State of)	115.6
Antigua and Barbuda	
Ecuador	
Grenada	
Saint Kitts and Nevis	

SEAR

Country	Rate
Democratic People's Republic of Korea	0.7
Maldives	13.7
Sri Lanka	20.3
India	28.1
Bhutan	28.4
Myanmar	30.3
Indonesia	47.0
Timor-Leste	50.0
Thailand	60.0
Nepal	71.0
Bangladesh	113.0

EUR

Country	Rate
San Marino[2]	1.3
Switzerland	2.0
Denmark	2.4
Cyprus	4.2
Andorra	4.4
Netherlands	4.5
Slovenia	4.6
Norway	5.0
Sweden	5.1
Italy	5.8
France	6.2
Luxembourg	6.4
Iceland	7.1
Belgium	7.2
Finland	7.3
Germany	7.8
Austria	7.9
Greece	8.3
Spain	8.4
Ireland	9.2
Israel	10.2
Portugal	10.5
Bosnia and Herzegovina	11.0
Czechia	11.1
Croatia	11.8
Malta	13.1
Montenegro	13.4
Lithuania	13.9
Poland	14.0
Latvia	15.3
Estonia	15.6
The Former Yugoslav Republic of Macedonia	18.7
United Kingdom	19.3
Albania	19.7
Hungary	19.8
Turkmenistan	21.0
Slovakia	21.2
Belarus	21.6
Serbia	22.0
Armenia	22.7
Russian Federation	26.6
Republic of Moldova	26.7
Ukraine	27.2
Turkey	29.0
Uzbekistan	29.5
Kazakhstan	36.4
Romania	38.9
Bulgaria	40.8
Georgia	41.5
Kyrgyzstan	42.1
Azerbaijan	47.2
Tajikistan	54.0
Monaco	

EMR

Country	Rate
Libya	6.0
Tunisia[2]	6.7
Kuwait	7.1
Qatar	13.4
Oman	13.5
Bahrain	13.8
Saudi Arabia	17.6
Djibouti	20.6
Jordan	26.0
Morocco	32.0
United Arab Emirates	34.2
Iran (Islamic Republic of)	37.7
Pakistan	44.0
Afghanistan	51.9
Syrian Arab Republic	54.0
Egypt	56.0
Somalia	64.0
Yemen	67.0
Iraq	82.0
Sudan	87.0
Lebanon	

WPR

Country	Rate
Republic of Korea	1.7
Singapore	2.7
Japan	4.4
China	6.2
Malaysia	12.7
Australia	14.2
Niue	14.3
Brunei Darussalam	16.6
New Zealand	19.1
Mongolia	26.7
Palau	27.0
Fiji	27.5
Tonga	30.0
Micronesia (Federated States of)	32.6
Viet Nam	36.0
Tuvalu	42.0
Samoa	44.0
Kiribati	49.9
Cook Islands	56.0
Cambodia	57.0
Philippines	57.0
Solomon Islands	62.0
Vanuatu	78.0
Marshall Islands	85.0
Lao People's Democratic Republic	94.0
Nauru[2]	105.3
Papua New Guinea	

[1] World Fertility Data 2015 [online database]. New York (NY): United Nations, Department of Economic and Social Affairs, Population Division; 2015 (http://www.un.org/en/development/desa/population/publications/dataset/fertility/wfd2015.shtml). Data shown are the latest available for 2005–2014. Data from 2005–2009 are shown in pale orange.

[2] Updated estimate.

MORTALITY DUE TO AIR POLLUTION

SDG Target 3.9
By 2030, substantially reduce the number of deaths and illnesses from hazardous chemicals and air, water and soil pollution and contamination

Indicator 3.9.1: Mortality rate attributed to household and ambient air pollution

Mortality rate attributed to household and ambient air pollution (per 100 000 population), 2012[1]

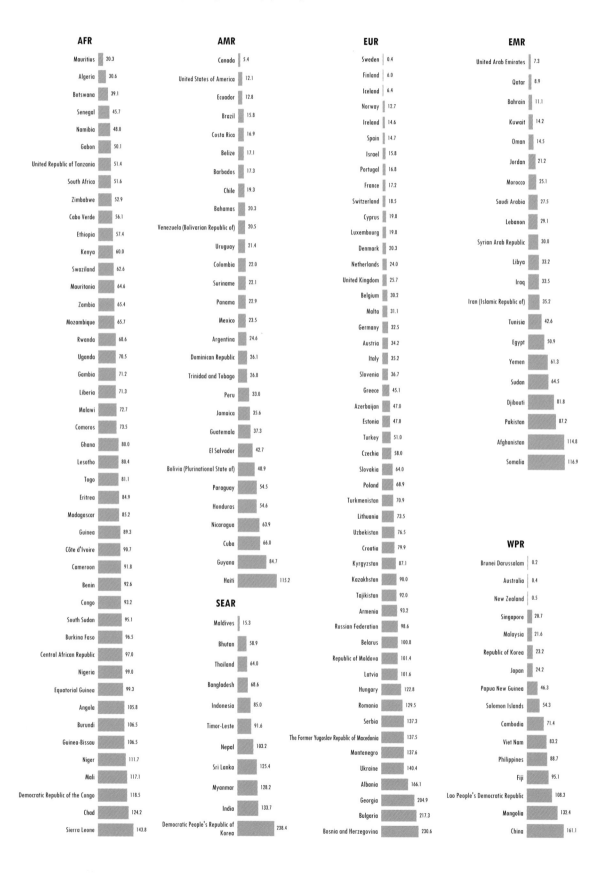

AFR		AMR		EUR		EMR	
Mauritius	20.3	Canada	5.4	Sweden	0.4	United Arab Emirates	7.3
Algeria	30.6	United States of America	12.1	Finland	6.0	Qatar	8.9
Botswana	39.1	Ecuador	12.8	Iceland	6.4	Bahrain	11.1
Senegal	45.7	Brazil	15.8	Norway	12.7	Kuwait	14.2
Namibia	48.0	Costa Rica	16.9	Ireland	14.6	Oman	14.5
Gabon	50.1	Belize	17.1	Spain	14.7	Jordan	21.2
United Republic of Tanzania	51.4	Barbados	17.3	Israel	15.8	Morocco	25.1
South Africa	51.6	Chile	19.3	Portugal	16.8	Saudi Arabia	27.5
Zimbabwe	52.9	Bahamas	20.3	France	17.2	Lebanon	29.1
Cabo Verde	56.1	Venezuela (Bolivarian Republic of)	20.5	Switzerland	18.5	Syrian Arab Republic	30.0
Ethiopia	57.4	Uruguay	21.4	Cyprus	19.8	Libya	33.2
Kenya	60.0	Colombia	22.0	Luxembourg	19.8	Iraq	33.5
Swaziland	62.6	Suriname	22.1	Denmark	20.3	Iran (Islamic Republic of)	35.2
Mauritania	64.6	Panama	22.9	Netherlands	24.0	Tunisia	42.6
Zambia	65.4	Mexico	23.5	United Kingdom	25.7	Egypt	50.9
Mozambique	65.7	Argentina	24.6	Belgium	30.2	Yemen	61.3
Rwanda	68.6	Dominican Republic	26.1	Malta	31.1	Sudan	64.5
Uganda	70.5	Trinidad and Tobago	26.8	Germany	32.5	Djibouti	81.8
Gambia	71.2	Peru	33.0	Austria	34.2	Pakistan	87.2
Liberia	71.3	Jamaica	35.6	Italy	35.2	Afghanistan	114.8
Malawi	72.7	Guatemala	37.3	Slovenia	36.7	Somalia	116.9
Comoros	73.5	El Salvador	42.7	Greece	45.1		
Ghana	80.0	Bolivia (Plurinational State of)	48.9	Azerbaijan	47.0		
Lesotho	80.4	Paraguay	54.5	Estonia	47.0		
Togo	81.1	Honduras	54.6	Turkey	51.0		
Eritrea	84.9	Nicaragua	63.9	Czechia	58.0		
Madagascar	85.2	Cuba	66.0	Slovakia	64.0		
Guinea	89.3	Guyana	84.7	Poland	68.9		
Côte d'Ivoire	90.7	Haiti	115.2	Turkmenistan	70.9		
Cameroon	91.8			Lithuania	73.5		
Benin	92.6	**SEAR**		Uzbekistan	76.5	**WPR**	
Congo	93.2	Maldives	15.3	Croatia	79.9	Brunei Darussalam	0.2
South Sudan	95.1	Bhutan	58.9	Kyrgyzstan	87.1	Australia	0.4
Burkina Faso	96.5	Thailand	64.0	Kazakhstan	90.0	New Zealand	0.5
Central African Republic	97.0	Bangladesh	68.6	Tajikistan	92.0	Singapore	20.7
Nigeria	99.0	Indonesia	85.0	Armenia	93.2	Malaysia	21.6
Equatorial Guinea	99.3	Timor-Leste	91.6	Russian Federation	98.6	Republic of Korea	23.2
Angola	105.8	Nepal	103.2	Belarus	100.8	Japan	24.2
Burundi	106.5	Sri Lanka	125.4	Republic of Moldova	101.4	Papua New Guinea	46.3
Guinea-Bissau	106.5	Myanmar	128.2	Latvia	101.6	Solomon Islands	54.3
Niger	111.7	India	133.7	Hungary	122.8	Cambodia	71.4
Mali	117.1	Democratic People's Republic of Korea	238.4	Romania	129.5	Viet Nam	83.2
Democratic Republic of the Congo	118.5			Serbia	137.3	Philippines	88.7
Chad	124.2			The Former Yugoslav Republic of Macedonia	137.5	Fiji	95.1
Sierra Leone	143.8			Montenegro	137.6	Lao People's Democratic Republic	108.3
				Ukraine	140.4	Mongolia	132.4
				Albania	166.1	China	161.1
				Georgia	204.9		
				Bulgaria	217.3		
				Bosnia and Herzegovina	230.6		

[1] Public health and environment [online database]. Global Health Observatory (GHO) data. Geneva: World Health Organization (http://www.who.int/gho/phe/en/). WHO Member States with a population of less than 250 000 population in 2012 were not included in the analysis.

MORTALITY DUE TO UNSAFE WASH SERVICES

SDG Target 3.9
By 2030, substantially reduce the number of deaths and illnesses from hazardous chemicals and air, water and soil pollution and contamination

Indicator 3.9.2: Mortality rate attributed to unsafe water, unsafe sanitation and lack of hygiene (exposure to unsafe Water, Sanitation and Hygiene for All (WASH) services)

Mortality rate attributed to exposure to unsafe WASH services (per 100 000 population), 2012[1]

AFR

Mauritius	0.9
Algeria	2.4
Cabo Verde	4.5
Botswana	9.2
Namibia	9.8
South Africa	12.1
Rwanda	19.4
Ghana	20.0
Gambia	21.0
Swaziland	22.7
Zambia	24.5
Liberia	25.0
Senegal	25.4
Malawi	26.1
Madagascar	26.6
Zimbabwe	27.1
United Republic of Tanzania	27.6
Gabon	28.1
Lesotho	28.3
Comoros	28.6
Mauritania	28.9
Ethiopia	29.6
Uganda	30.3
Benin	32.2
Kenya	32.5
Eritrea	34.9
Mozambique	37.9
Togo	37.9
Guinea	40.7
Burkina Faso	40.9
Cameroon	40.9
Côte d'Ivoire	44.1
Congo	48.1
Guinea-Bissau	48.9
South Sudan	50.0
Nigeria	50.9
Equatorial Guinea	57.3
Mali	61.1
Burundi	68.4
Niger	69.2
Sierra Leone	90.4
Chad	92.8
Central African Republic	102.3
Democratic Republic of the Congo	107.8
Angola	111.2

AMR

Bahamas	0.1
Barbados	0.2
Chile	0.2
Trinidad and Tobago	0.2
Uruguay	0.3
Canada	0.6
United States of America	0.6
Argentina	0.7
Costa Rica	0.7
Cuba	0.7
Colombia	0.8
Suriname	0.8
Brazil	1.1
Mexico	1.1
Belize	1.2
Peru	1.3
Venezuela (Bolivarian Republic of)	1.3
Ecuador	1.8
Dominican Republic	1.9
Jamaica	1.9
Paraguay	2.3
El Salvador	2.4
Nicaragua	3.5
Guyana	4.0
Panama	4.1
Bolivia (Plurinational State of)	7.0
Honduras	7.9
Guatemala	9.2
Haiti	28.5

SEAR

Maldives	0.6
Democratic People's Republic of Korea	1.4
Thailand	1.9
Sri Lanka	3.3
Indonesia	3.6
Bangladesh	6.0
Bhutan	7.1
Timor-Leste	10.3
Myanmar	10.4
Nepal	12.9
India	27.4

EUR

Hungary	0.0
Bosnia and Herzegovina	<0.1
Bulgaria	<0.1
Croatia	<0.1
Estonia	<0.1
Greece	<0.1
Iceland	<0.1
Latvia	<0.1
Lithuania	<0.1
Malta	<0.1
Montenegro	<0.1
Poland	<0.1
Republic of Moldova	<0.1
Romania	<0.1
Slovakia	<0.1
Slovenia	<0.1
The Former Yugoslav Republic of Macedonia	<0.1
Austria	0.1
Italy	0.1
Luxembourg	0.1
Portugal	0.1
Albania	0.2
Belarus	0.2
Finland	0.2
Georgia	0.2
Netherlands	0.2
Russian Federation	0.2
Cyprus	0.3
Ireland	0.3
Serbia	0.3
Spain	0.3
Switzerland	0.3
Ukraine	0.4
United Kingdom	0.4
Belgium	0.5
Czechia	0.5
France	0.5
Israel	0.5
Norway	0.5
Denmark	0.8
Turkey	0.8
Germany	0.9
Armenia	1.1
Sweden	1.1
Kazakhstan	1.2
Kyrgyzstan	1.8
Azerbaijan	2.1
Uzbekistan	2.4
Turkmenistan	5.8
Tajikistan	7.5

EMR

Kuwait	<0.1
Qatar	<0.1
United Arab Emirates	<0.1
Bahrain	0.1
Saudi Arabia	0.2
Lebanon	0.4
Oman	0.4
Libya	0.6
Tunisia	0.8
Iran (Islamic Republic of)	0.9
Jordan	1.0
Egypt	1.6
Syrian Arab Republic	1.8
Morocco	3.4
Iraq	3.9
Yemen	13.0
Pakistan	20.7
Djibouti	26.4
Afghanistan	34.6
Sudan	34.6
Somalia	98.8

WPR

Australia	<0.1
Brunei Darussalam	<0.1
Japan	0.1
Singapore	0.1
Republic of Korea	0.2
China	0.4
Malaysia	0.4
New Zealand	0.6
Viet Nam	2.0
Fiji	3.0
Mongolia	3.1
Philippines	5.1
Cambodia	5.6
Solomon Islands	10.4
Papua New Guinea	12.4
Lao People's Democratic Republic	13.9

[1] Preventing disease through healthy environments. A global assessment of the burden of disease from environmental risks. Geneva: World Health Organization; 2016 (http://apps.who.int/iris/bitstream/10665/204585/1/9789241565196_eng.pdf?ua=1, accessed 23 March 2017); and: Preventing diarrhoea through better water, sanitation and hygiene. Exposures and impacts in low- and middle-income countries. Geneva: World Health Organization; 2014 (http://apps.who.int/iris/bitstream/10665/150112/1/9789241564823_eng.pdf?ua=1&ua=1, accessed 23 March 2017). WHO Member States with a population of less than 250 000 in 2012 were not included in the analysis.

MORTALITY DUE TO UNINTENTIONAL POISONING

SDG Target 3.9
By 2030, substantially reduce the number of deaths and illnesses from hazardous chemicals and air, water and soil pollution and contamination

Indicator 3.9.3: Mortality rate attributed to unintentional poisoning

Mortality rate attributed to unintentional poisoning (per 100 000 population), 2015[1]

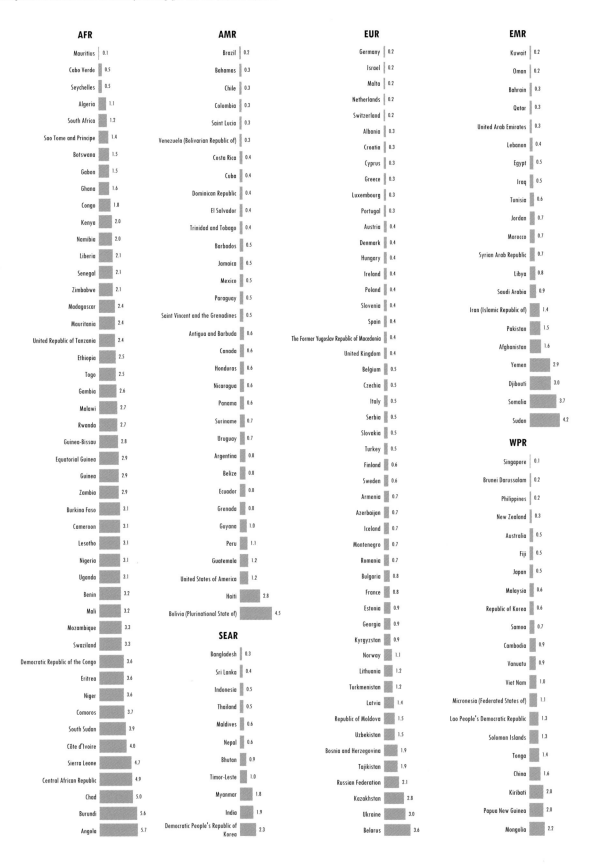

AFR	
Mauritius	0.1
Cabo Verde	0.5
Seychelles	0.5
Algeria	1.1
South Africa	1.2
Sao Tome and Principe	1.4
Botswana	1.5
Gabon	1.5
Ghana	1.6
Congo	1.8
Kenya	2.0
Namibia	2.0
Liberia	2.1
Senegal	2.1
Zimbabwe	2.1
Madagascar	2.4
Mauritania	2.4
United Republic of Tanzania	2.4
Ethiopia	2.5
Togo	2.5
Gambia	2.6
Malawi	2.7
Rwanda	2.7
Guinea-Bissau	2.8
Equatorial Guinea	2.9
Guinea	2.9
Zambia	2.9
Burkina Faso	3.1
Cameroon	3.1
Lesotho	3.1
Nigeria	3.1
Uganda	3.1
Benin	3.2
Mali	3.2
Mozambique	3.3
Swaziland	3.3
Democratic Republic of the Congo	3.6
Eritrea	3.6
Niger	3.6
Comoros	3.7
South Sudan	3.9
Côte d'Ivoire	4.0
Sierra Leone	4.7
Central African Republic	4.9
Chad	5.0
Burundi	5.6
Angola	5.7

AMR	
Brazil	0.2
Bahamas	0.3
Chile	0.3
Colombia	0.3
Saint Lucia	0.3
Venezuela (Bolivarian Republic of)	0.3
Costa Rica	0.4
Cuba	0.4
Dominican Republic	0.4
El Salvador	0.4
Trinidad and Tobago	0.4
Barbados	0.5
Jamaica	0.5
Mexico	0.5
Paraguay	0.5
Saint Vincent and the Grenadines	0.5
Antigua and Barbuda	0.6
Canada	0.6
Honduras	0.6
Nicaragua	0.6
Panama	0.6
Suriname	0.7
Uruguay	0.7
Argentina	0.8
Belize	0.8
Ecuador	0.8
Grenada	0.8
Guyana	1.0
Peru	1.1
Guatemala	1.2
United States of America	1.2
Haiti	2.8
Bolivia (Plurinational State of)	4.5

SEAR	
Bangladesh	0.3
Sri Lanka	0.4
Indonesia	0.5
Thailand	0.5
Maldives	0.6
Nepal	0.6
Bhutan	0.9
Timor-Leste	1.0
Myanmar	1.8
India	1.9
Democratic People's Republic of Korea	2.3

EUR	
Germany	0.2
Israel	0.2
Malta	0.2
Netherlands	0.2
Switzerland	0.2
Albania	0.3
Croatia	0.3
Cyprus	0.3
Greece	0.3
Luxembourg	0.3
Portugal	0.3
Austria	0.4
Denmark	0.4
Hungary	0.4
Ireland	0.4
Poland	0.4
Slovenia	0.4
Spain	0.4
The Former Yugoslav Republic of Macedonia	0.4
United Kingdom	0.4
Belgium	0.5
Czechia	0.5
Italy	0.5
Serbia	0.5
Slovakia	0.5
Turkey	0.5
Finland	0.6
Sweden	0.6
Armenia	0.7
Azerbaijan	0.7
Iceland	0.7
Montenegro	0.7
Romania	0.7
Bulgaria	0.8
France	0.8
Estonia	0.9
Georgia	0.9
Kyrgyzstan	0.9
Norway	1.1
Lithuania	1.2
Turkmenistan	1.2
Latvia	1.4
Republic of Moldova	1.5
Uzbekistan	1.5
Bosnia and Herzegovina	1.9
Tajikistan	1.9
Russian Federation	2.1
Kazakhstan	2.8
Ukraine	3.0
Belarus	3.6

EMR	
Kuwait	0.2
Oman	0.2
Bahrain	0.3
Qatar	0.3
United Arab Emirates	0.3
Lebanon	0.4
Egypt	0.5
Iraq	0.5
Tunisia	0.6
Jordan	0.7
Morocco	0.7
Syrian Arab Republic	0.7
Libya	0.8
Saudi Arabia	0.9
Iran (Islamic Republic of)	1.4
Pakistan	1.5
Afghanistan	1.6
Yemen	2.9
Djibouti	3.0
Somalia	3.7
Sudan	4.2

WPR	
Singapore	0.1
Brunei Darussalam	0.2
Philippines	0.2
New Zealand	0.3
Australia	0.5
Fiji	0.5
Japan	0.5
Malaysia	0.6
Republic of Korea	0.6
Samoa	0.7
Cambodia	0.9
Vanuatu	0.9
Viet Nam	1.0
Micronesia (Federated States of)	1.1
Lao People's Democratic Republic	1.3
Solomon Islands	1.3
Tonga	1.4
China	1.6
Kiribati	2.0
Papua New Guinea	2.0
Mongolia	2.2

[1] Global Health Estimates 2015: Deaths by cause, age, sex, by country and by region, 2000–2015. Geneva: World Health Organization; 2016 (http://www.who.int/healthinfo/global_burden_disease/estimates/en/index1.html, accessed 22 March 2017). WHO Member States with a population of less than 90 000 in 2015 were not included in this analysis.

TOBACCO USE

SDG Target 3.a
Strengthen the implementation of the WHO Framework Convention on Tobacco Control in all countries, as appropriate

Indicator 3.a.1: Age-standardized prevalence of current tobacco use among persons aged 15 years and older

Age-standardized prevalence of tobacco smoking among persons 15 years and older, by sex, 2015[1]

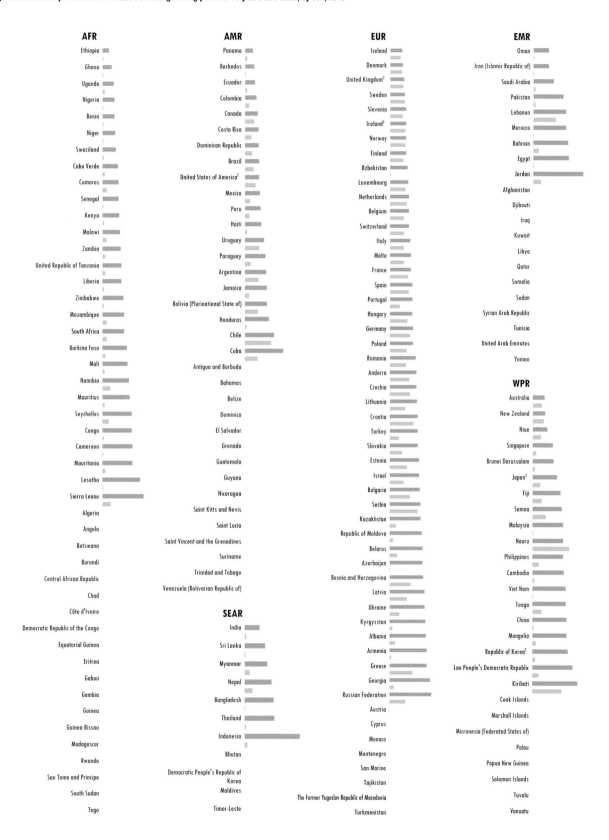

¹ WHO global report on trends in prevalence of tobacco smoking 2015. Geneva: World Health Organization; 2015 (http://apps.who.int/iris/bitstream/10665/156262/1/9789241564922_eng. pdf, accessed 22 March 2017). Darker orange bars represent the prevalence among males. Pale orange bars represent the prevalence among females.

² Cigarette smoking only.

SDG Target 3.b
Support the research and development of vaccines and medicines for the communicable and noncommunicable diseases that primarily affect developing countries, provide access to affordable essential medicines and vaccines, in accordance with the Doha Declaration on the TRIPS Agreement and Public Health, which affirms the right of developing countries to use to the full the provisions in the Agreement on Trade-Related Aspects of Intellectual Property Rights regarding flexibilities to protect public health, and, in particular, provide access to medicines for all

Indicator 3.b.1: Proportion of the target population covered by all vaccines included in their national programme

Diphtheria-tetanus-pertussis (DTP3) immunization coverage among 1-year-olds (%), 2015[1]

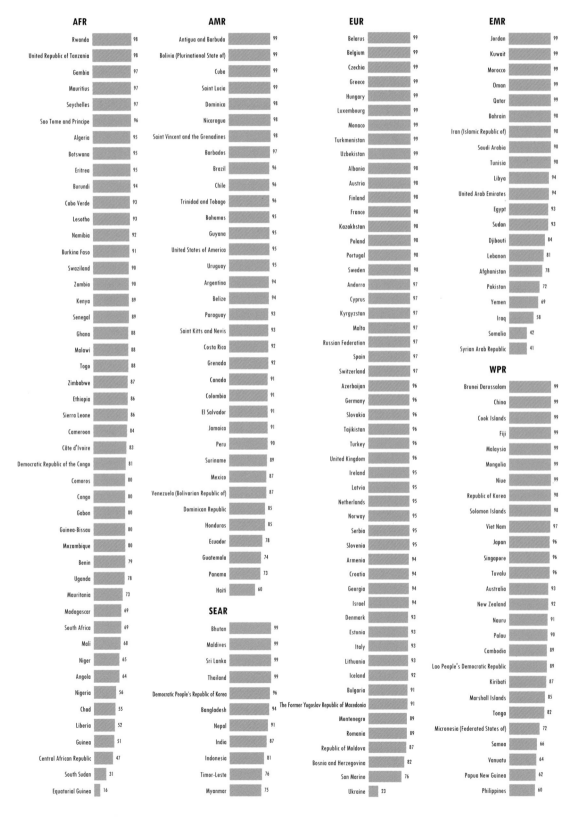

AFR

Country	%
Rwanda	98
United Republic of Tanzania	98
Gambia	97
Mauritius	97
Seychelles	97
Sao Tome and Principe	96
Algeria	95
Botswana	95
Eritrea	95
Burundi	94
Cabo Verde	93
Lesotho	93
Namibia	92
Burkina Faso	91
Swaziland	90
Zambia	90
Kenya	89
Senegal	89
Ghana	88
Malawi	88
Togo	88
Zimbabwe	87
Ethiopia	86
Sierra Leone	86
Cameroon	84
Côte d'Ivoire	83
Democratic Republic of the Congo	81
Comoros	80
Congo	80
Gabon	80
Guinea-Bissau	80
Mozambique	80
Benin	79
Uganda	78
Mauritania	73
Madagascar	69
South Africa	69
Mali	68
Niger	65
Angola	64
Nigeria	56
Chad	55
Liberia	52
Guinea	51
Central African Republic	47
South Sudan	31
Equatorial Guinea	16

AMR

Country	%
Antigua and Barbuda	99
Bolivia (Plurinational State of)	99
Cuba	99
Saint Lucia	99
Dominica	98
Nicaragua	98
Saint Vincent and the Grenadines	98
Barbados	97
Brazil	96
Chile	96
Trinidad and Tobago	96
Bahamas	95
Guyana	95
United States of America	95
Uruguay	95
Argentina	94
Belize	94
Paraguay	93
Saint Kitts and Nevis	93
Costa Rica	92
Grenada	92
Canada	91
Colombia	91
El Salvador	91
Jamaica	91
Peru	90
Suriname	89
Mexico	87
Venezuela (Bolivarian Republic of)	87
Dominican Republic	85
Honduras	85
Ecuador	78
Guatemala	74
Panama	73
Haiti	60

SEAR

Country	%
Bhutan	99
Maldives	99
Sri Lanka	99
Thailand	99
Democratic People's Republic of Korea	96
Bangladesh	94
Nepal	91
India	87
Indonesia	81
Timor-Leste	76
Myanmar	75

EUR

Country	%
Belarus	99
Belgium	99
Czechia	99
Greece	99
Hungary	99
Luxembourg	99
Monaco	99
Turkmenistan	99
Uzbekistan	99
Albania	98
Austria	98
Finland	98
France	98
Kazakhstan	98
Poland	98
Portugal	98
Sweden	98
Andorra	97
Cyprus	97
Kyrgyzstan	97
Malta	97
Russian Federation	97
Spain	97
Switzerland	97
Azerbaijan	96
Germany	96
Slovakia	96
Tajikistan	96
Turkey	96
United Kingdom	96
Ireland	95
Latvia	95
Netherlands	95
Norway	95
Serbia	95
Slovenia	95
Armenia	94
Croatia	94
Georgia	94
Israel	94
Denmark	93
Estonia	93
Italy	93
Lithuania	93
Iceland	92
Bulgaria	91
The Former Yugoslav Republic of Macedonia	91
Montenegro	89
Romania	89
Republic of Moldova	87
Bosnia and Herzegovina	82
San Marino	76
Ukraine	23

EMR

Country	%
Jordan	99
Kuwait	99
Morocco	99
Oman	99
Qatar	99
Bahrain	98
Iran (Islamic Republic of)	98
Saudi Arabia	98
Tunisia	98
Libya	94
United Arab Emirates	94
Egypt	93
Sudan	93
Djibouti	84
Lebanon	81
Afghanistan	78
Pakistan	72
Yemen	69
Iraq	58
Somalia	42
Syrian Arab Republic	41

WPR

Country	%
Brunei Darussalam	99
China	99
Cook Islands	99
Fiji	99
Malaysia	99
Mongolia	99
Niue	99
Republic of Korea	98
Solomon Islands	98
Viet Nam	97
Japan	96
Singapore	96
Tuvalu	96
Australia	93
New Zealand	92
Nauru	91
Palau	90
Cambodia	89
Lao People's Democratic Republic	89
Kiribati	87
Marshall Islands	85
Tonga	82
Micronesia (Federated States of)	72
Samoa	66
Vanuatu	64
Papua New Guinea	62
Philippines	60

[1] This indicator is used here as a proxy for the SDG indicator. Data source: WHO/UNICEF estimates of national immunization coverage. July 2016 revision (see: http://www.who.int/immunization/monitoring_surveillance/routine/coverage/en/index4.html, accessed 22 March 2017).

DEVELOPMENT ASSISTANCE FOR HEALTH

SDG Target 3.b
Support the research and development of vaccines and medicines for the communicable and noncommunicable diseases that primarily affect developing countries, provide access to affordable essential medicines and vaccines, in accordance with the Doha Declaration on the TRIPS Agreement and Public Health, which affirms the right of developing countries to use to the full the provisions in the Agreement on Trade-Related Aspects of Intellectual Property Rights regarding flexibilities to protect public health, and, in particular, provide access to medicines for all

Indicator 3.b.2: Total net official development assistance to the medical research and basic health sectors

Total net official development assistance to medical research and basic health sector per capita (constant 2014 US$), by recipient country, 2014[1]

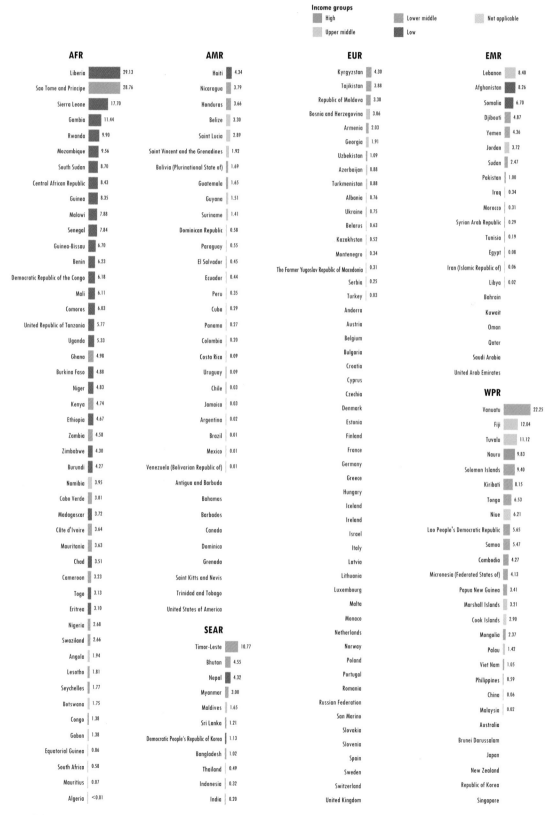

[1] United Nations' SDG indicators global database (https://unstats.un.org/sdgs/indicators/database/?indicator=3.b.2, accessed 6 April 2017) based on the Creditor Reporting System database of the Organisation for Economic Co-operation and Development, 2016. See section 1.5 for more data. Income classification is based on the World Bank analytical income of economies (July 2016).

SDG Target 3.c
Substantially increase health financing and the recruitment, development, training and retention of the health workforce in developing countries, especially in least-developed countries and small-island developing States

Indicator 3.c.1: Health worker density and distribution

Skilled health professionals density (per 10 000 population), 2005–2015[1]

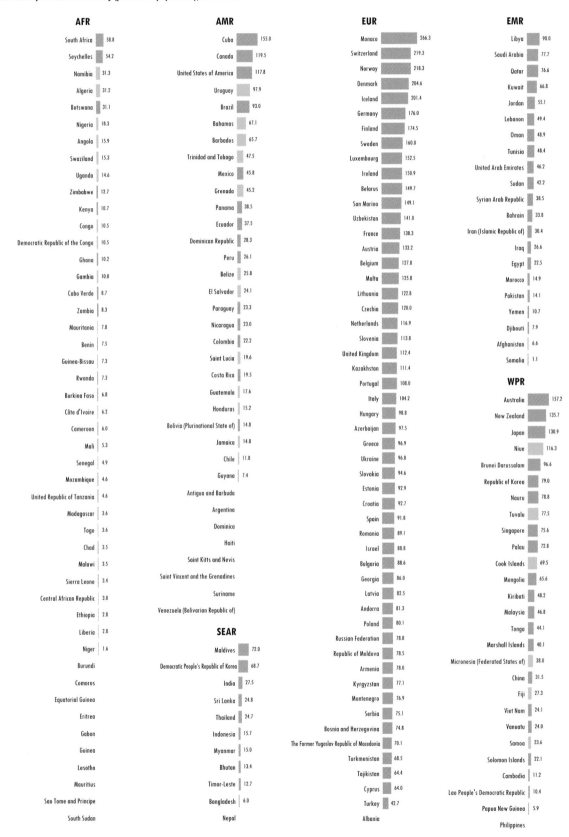

AFR

South Africa	58.8
Seychelles	54.2
Namibia	31.3
Algeria	31.2
Botswana	31.1
Nigeria	18.3
Angola	15.9
Swaziland	15.3
Uganda	14.6
Zimbabwe	12.7
Kenya	10.7
Congo	10.5
Democratic Republic of the Congo	10.5
Ghana	10.2
Gambia	10.0
Cabo Verde	8.7
Zambia	8.3
Mauritania	7.8
Benin	7.5
Guinea-Bissau	7.3
Rwanda	7.3
Burkina Faso	6.8
Côte d'Ivoire	6.2
Cameroon	6.0
Mali	5.3
Senegal	4.9
Mozambique	4.6
United Republic of Tanzania	4.6
Madagascar	3.6
Togo	3.6
Chad	3.5
Malawi	3.5
Sierra Leone	3.4
Central African Republic	3.0
Ethiopia	2.8
Liberia	2.8
Niger	1.6
Burundi	
Comoros	
Equatorial Guinea	
Eritrea	
Gabon	
Guinea	
Lesotho	
Mauritius	
Sao Tome and Principe	
South Sudan	

AMR

Cuba	155.0
Canada	119.5
United States of America	117.8
Uruguay	97.9
Brazil	93.0
Bahamas	67.1
Barbados	65.7
Trinidad and Tobago	47.5
Mexico	45.8
Grenada	45.2
Panama	38.5
Ecuador	37.5
Dominican Republic	28.3
Peru	26.1
Belize	25.8
El Salvador	24.1
Paraguay	23.3
Nicaragua	23.0
Colombia	22.2
Saint Lucia	19.6
Costa Rica	19.5
Guatemala	17.6
Honduras	15.2
Bolivia (Plurinational State of)	14.8
Jamaica	14.8
Chile	11.8
Guyana	7.4
Antigua and Barbuda	
Argentina	
Dominica	
Haiti	
Saint Kitts and Nevis	
Saint Vincent and the Grenadines	
Suriname	
Venezuela (Bolivarian Republic of)	

SEAR

Maldives	72.0
Democratic People's Republic of Korea	68.7
India	27.5
Sri Lanka	24.8
Thailand	24.7
Indonesia	15.7
Myanmar	15.0
Bhutan	13.4
Timor-Leste	12.7
Bangladesh	6.0
Nepal	

EUR

Monaco	266.3
Switzerland	219.3
Norway	218.3
Denmark	204.6
Iceland	201.4
Germany	176.0
Finland	174.5
Sweden	160.0
Luxembourg	152.5
Ireland	150.9
Belarus	149.7
San Marino	149.1
Uzbekistan	141.0
France	138.3
Austria	133.2
Belgium	127.8
Malta	125.8
Lithuania	122.8
Czechia	120.0
Netherlands	116.9
Slovenia	113.8
United Kingdom	112.4
Kazakhstan	111.4
Portugal	108.0
Italy	104.2
Hungary	98.8
Azerbaijan	97.5
Greece	96.9
Ukraine	96.8
Slovakia	94.6
Estonia	92.9
Croatia	92.7
Spain	91.8
Romania	89.1
Israel	88.8
Bulgaria	88.6
Georgia	86.0
Latvia	82.5
Andorra	81.3
Poland	80.1
Russian Federation	78.8
Republic of Moldova	78.5
Armenia	78.0
Kyrgyzstan	77.1
Montenegro	76.9
Serbia	75.1
Bosnia and Herzegovina	74.8
The Former Yugoslav Republic of Macedonia	70.1
Turkmenistan	68.5
Tajikistan	64.4
Cyprus	64.0
Turkey	42.7
Albania	

EMR

Libya	90.0
Saudi Arabia	77.7
Qatar	76.6
Kuwait	66.8
Jordan	55.1
Lebanon	49.4
Oman	48.9
Tunisia	48.4
United Arab Emirates	46.2
Sudan	42.2
Syrian Arab Republic	38.5
Bahrain	33.8
Iran (Islamic Republic of)	30.4
Iraq	26.6
Egypt	22.5
Morocco	14.9
Pakistan	14.1
Yemen	10.7
Djibouti	7.9
Afghanistan	6.6
Somalia	1.1

WPR

Australia	157.2
New Zealand	135.7
Japan	130.9
Niue	116.3
Brunei Darussalam	96.6
Republic of Korea	79.0
Nauru	78.8
Tuvalu	77.5
Singapore	75.6
Palau	72.8
Cook Islands	69.5
Mongolia	65.6
Kiribati	48.2
Malaysia	46.8
Tonga	44.1
Marshall Islands	40.1
Micronesia (Federated States of)	38.0
China	31.5
Fiji	27.3
Viet Nam	24.1
Vanuatu	24.0
Samoa	23.6
Solomon Islands	22.1
Cambodia	11.2
Lao People's Democratic Republic	10.4
Papua New Guinea	5.9
Philippines	

[1] Figures shown for skilled health professionals refer to the latest available values (2005–2015) given in: WHO Global Health Workforce Statistics. 2016 update [online database]. Geneva: World Health Organization (http://who.int/hrh/statistics/hwfstats/en/) aggregated across physicians and nurses/midwives. Please refer to this source for the latest values, and disaggregation and metadata descriptors. Data from 2005–2009 are shown in pale orange.

IHR CAPACITY AND HEALTH EMERGENCY PREPAREDNESS

SDG Target 3.d
Strengthen the capacity of all countries, in particular developing countries, for early warning, risk reduction and management of national and global health risks

Indicator 3.d.1: International Health Regulations (IHR) capacity and health emergency preparedness

International Health Regulations implementation: average of 13 core capacity scores, 2010–2016[1]

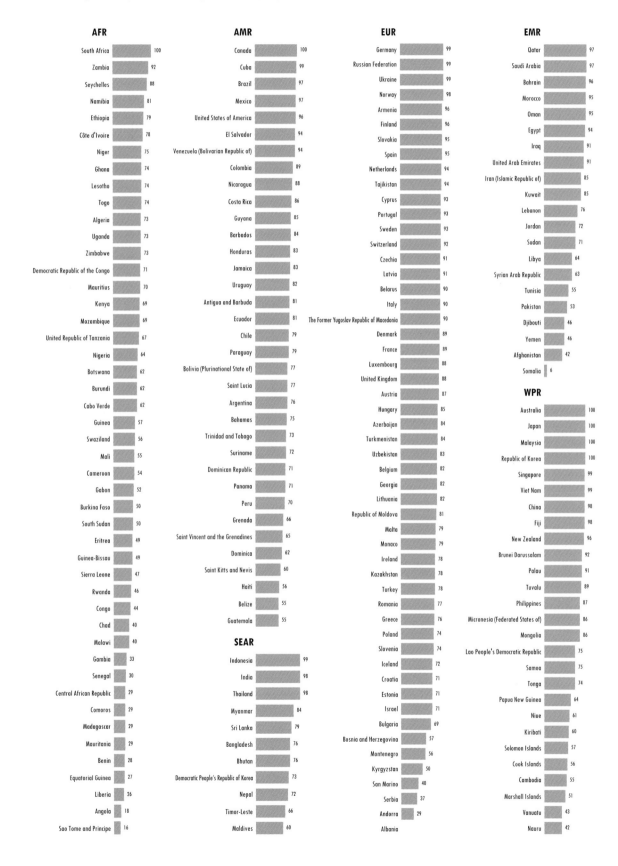

AFR

Country	Score
South Africa	100
Zambia	92
Seychelles	88
Namibia	81
Ethiopia	79
Côte d'Ivoire	78
Niger	75
Ghana	74
Lesotho	74
Togo	74
Algeria	73
Uganda	73
Zimbabwe	73
Democratic Republic of the Congo	71
Mauritius	70
Kenya	69
Mozambique	69
United Republic of Tanzania	67
Nigeria	64
Botswana	62
Burundi	62
Cabo Verde	62
Guinea	57
Swaziland	56
Mali	55
Cameroon	54
Gabon	52
Burkina Faso	50
South Sudan	50
Eritrea	49
Guinea-Bissau	49
Sierra Leone	47
Rwanda	46
Congo	44
Chad	40
Malawi	40
Gambia	33
Senegal	30
Central African Republic	29
Comoros	29
Madagascar	29
Mauritania	29
Benin	28
Equatorial Guinea	27
Liberia	26
Angola	18
Sao Tome and Principe	16

AMR

Country	Score
Canada	100
Cuba	99
Brazil	97
Mexico	97
United States of America	96
El Salvador	94
Venezuela (Bolivarian Republic of)	94
Colombia	89
Nicaragua	88
Costa Rica	86
Guyana	85
Barbados	84
Honduras	83
Jamaica	83
Uruguay	82
Antigua and Barbuda	81
Ecuador	81
Chile	79
Paraguay	79
Bolivia (Plurinational State of)	77
Saint Lucia	77
Argentina	76
Bahamas	75
Trinidad and Tobago	73
Suriname	72
Dominican Republic	71
Panama	71
Peru	70
Grenada	66
Saint Vincent and the Grenadines	65
Dominica	62
Saint Kitts and Nevis	60
Haiti	56
Belize	55
Guatemala	55

SEAR

Country	Score
Indonesia	99
India	98
Thailand	98
Myanmar	84
Sri Lanka	79
Bangladesh	76
Bhutan	76
Democratic People's Republic of Korea	73
Nepal	72
Timor-Leste	66
Maldives	60

EUR

Country	Score
Germany	99
Russian Federation	99
Ukraine	99
Norway	98
Armenia	96
Finland	96
Slovakia	95
Spain	95
Netherlands	94
Tajikistan	94
Cyprus	93
Portugal	93
Sweden	93
Switzerland	92
Czechia	91
Latvia	91
Belarus	90
Italy	90
The Former Yugoslav Republic of Macedonia	90
Denmark	89
France	89
Luxembourg	88
United Kingdom	88
Austria	87
Hungary	85
Azerbaijan	84
Turkmenistan	84
Uzbekistan	83
Belgium	82
Georgia	82
Lithuania	82
Republic of Moldova	81
Malta	79
Monaco	79
Ireland	78
Kazakhstan	78
Turkey	78
Romania	77
Greece	76
Poland	74
Slovenia	74
Iceland	72
Croatia	71
Estonia	71
Israel	71
Bulgaria	69
Bosnia and Herzegovina	57
Montenegro	56
Kyrgyzstan	50
San Marino	40
Serbia	37
Andorra	29
Albania	

EMR

Country	Score
Qatar	97
Saudi Arabia	97
Bahrain	96
Morocco	95
Oman	95
Egypt	94
Iraq	91
United Arab Emirates	91
Iran (Islamic Republic of)	85
Kuwait	85
Lebanon	76
Jordan	72
Sudan	71
Libya	64
Syrian Arab Republic	63
Tunisia	55
Pakistan	53
Djibouti	46
Yemen	46
Afghanistan	42
Somalia	6

WPR

Country	Score
Australia	100
Japan	100
Malaysia	100
Republic of Korea	100
Singapore	99
Viet Nam	99
China	98
Fiji	98
New Zealand	96
Brunei Darussalam	92
Palau	91
Tuvalu	89
Philippines	87
Micronesia (Federated States of)	86
Mongolia	86
Lao People's Democratic Republic	75
Samoa	75
Tonga	74
Papua New Guinea	64
Niue	61
Kiribati	60
Solomon Islands	57
Cook Islands	56
Cambodia	55
Marshall Islands	51
Vanuatu	43
Nauru	42

[1] International Health Regulations (2005) Monitoring Framework [online database]. Global Health Observatory (GHO) data. Geneva: World Health Organization (http://www.who.int/gho/ihr/en/).
Data shown are the latest available for 2010–2016.

GOVERNMENT SPENDING ON ESSENTIAL SERVICES, INCLUDING HEALTH

SDG Target 1.a
Ensure significant mobilization of resources from a variety of sources, including through enhanced development cooperation, in order to provide adequate and predictable means for developing countries, in particular least-developed countries, to implement programmes and policies to end poverty in all its dimensions

Indicator 1.a.2: Proportion of total government spending on essential services (education, health and social protection)

General government health expenditure as % of general government expenditure, 2014[1]

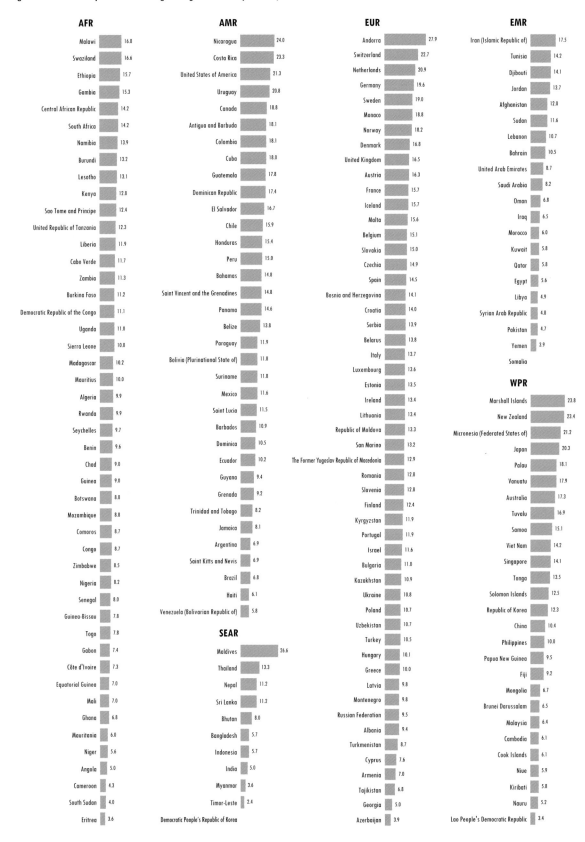

AFR		AMR		EUR		EMR	
Malawi	16.8	Nicaragua	24.0	Andorra	27.9	Iran (Islamic Republic of)	17.5
Swaziland	16.6	Costa Rica	23.3	Switzerland	22.7	Tunisia	14.2
Ethiopia	15.7	United States of America	21.3	Netherlands	20.9	Djibouti	14.1
Gambia	15.3	Uruguay	20.8	Germany	19.6	Jordan	13.7
Central African Republic	14.2	Canada	18.8	Sweden	19.0	Afghanistan	12.0
South Africa	14.2	Antigua and Barbuda	18.1	Monaco	18.8	Sudan	11.6
Namibia	13.9	Colombia	18.1	Norway	18.2	Lebanon	10.7
Burundi	13.2	Cuba	18.0	Denmark	16.8	Bahrain	10.5
Lesotho	13.1	Guatemala	17.8	United Kingdom	16.5	United Arab Emirates	8.7
Kenya	12.8	Dominican Republic	17.4	Austria	16.3	Saudi Arabia	8.2
Sao Tome and Principe	12.4	El Salvador	16.7	France	15.7	Oman	6.8
United Republic of Tanzania	12.3	Chile	15.9	Iceland	15.7	Iraq	6.5
Liberia	11.9	Honduras	15.4	Malta	15.6	Morocco	6.0
Cabo Verde	11.7	Peru	15.0	Belgium	15.1	Kuwait	5.8
Zambia	11.3	Bahamas	14.8	Slovakia	15.0	Qatar	5.8
Burkina Faso	11.2	Saint Vincent and the Grenadines	14.8	Czechia	14.9	Egypt	5.6
Democratic Republic of the Congo	11.1	Panama	14.6	Spain	14.5	Libya	4.9
Uganda	11.0	Belize	13.8	Bosnia and Herzegovina	14.1	Syrian Arab Republic	4.8
Sierra Leone	10.8	Paraguay	11.9	Croatia	14.0	Pakistan	4.7
Madagascar	10.2	Bolivia (Plurinational State of)	11.8	Serbia	13.9	Yemen	3.9
Mauritius	10.0	Suriname	11.8	Belarus	13.8	Somalia	
Algeria	9.9	Mexico	11.6	Italy	13.7		
Rwanda	9.9	Saint Lucia	11.5	Luxembourg	13.6	**WPR**	
Seychelles	9.7	Barbados	10.9	Estonia	13.5	Marshall Islands	23.8
Benin	9.6	Dominica	10.5	Ireland	13.4	New Zealand	23.4
Chad	9.0	Ecuador	10.2	Lithuania	13.4	Micronesia (Federated States of)	21.2
Guinea	9.0	Guyana	9.4	Republic of Moldova	13.3	Japan	20.3
Botswana	8.8	Grenada	9.2	San Marino	13.2	Palau	18.1
Mozambique	8.8	Trinidad and Tobago	8.2	The Former Yugoslav Republic of Macedonia	12.9	Vanuatu	17.9
Comoros	8.7	Jamaica	8.1	Romania	12.8	Australia	17.3
Congo	8.7	Argentina	6.9	Slovenia	12.8	Tuvalu	16.9
Zimbabwe	8.5	Saint Kitts and Nevis	6.9	Finland	12.4	Samoa	15.1
Nigeria	8.2	Brazil	6.8	Kyrgyzstan	11.9	Viet Nam	14.2
Senegal	8.0	Haiti	6.1	Portugal	11.9	Singapore	14.1
Guinea-Bissau	7.8	Venezuela (Bolivarian Republic of)	5.8	Israel	11.6	Tonga	13.5
Togo	7.8			Bulgaria	11.0	Solomon Islands	12.5
Gabon	7.4	**SEAR**		Kazakhstan	10.9	Republic of Korea	12.3
Côte d'Ivoire	7.3	Maldives	26.6	Ukraine	10.8	China	10.4
Equatorial Guinea	7.0	Thailand	13.3	Poland	10.7	Philippines	10.0
Mali	7.0	Nepal	11.2	Uzbekistan	10.7	Papua New Guinea	9.5
Ghana	6.8	Sri Lanka	11.2	Turkey	10.5	Fiji	9.2
Mauritania	6.0	Bhutan	8.0	Hungary	10.1	Mongolia	6.7
Niger	5.6	Bangladesh	5.7	Greece	10.0	Brunei Darussalam	6.5
Angola	5.0	Indonesia	5.7	Latvia	9.8	Malaysia	6.4
Cameroon	4.3	India	5.0	Montenegro	9.8	Cambodia	6.1
South Sudan	4.0	Myanmar	3.6	Russian Federation	9.5	Cook Islands	6.1
Eritrea	3.6	Timor-Leste	2.4	Albania	9.4	Niue	5.9
		Democratic People's Republic of Korea		Turkmenistan	8.7	Kiribati	5.8
				Cyprus	7.6	Nauru	5.2
				Armenia	7.0	Lao People's Democratic Republic	3.4
				Tajikistan	6.8		
				Georgia	5.0		
				Azerbaijan	3.9		

[1] The indicator here reflects the health-related portion of the SDG indicator. Data source: Global Health Expenditure Database [online database]. Geneva. World Health Organization. 2017 (http://apps.who.int/nha/database/Select/Indicators/en, accessed 23 March, 2017).

STUNTING AMONG CHILDREN

SDG Target 2.2
By 2030, end all forms of malnutrition, including achieving, by 2025, the internationally agreed targets on stunting and wasting in children under 5 years of age, and address the nutritional needs of adolescent girls, pregnant and lactating women and older persons

Indicator 2.2.1: Prevalence of stunting (height for age <-2 standard deviation from the median of the World Health Organization (WHO) Child Growth Standards) among children under 5 years of age

Prevalence of stunting among children under 5 years of age (%), 2005–2016[1]

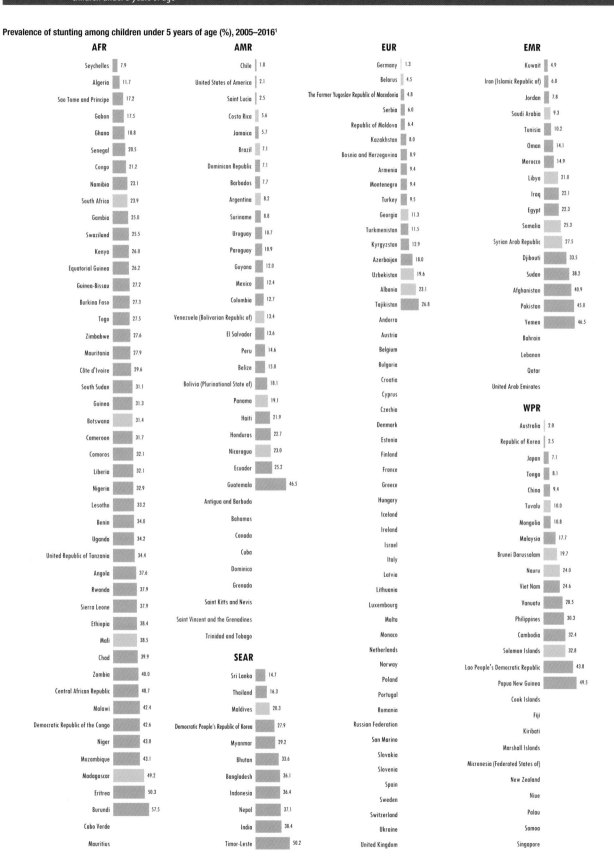

AFR

Country	%
Seychelles	7.9
Algeria	11.7
Sao Tome and Principe	17.2
Gabon	17.5
Ghana	18.8
Senegal	20.5
Congo	21.2
Namibia	23.1
South Africa	23.9
Gambia	25.0
Swaziland	25.5
Kenya	26.0
Equatorial Guinea	26.2
Guinea-Bissau	27.2
Burkina Faso	27.3
Togo	27.5
Zimbabwe	27.6
Mauritania	27.9
Côte d'Ivoire	29.6
South Sudan	31.1
Guinea	31.3
Botswana	31.4
Cameroon	31.7
Comoros	32.1
Liberia	32.1
Nigeria	32.9
Lesotho	33.2
Benin	34.0
Uganda	34.2
United Republic of Tanzania	34.4
Angola	37.6
Rwanda	37.9
Sierra Leone	37.9
Ethiopia	38.4
Mali	38.5
Chad	39.9
Zambia	40.0
Central African Republic	40.7
Malawi	42.4
Democratic Republic of the Congo	42.6
Niger	43.0
Mozambique	43.1
Madagascar	49.2
Eritrea	50.3
Burundi	57.5
Cabo Verde	
Mauritius	

AMR

Country	%
Chile	1.8
United States of America	2.1
Saint Lucia	2.5
Costa Rica	5.6
Jamaica	5.7
Brazil	7.1
Dominican Republic	7.1
Barbados	7.7
Argentina	8.2
Suriname	8.8
Uruguay	10.7
Paraguay	10.9
Guyana	12.0
Mexico	12.4
Colombia	12.7
Venezuela (Bolivarian Republic of)	13.4
El Salvador	13.6
Peru	14.6
Belize	15.0
Bolivia (Plurinational State of)	18.1
Panama	19.1
Haiti	21.9
Honduras	22.7
Nicaragua	23.0
Ecuador	25.2
Guatemala	46.5
Antigua and Barbuda	
Bahamas	
Canada	
Cuba	
Dominica	
Grenada	
Saint Kitts and Nevis	
Saint Vincent and the Grenadines	
Trinidad and Tobago	

SEAR

Country	%
Sri Lanka	14.7
Thailand	16.3
Maldives	20.3
Democratic People's Republic of Korea	27.9
Myanmar	29.2
Bhutan	33.6
Bangladesh	36.1
Indonesia	36.4
Nepal	37.1
India	38.4
Timor-Leste	50.2

EUR

Country	%
Germany	1.3
Belarus	4.5
The Former Yugoslav Republic of Macedonia	4.8
Serbia	6.0
Republic of Moldova	6.4
Kazakhstan	8.0
Bosnia and Herzegovina	8.9
Armenia	9.4
Montenegro	9.4
Turkey	9.5
Georgia	11.3
Turkmenistan	11.5
Kyrgyzstan	12.9
Azerbaijan	18.0
Uzbekistan	19.6
Albania	23.1
Tajikistan	26.8
Andorra	
Austria	
Belgium	
Bulgaria	
Croatia	
Cyprus	
Czechia	
Denmark	
Estonia	
Finland	
France	
Greece	
Hungary	
Iceland	
Ireland	
Israel	
Italy	
Latvia	
Lithuania	
Luxembourg	
Malta	
Monaco	
Netherlands	
Norway	
Poland	
Portugal	
Romania	
Russian Federation	
San Marino	
Slovakia	
Slovenia	
Spain	
Sweden	
Switzerland	
Ukraine	
United Kingdom	

EMR

Country	%
Kuwait	4.9
Iran (Islamic Republic of)	6.8
Jordan	7.8
Saudi Arabia	9.3
Tunisia	10.2
Oman	14.1
Morocco	14.9
Libya	21.0
Iraq	22.1
Egypt	22.3
Somalia	25.3
Syrian Arab Republic	27.5
Djibouti	33.5
Sudan	38.2
Afghanistan	40.9
Pakistan	45.0
Yemen	46.5
Bahrain	
Lebanon	
Qatar	
United Arab Emirates	

WPR

Country	%
Australia	2.0
Republic of Korea	2.5
Japan	7.1
Tonga	8.1
China	9.4
Tuvalu	10.0
Mongolia	10.8
Malaysia	17.7
Brunei Darussalam	19.7
Nauru	24.0
Viet Nam	24.6
Vanuatu	28.5
Philippines	30.3
Cambodia	32.4
Solomon Islands	32.8
Lao People's Democratic Republic	43.8
Papua New Guinea	49.5
Cook Islands	
Fiji	
Kiribati	
Marshall Islands	
Micronesia (Federated States of)	
New Zealand	
Niue	
Palau	
Samoa	
Singapore	

[1] United Nations Children's Fund, World Health Organization, the World Bank Group. Levels and trends in child malnutrition. UNICEF/WHO/World Bank Group Joint Child Malnutrition Estimates. UNICEF, New York; WHO, Geneva; the World Bank Group, Washington (DC); May 2017. Data shown are the latest available for 2005–2016. Data from 2005–2009 are shown in pale orange.

WASTING AND OVERWEIGHT AMONG CHILDREN

SDG Target 2.2
By 2030, end all forms of malnutrition, including achieving, by 2025, the internationally agreed targets on stunting and wasting in children under 5 years of age, and address the nutritional needs of adolescent girls, pregnant and lactating women and older persons

Indicator 2.2.2: Prevalence of malnutrition (weight for height >+2 or <-2 standard deviation from the median of the WHO Child Growth Standards) among children under 5 years of age, by type (wasting and overweight)

Prevalence of wasting (green bar) and of overweight (orange bar) in children under 5 years of age (%), 2005–2016[1]

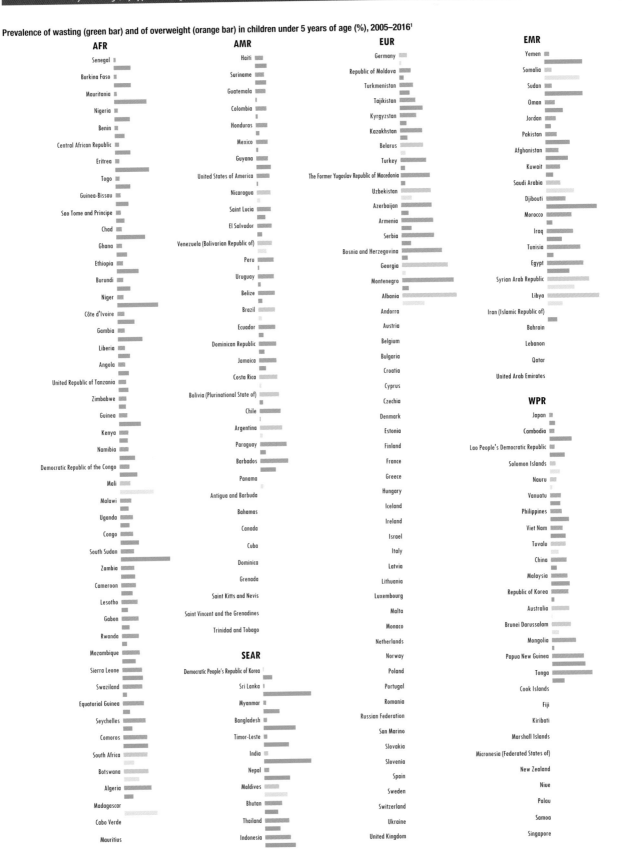

[1] United Nations Children's Fund, World Health Organization, the World Bank Group. Levels and trends in child malnutrition. UNICEF/WHO/World Bank Group Joint Child Malnutrition Estimates. UNICEF, New York; WHO, Geneva; the World Bank Group, Washington (DC); May 2017. Data shown are the latest available for 2005–2016. Data from 2005–2009 are shown in pale orange and green.

SAFELY MANAGED DRINKING-WATER SERVICES

SDG Target 6.1
By 2030, achieve universal and equitable access to safe and affordable drinking-water for all

Indicator 6.1.1: Proportion of population using safely managed drinking-water services

Proportion of population using improved drinking-water sources (%), 2015[1]

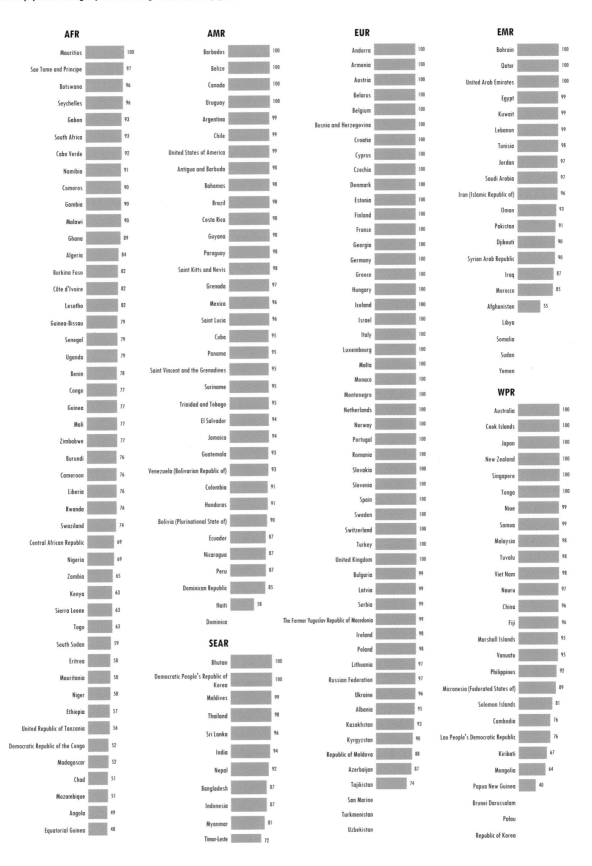

AFR

Mauritius	100
Sao Tome and Principe	97
Botswana	96
Seychelles	96
Gabon	93
South Africa	93
Cabo Verde	92
Namibia	91
Comoros	90
Gambia	90
Malawi	90
Ghana	89
Algeria	84
Burkina Faso	82
Côte d'Ivoire	82
Lesotho	82
Guinea-Bissau	79
Senegal	79
Uganda	79
Benin	78
Congo	77
Guinea	77
Mali	77
Zimbabwe	77
Burundi	76
Cameroon	76
Liberia	76
Rwanda	76
Swaziland	74
Central African Republic	69
Nigeria	69
Zambia	65
Kenya	63
Sierra Leone	63
Togo	63
South Sudan	59
Eritrea	58
Mauritania	58
Niger	58
Ethiopia	57
United Republic of Tanzania	56
Democratic Republic of the Congo	52
Madagascar	52
Chad	51
Mozambique	51
Angola	49
Equatorial Guinea	48

AMR

Barbados	100
Belize	100
Canada	100
Uruguay	100
Argentina	99
Chile	99
United States of America	99
Antigua and Barbuda	98
Bahamas	98
Brazil	98
Costa Rica	98
Guyana	98
Paraguay	98
Saint Kitts and Nevis	98
Grenada	97
Mexico	96
Saint Lucia	96
Cuba	95
Panama	95
Saint Vincent and the Grenadines	95
Suriname	95
Trinidad and Tobago	95
El Salvador	94
Jamaica	94
Guatemala	93
Venezuela (Bolivarian Republic of)	93
Colombia	91
Honduras	91
Bolivia (Plurinational State of)	90
Ecuador	87
Nicaragua	87
Peru	87
Dominican Republic	85
Haiti	58
Dominica	

SEAR

Bhutan	100
Democratic People's Republic of Korea	100
Maldives	99
Thailand	98
Sri Lanka	96
India	94
Nepal	92
Bangladesh	87
Indonesia	87
Myanmar	81
Timor-Leste	72

EUR

Andorra	100
Armenia	100
Austria	100
Belarus	100
Belgium	100
Bosnia and Herzegovina	100
Croatia	100
Cyprus	100
Czechia	100
Denmark	100
Estonia	100
Finland	100
France	100
Georgia	100
Germany	100
Greece	100
Hungary	100
Iceland	100
Israel	100
Italy	100
Luxembourg	100
Malta	100
Monaco	100
Montenegro	100
Netherlands	100
Norway	100
Portugal	100
Romania	100
Slovakia	100
Slovenia	100
Spain	100
Sweden	100
Switzerland	100
Turkey	100
United Kingdom	100
Bulgaria	99
Latvia	99
Serbia	99
The Former Yugoslav Republic of Macedonia	99
Ireland	98
Poland	98
Lithuania	97
Russian Federation	97
Ukraine	96
Albania	95
Kazakhstan	93
Kyrgyzstan	90
Republic of Moldova	88
Azerbaijan	87
Tajikistan	74
San Marino	
Turkmenistan	
Uzbekistan	

EMR

Bahrain	100
Qatar	100
United Arab Emirates	100
Egypt	99
Kuwait	99
Lebanon	99
Tunisia	98
Jordan	97
Saudi Arabia	97
Iran (Islamic Republic of)	96
Oman	93
Pakistan	91
Djibouti	90
Syrian Arab Republic	90
Iraq	87
Morocco	85
Afghanistan	55
Libya	
Somalia	
Sudan	
Yemen	

WPR

Australia	100
Cook Islands	100
Japan	100
New Zealand	100
Singapore	100
Tonga	100
Niue	99
Samoa	99
Malaysia	98
Tuvalu	98
Viet Nam	98
Nauru	97
China	96
Fiji	96
Marshall Islands	95
Vanuatu	95
Philippines	92
Micronesia (Federated States of)	89
Solomon Islands	81
Cambodia	76
Lao People's Democratic Republic	76
Kiribati	67
Mongolia	64
Papua New Guinea	40
Brunei Darussalam	
Palau	
Republic of Korea	

[1] This indicator is used here as a proxy for the SDG indicator. Data source: Progress on sanitation and drinking water – 2015 update and MDG assessment. New York (NY): UNICEF; and Geneva: World Health Organization; 2015 (http://apps.who.int/iris/bitstream/10665/177752/1/9789241509145_eng.pdf?ua=1, accessed 23 March 2017).

SAFELY MANAGED SANITATION SERVICES

SDG Target 6.2
By 2030, achieve access to adequate and equitable sanitation and hygiene for all and end open defecation, paying special attention to the needs of women and girls and those in vulnerable situations

Indicator 6.2.1: Proportion of population using safely managed sanitation services, including a hand-washing facility with soap and water

Proportion of population using improved sanitation (%), 2015[1]

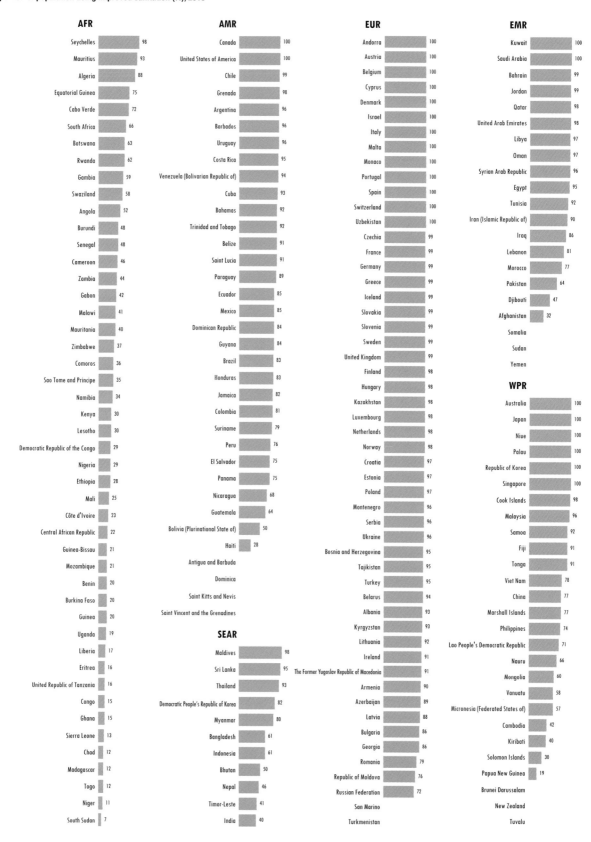

AFR

Seychelles	98
Mauritius	93
Algeria	88
Equatorial Guinea	75
Cabo Verde	72
South Africa	66
Botswana	63
Rwanda	62
Gambia	59
Swaziland	58
Angola	52
Burundi	48
Senegal	48
Cameroon	46
Zambia	44
Gabon	42
Malawi	41
Mauritania	40
Zimbabwe	37
Comoros	36
Sao Tome and Principe	35
Namibia	34
Kenya	30
Lesotho	30
Democratic Republic of the Congo	29
Nigeria	29
Ethiopia	28
Mali	25
Côte d'Ivoire	23
Central African Republic	22
Guinea-Bissau	21
Mozambique	21
Benin	20
Burkina Faso	20
Guinea	20
Uganda	19
Liberia	17
Eritrea	16
United Republic of Tanzania	16
Congo	15
Ghana	15
Sierra Leone	13
Chad	12
Madagascar	12
Togo	12
Niger	11
South Sudan	7

AMR

Canada	100
United States of America	100
Chile	99
Grenada	98
Argentina	96
Barbados	96
Uruguay	96
Costa Rica	95
Venezuela (Bolivarian Republic of)	94
Cuba	93
Bahamas	92
Trinidad and Tobago	92
Belize	91
Saint Lucia	91
Paraguay	89
Ecuador	85
Mexico	85
Dominican Republic	84
Guyana	84
Brazil	83
Honduras	83
Jamaica	82
Colombia	81
Suriname	79
Peru	76
El Salvador	75
Panama	75
Nicaragua	68
Guatemala	64
Bolivia (Plurinational State of)	50
Haiti	28
Antigua and Barbuda	
Dominica	
Saint Kitts and Nevis	
Saint Vincent and the Grenadines	

SEAR

Maldives	98
Sri Lanka	95
Thailand	93
Democratic People's Republic of Korea	82
Myanmar	80
Bangladesh	61
Indonesia	61
Bhutan	50
Nepal	46
Timor-Leste	41
India	40

EUR

Andorra	100
Austria	100
Belgium	100
Cyprus	100
Denmark	100
Israel	100
Italy	100
Malta	100
Monaco	100
Portugal	100
Spain	100
Switzerland	100
Uzbekistan	100
Czechia	99
France	99
Germany	99
Greece	99
Iceland	99
Slovakia	99
Slovenia	99
Sweden	99
United Kingdom	99
Finland	98
Hungary	98
Kazakhstan	98
Luxembourg	98
Netherlands	98
Norway	98
Croatia	97
Estonia	97
Poland	97
Montenegro	96
Serbia	96
Ukraine	96
Bosnia and Herzegovina	95
Tajikistan	95
Turkey	95
Belarus	94
Albania	93
Kyrgyzstan	93
Lithuania	92
Ireland	91
The Former Yugoslav Republic of Macedonia	91
Armenia	90
Azerbaijan	89
Latvia	88
Bulgaria	86
Georgia	86
Romania	79
Republic of Moldova	76
Russian Federation	72
San Marino	
Turkmenistan	

EMR

Kuwait	100
Saudi Arabia	100
Bahrain	99
Jordan	99
Qatar	98
United Arab Emirates	98
Libya	97
Oman	97
Syrian Arab Republic	96
Egypt	95
Tunisia	92
Iran (Islamic Republic of)	90
Iraq	86
Lebanon	81
Morocco	77
Pakistan	64
Djibouti	47
Afghanistan	32
Somalia	
Sudan	
Yemen	

WPR

Australia	100
Japan	100
Niue	100
Palau	100
Republic of Korea	100
Singapore	100
Cook Islands	98
Malaysia	96
Samoa	92
Fiji	91
Tonga	91
Viet Nam	78
China	77
Marshall Islands	77
Philippines	74
Lao People's Democratic Republic	71
Nauru	66
Mongolia	60
Vanuatu	58
Micronesia (Federated States of)	57
Cambodia	42
Kiribati	40
Solomon Islands	30
Papua New Guinea	19
Brunei Darussalam	
New Zealand	
Tuvalu	

[1] This indicator is used here as a proxy for the SDG indicator. Data source: Progress on sanitation and drinking water – 2015 update and MDG assessment. New York (NY): UNICEF; and Geneva: World Health Organization; 2015 (http://apps.who.int/iris/bitstream/10665/177752/1/9789241509145_eng.pdf?ua=1, accessed 23 March 2017).

CLEAN HOUSEHOLD ENERGY

SDG Target 7.1
By 2030, ensure universal access to affordable, reliable and modern energy services

Indicator 7.1.2: Proportion of population with primary reliance on clean fuels and technology

Proportion of population with primary reliance on clean fuels (%), 2014[1]

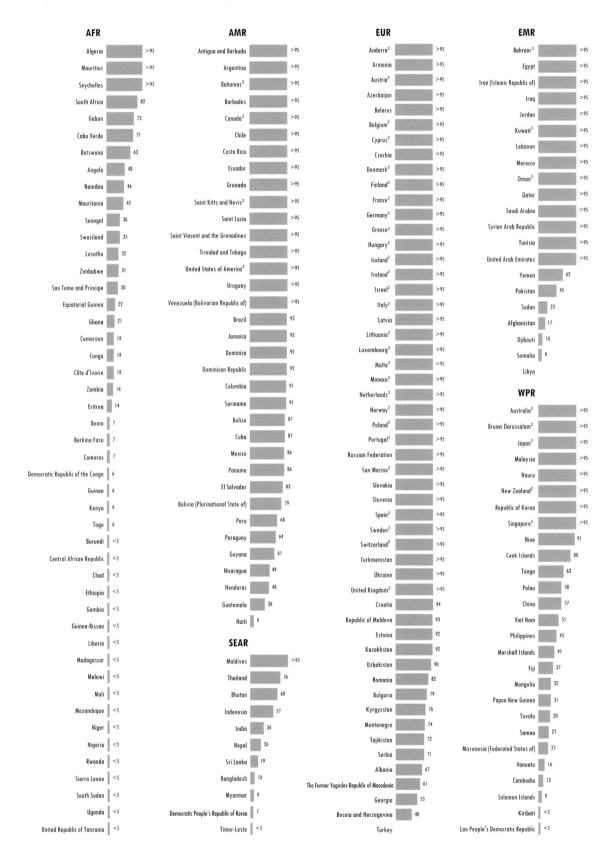

AFR

Country	%
Algeria	>95
Mauritius	>95
Seychelles	>95
South Africa	82
Gabon	73
Cabo Verde	71
Botswana	63
Angola	48
Namibia	46
Mauritania	45
Senegal	36
Swaziland	35
Lesotho	32
Zimbabwe	31
Sao Tome and Principe	30
Equatorial Guinea	22
Ghana	21
Cameroon	18
Congo	18
Côte d'Ivoire	18
Zambia	16
Eritrea	14
Benin	7
Burkina Faso	7
Comoros	7
Democratic Republic of the Congo	6
Guinea	6
Kenya	6
Togo	6
Burundi	<5
Central African Republic	<5
Chad	<5
Ethiopia	<5
Gambia	<5
Guinea-Bissau	<5
Liberia	<5
Madagascar	<5
Malawi	<5
Mali	<5
Mozambique	<5
Niger	<5
Nigeria	<5
Rwanda	<5
Sierra Leone	<5
South Sudan	<5
Uganda	<5
United Republic of Tanzania	<5

AMR

Country	%
Antigua and Barbuda	>95
Argentina	>95
Bahamas[2]	>95
Barbados	>95
Canada[2]	>95
Chile	>95
Costa Rica	>95
Ecuador	>95
Grenada	>95
Saint Kitts and Nevis[2]	>95
Saint Lucia	>95
Saint Vincent and the Grenadines	>95
Trinidad and Tobago	>95
United States of America[2]	>95
Uruguay	>95
Venezuela (Bolivarian Republic of)	>95
Brazil	93
Jamaica	93
Dominica	92
Dominican Republic	92
Colombia	91
Suriname	91
Belize	87
Cuba	87
Mexico	86
Panama	86
El Salvador	83
Bolivia (Plurinational State of)	79
Peru	68
Paraguay	64
Guyana	61
Nicaragua	49
Honduras	48
Guatemala	36
Haiti	9

SEAR

Country	%
Maldives	>95
Thailand	76
Bhutan	68
Indonesia	57
India	34
Nepal	26
Sri Lanka	19
Bangladesh	10
Myanmar	9
Democratic People's Republic of Korea	7
Timor-Leste	<5

EUR

Country	%
Andorra[2]	>95
Armenia	>95
Austria[2]	>95
Azerbaijan	>95
Belarus	>95
Belgium[2]	>95
Cyprus[2]	>95
Czechia	>95
Denmark[2]	>95
Finland[2]	>95
France[2]	>95
Germany[2]	>95
Greece[2]	>95
Hungary[2]	>95
Iceland[2]	>95
Ireland[2]	>95
Israel[2]	>95
Italy[2]	>95
Latvia	>95
Lithuania[2]	>95
Luxembourg[2]	>95
Malta[2]	>95
Monaco[2]	>95
Netherlands[2]	>95
Norway[2]	>95
Poland[2]	>95
Portugal[2]	>95
Russian Federation	>95
San Marino[2]	>95
Slovakia	>95
Slovenia	>95
Spain[2]	>95
Sweden[2]	>95
Switzerland[2]	>95
Turkmenistan	>95
Ukraine	>95
United Kingdom[2]	>95
Croatia	94
Republic of Moldova	93
Estonia	92
Kazakhstan	92
Uzbekistan	90
Romania	82
Bulgaria	79
Kyrgyzstan	76
Montenegro	74
Tajikistan	72
Serbia	71
Albania	67
The Former Yugoslav Republic of Macedonia	61
Georgia	55
Bosnia and Herzegovina	40
Turkey	

EMR

Country	%
Bahrain[2]	>95
Egypt	>95
Iran (Islamic Republic of)	>95
Iraq	>95
Jordan	>95
Kuwait[2]	>95
Lebanon	>95
Morocco	>95
Oman[2]	>95
Qatar	>95
Saudi Arabia	>95
Syrian Arab Republic	>95
Tunisia	>95
United Arab Emirates	>95
Yemen	62
Pakistan	45
Sudan	23
Afghanistan	17
Djibouti	10
Somalia	9
Libya	

WPR

Country	%
Australia[2]	>95
Brunei Darussalam[2]	>95
Japan[2]	>95
Malaysia	>95
Nauru	>95
New Zealand[2]	>95
Republic of Korea	>95
Singapore[2]	>95
Niue	91
Cook Islands	80
Tonga	63
Palau	58
China	57
Viet Nam	51
Philippines	45
Marshall Islands	41
Fiji	37
Mongolia	32
Papua New Guinea	31
Tuvalu	30
Samoa	27
Micronesia (Federated States of)	25
Vanuatu	16
Cambodia	13
Solomon Islands	9
Kiribati	<5
Lao People's Democratic Republic	<5

[1] Burning opportunity: clean household energy for health, sustainable development, and wellbeing of women and children. Geneva: World Health Organization; 2016 (http://apps.who.int/iris/bitstream/10665/204717/1/9789241565233_eng.pdf, accessed 23 March 2017).

[2] For high-income countries with no information on clean fuel use, usage is assumed to be >95%.

AIR POLLUTION

SDG Target 11.6
By 2030, reduce the adverse per capita environmental impact of cities, including by paying special attention to air quality and municipal and other waste management

Indicator 11.6.2: Annual mean levels of fine particulate matter (e.g. $PM_{2.5}$ and PM_{10}) in cities (population weighted)

Annual mean levels of fine particulate matter ($PM_{2.5}$) in urban areas (µg/m³), 2014[1]

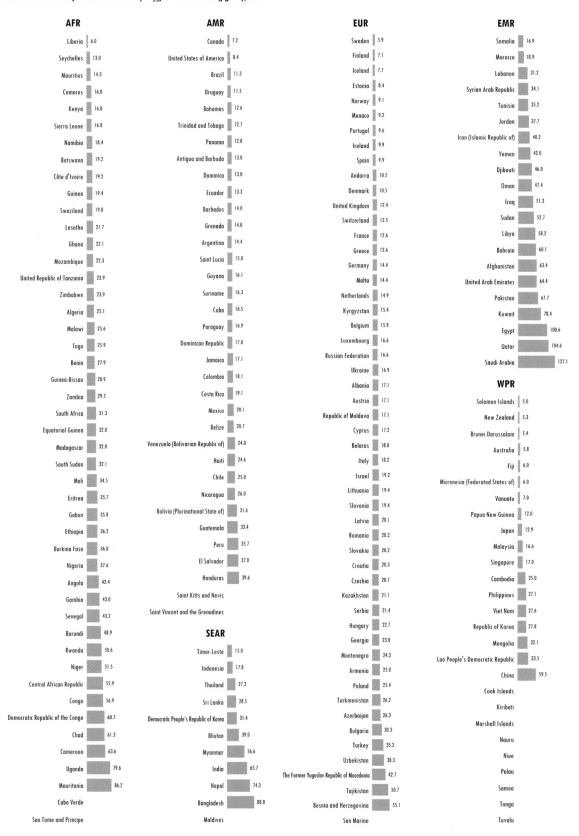

AFR

Liberia	6.0
Seychelles	13.0
Mauritius	14.3
Comoros	16.0
Kenya	16.8
Sierra Leone	16.8
Namibia	18.4
Botswana	19.2
Côte d'Ivoire	19.2
Guinea	19.4
Swaziland	19.8
Lesotho	21.7
Ghana	22.1
Mozambique	22.3
United Republic of Tanzania	23.9
Zimbabwe	23.9
Algeria	25.1
Malawi	25.6
Togo	25.9
Benin	27.9
Guinea-Bissau	28.9
Zambia	29.5
South Africa	31.3
Equatorial Guinea	32.0
Madagascar	32.0
South Sudan	32.1
Mali	34.5
Eritrea	35.7
Gabon	35.8
Ethiopia	36.2
Burkina Faso	36.8
Nigeria	37.6
Angola	42.4
Gambia	43.0
Senegal	43.2
Burundi	48.9
Rwanda	50.6
Niger	51.5
Central African Republic	55.9
Congo	56.9
Democratic Republic of the Congo	60.7
Chad	61.3
Cameroon	63.6
Uganda	79.6
Mauritania	86.2
Cabo Verde	
Sao Tome and Principe	

AMR

Canada	7.2
United States of America	8.4
Brazil	11.3
Uruguay	11.5
Bahamas	12.6
Trinidad and Tobago	12.7
Panama	12.8
Antigua and Barbuda	13.0
Dominica	13.0
Ecuador	13.3
Barbados	14.0
Grenada	14.0
Argentina	14.4
Saint Lucia	15.0
Guyana	16.1
Suriname	16.3
Cuba	16.5
Paraguay	16.9
Dominican Republic	17.0
Jamaica	17.1
Colombia	18.1
Costa Rica	19.1
Mexico	20.1
Belize	20.7
Venezuela (Bolivarian Republic of)	24.0
Haiti	24.6
Chile	25.0
Nicaragua	26.0
Bolivia (Plurinational State of)	31.6
Guatemala	33.4
Peru	35.7
El Salvador	37.0
Honduras	39.6
Saint Kitts and Nevis	
Saint Vincent and the Grenadines	

SEAR

Timor-Leste	15.0
Indonesia	17.8
Thailand	27.3
Sri Lanka	28.5
Democratic People's Republic of Korea	31.4
Bhutan	39.0
Myanmar	56.6
India	65.7
Nepal	74.3
Bangladesh	88.8
Maldives	

EUR

Sweden	5.9
Finland	7.1
Iceland	7.7
Estonia	8.4
Norway	9.1
Monaco	9.2
Portugal	9.6
Ireland	9.9
Spain	9.9
Andorra	10.5
Denmark	10.5
United Kingdom	12.4
Switzerland	12.5
France	12.6
Greece	12.6
Germany	14.4
Malta	14.4
Netherlands	14.9
Kyrgyzstan	15.4
Belgium	15.9
Luxembourg	16.6
Russian Federation	16.6
Ukraine	16.9
Albania	17.1
Austria	17.1
Republic of Moldova	17.1
Cyprus	17.2
Belarus	18.0
Italy	18.2
Israel	19.2
Lithuania	19.4
Slovenia	19.4
Latvia	20.1
Romania	20.2
Slovakia	20.2
Croatia	20.3
Czechia	20.7
Kazakhstan	21.1
Serbia	21.4
Hungary	22.7
Georgia	23.0
Montenegro	24.3
Armenia	25.0
Poland	25.4
Turkmenistan	26.2
Azerbaijan	26.3
Bulgaria	30.3
Turkey	35.2
Uzbekistan	38.3
The Former Yugoslav Republic of Macedonia	42.7
Tajikistan	50.7
Bosnia and Herzegovina	55.1
San Marino	

EMR

Somalia	16.9
Morocco	18.9
Lebanon	31.2
Syrian Arab Republic	34.1
Tunisia	35.2
Jordan	37.7
Iran (Islamic Republic of)	40.2
Yemen	42.0
Djibouti	46.0
Oman	47.4
Iraq	51.3
Sudan	52.7
Libya	58.2
Bahrain	60.1
Afghanistan	63.4
United Arab Emirates	64.4
Pakistan	67.7
Kuwait	78.4
Egypt	100.6
Qatar	104.6
Saudi Arabia	127.1

WPR

Solomon Islands	5.0
New Zealand	5.3
Brunei Darussalam	5.4
Australia	5.8
Fiji	6.0
Micronesia (Federated States of)	6.0
Vanuatu	7.0
Papua New Guinea	12.0
Japan	12.9
Malaysia	16.6
Singapore	17.0
Cambodia	25.0
Philippines	27.1
Viet Nam	27.6
Republic of Korea	27.8
Mongolia	32.1
Lao People's Democratic Republic	33.5
China	59.5
Cook Islands	
Kiribati	
Marshall Islands	
Nauru	
Niue	
Palau	
Samoa	
Tonga	
Tuvalu	

[1] Ambient air pollution: a global assessment of exposure and burden of disease. Geneva: World Health Organization; 2016 (see: http://who.int/phe/publications/air-pollution-global-assessment/en/, accessed 23 March 2017).

MORTALITY DUE TO DISASTERS

SDG Target 13.1
Strengthen resilience and adaptive capacity to climate-related hazards and natural disasters in all countries

Indicator 13.1.1: Number of deaths, missing persons and directly affected persons attributed to disasters per 100 000 population

Average death rate due to natural disasters (per 100 000 population), 2011–2015[1]

AFR		AMR		EUR		EMR	
Cabo Verde	0.0	Antigua and Barbuda	0.0	Albania	0.0	Bahrain	0.0
Central African Republic	0.0	Bahamas	0.0	Armenia	0.0	Djibouti	0.0
Equatorial Guinea	0.0	Barbados	0.0	Azerbaijan	0.0	Egypt	0.0
Eritrea	0.0	Belize	0.0	Belarus	0.0	Jordan	0.0
Ethiopia	0.0	Grenada	0.0	Cyprus	0.0	Kuwait	0.0
Gabon	0.0	Guyana	0.0	Estonia	0.0	Lebanon	0.0
Guinea	0.0	Jamaica	0.0	Finland	0.0	Qatar	0.0
Guinea-Bissau	0.0	Suriname	0.0	Hungary	0.0	Syrian Arab Republic	0.0
Liberia	0.0	Trinidad and Tobago	0.0	Iceland	0.0	Tunisia	0.0
Sao Tome and Principe	0.0	Uruguay	0.0	Kyrgyzstan	0.0	United Arab Emirates	0.0
Seychelles	0.0	Dominican Republic	<0.1	Latvia	0.0	Iraq	<0.1
Togo	0.0	Paraguay	<0.1	Lithuania	0.0	Morocco	<0.1
Zambia	0.0	Venezuela (Bolivarian Republic of)	<0.1	Luxembourg	0.0	Saudi Arabia	<0.1
Algeria	<0.1	Argentina	0.1	Malta	0.0	Yemen	<0.1
Benin	<0.1	Canada	0.1	Montenegro	0.0	Iran (Islamic Republic of)	0.1
Burkina Faso	<0.1	Chile	0.1	Republic of Moldova	0.0	Libya	0.1
Cameroon	<0.1	Costa Rica	0.1	Slovakia	0.0	Oman	0.1
Chad	<0.1	El Salvador	0.1	The Former Yugoslav Republic of Macedonia	0.0	Sudan	0.1
Côte d'Ivoire	<0.1	Honduras	0.1	Turkmenistan	0.0	Pakistan	0.4
Democratic Republic of the Congo	<0.1	Peru	0.1	Belgium	<0.1	Somalia	0.4
Gambia	<0.1	Brazil	0.2	Denmark	<0.1	Afghanistan	0.8
Mali	<0.1	Cuba	0.2	Greece	<0.1		
Mauritania	<0.1	Ecuador	0.2	Ireland	<0.1	**WPR**	
Rwanda	<0.1	Guatemala	0.2	Israel	<0.1	Brunei Darussalam	0.0
Senegal	<0.1	Mexico	0.2	Kazakhstan	<0.1	Kiribati	0.0
South Africa	<0.1	Nicaragua	0.2	Netherlands	<0.1	Mongolia	0.0
Uganda	<0.1	Colombia	0.3	Poland	<0.1	Singapore	0.0
United Republic of Tanzania	<0.1	Panama	0.3	Russian Federation	<0.1	Tonga	0.0
Angola	0.1	Haiti	0.4	Slovenia	<0.1	Malaysia	<0.1
Botswana	0.1	United States of America	0.4	Switzerland	<0.1	Australia	0.1
Comoros	0.1	Bolivia (Plurinational State of)	0.5	Ukraine	<0.1	China	0.1
Congo	0.1	Saint Lucia	0.7	Bosnia and Herzegovina	0.1	Viet Nam	0.1
Kenya	0.1	Saint Vincent and the Grenadines	2.2	Bulgaria	0.1	Lao People's Democratic Republic	0.2
Nigeria	0.1			Croatia	0.1	Papua New Guinea	0.2
Sierra Leone	0.1	**SEAR**		Germany	0.1	Republic of Korea	0.3
Burundi	0.2	Bhutan	0.0	Italy	0.1	Fiji	0.4
Ghana	0.2	Maldives	0.0	Norway	0.1	Cambodia	0.7
Lesotho	0.2	Timor-Leste	0.0	Portugal	0.1	New Zealand	0.9
Madagascar	0.2	Bangladesh	0.1	Serbia	0.1	Vanuatu	0.9
Malawi	0.2	Indonesia	0.1	Spain	0.1	Micronesia (Federated States of)	1.3
Mauritius	0.2	Myanmar	0.1	Sweden	0.1	Solomon Islands	2.0
Mozambique	0.2	Democratic People's Republic of Korea	0.2	Tajikistan	0.1	Samoa	2.4
Niger	0.2	India	0.2	United Kingdom	0.1	Philippines	2.5
Swaziland	0.2	Thailand	0.3	Uzbekistan	0.1	Japan	4.2
Zimbabwe	0.2	Sri Lanka	0.4	Austria	0.2		
South Sudan	0.3	Nepal	7.2	Czechia	0.2		
Namibia	0.9			France	0.2		
				Georgia	0.2		
				Turkey	0.2		
				Romania	0.6		

[1] Global Health Estimates 2015: Deaths by cause, age, sex, by country and by region, 2000–2015. Geneva: World Health Organization; 2016 (http://www.who.int/healthinfo/global_burden_disease/estimates/en/index1.html, accessed 22 March 2017). WHO Member States with a population of less than 90 000 in 2015 were not included in this analysis. The death rate is an average over the five year period.

HOMICIDE

SDG Target 16.1
Significantly reduce all forms of violence and related death rates everywhere

Indicator 16.1.1: Number of victims of intentional homicide per 100 000 population, by sex and age

Mortality rate due to homicide (per 100 000 population), 2015[1]

AFR

Country	Rate
Malawi	1.7
Mauritius	2.7
Mozambique	3.0
Equatorial Guinea	3.2
Algeria	4.2
South Sudan	4.5
Rwanda	5.1
Cabo Verde	5.9
Benin	6.0
Burundi	6.2
Sao Tome and Principe	6.4
Senegal	7.3
Eritrea	7.5
Comoros	7.6
Ethiopia	7.6
United Republic of Tanzania	7.6
Madagascar	7.7
Kenya	8.2
Guinea	8.5
Chad	9.0
Gabon	9.0
Gambia	9.1
Togo	9.1
Guinea-Bissau	9.2
Angola	9.6
Zambia	9.7
Burkina Faso	9.8
Nigeria	9.8
Ghana	10.0
Niger	10.0
Congo	10.1
Mauritania	10.2
Seychelles	10.2
Liberia	10.4
Botswana	10.8
Mali	10.8
Cameroon	11.5
Côte d'Ivoire	11.8
Central African Republic	13.1
Uganda	13.1
Sierra Leone	13.2
Democratic Republic of the Congo	13.4
Namibia	14.6
Swaziland	20.0
South Africa	26.2
Zimbabwe	28.5
Lesotho	29.7

AMR

Country	Rate
Canada	1.8
Chile	4.6
Argentina	4.7
Antigua and Barbuda	4.8
Cuba	4.9
United States of America	5.3
Grenada	6.4
Paraguay	7.5
Uruguay	7.6
Costa Rica	9.2
Barbados	10.1
Ecuador	10.2
Suriname	10.7
Saint Lucia	13.5
Bolivia (Plurinational State of)	13.6
Peru	14.6
Nicaragua	15.0
Panama	18.7
Guyana	18.8
Mexico	19.0
Saint Vincent and the Grenadines	21.7
Bahamas	23.7
Haiti	28.1
Dominican Republic	30.2
Brazil	30.5
Trinidad and Tobago	32.8
Jamaica	35.2
Guatemala	36.2
Belize	37.2
Colombia	48.8
Venezuela (Bolivarian Republic of)	51.7
El Salvador	63.2
Honduras	85.7

SEAR

Country	Rate
Bhutan	1.5
Bangladesh	2.9
Sri Lanka	3.1
Nepal	3.3
Maldives	3.5
Myanmar	3.9
India	4.0
Thailand	4.0
Indonesia	4.3
Democratic People's Republic of Korea	4.4
Timor-Leste	4.4

EUR

Country	Rate
Luxembourg	0.4
Slovenia	0.6
Switzerland	0.6
Germany	0.7
Netherlands	0.7
Norway	0.7
Spain	0.8
Czechia	0.9
France	0.9
Ireland	0.9
Italy	0.9
Poland	0.9
Austria	1.0
Croatia	1.0
Belgium	1.1
Denmark	1.1
Portugal	1.1
Hungary	1.2
Sweden	1.2
Iceland	1.3
Slovakia	1.3
Tajikistan	1.3
United Kingdom	1.3
The Former Yugoslav Republic of Macedonia	1.4
Bulgaria	1.5
Romania	1.5
Finland	1.6
Armenia	1.7
Serbia	1.7
Greece	2.0
Israel	2.0
Azerbaijan	2.2
Cyprus	2.2
Turkey	2.4
Montenegro	2.6
Malta	2.9
Uzbekistan	3.0
Bosnia and Herzegovina	3.1
Albania	4.1
Georgia	4.2
Turkmenistan	4.2
Estonia	4.4
Republic of Moldova	5.5
Ukraine	6.0
Belarus	6.2
Latvia	6.7
Lithuania	6.8
Kyrgyzstan	7.7
Kazakhstan	9.0
Russian Federation	10.3

EMR

Country	Rate
Bahrain	0.7
Morocco	1.6
Tunisia	1.6
Kuwait	2.5
Libya	2.5
Syrian Arab Republic	2.5
Jordan	3.0
United Arab Emirates	3.7
Iran (Islamic Republic of)	4.1
Lebanon	4.2
Egypt	5.0
Oman	5.0
Somalia	5.6
Saudi Arabia	5.8
Yemen	6.1
Sudan	6.5
Djibouti	6.8
Afghanistan	7.0
Qatar	8.1
Pakistan	9.5
Iraq	12.7

WPR

Country	Rate
Japan	0.3
Australia	0.9
China	0.9
New Zealand	1.2
Brunei Darussalam	1.3
Republic of Korea	2.0
Vanuatu	2.1
Cambodia	2.2
Fiji	2.5
Singapore	2.7
Samoa	3.1
Malaysia	3.8
Tonga	3.8
Viet Nam	3.9
Solomon Islands	4.1
Micronesia (Federated States of)	4.7
Lao People's Democratic Republic	6.9
Mongolia	8.2
Kiribati	9.1
Philippines	11.6
Papua New Guinea	12.2

[1] Global Health Estimates 2015: Deaths by cause, age, sex, by country and by region, 2000–2015. Geneva: World Health Organization; 2016 (http://www.who.int/healthinfo/global_burden_disease/estimates/en/index1.html, accessed 22 March 2017). WHO Member States with a population of less than 90 000 in 2015 were not included in this analysis.

MORTALITY DUE TO CONFLICTS

SDG Target 16.1
Significantly reduce all forms of violence and related death rates everywhere

Indicator 16.1.2: Conflict-related deaths per 100 000 population, by sex, age and cause

Estimated deaths from major conflicts (per 100 000 population), 2001–2015[1]

■ 2011–2015   ■ 2006–2010   ■ 2001–2005

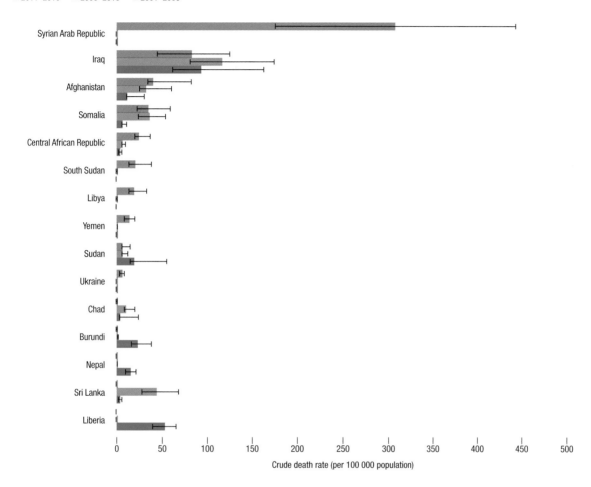

Crude death rate (per 100 000 population)

---

[1] Global Health Estimates 2015: Deaths by cause, age, sex, by country and by region, 2000–2015. Geneva: World Health Organization; 2016 (http://www.who.int/healthinfo/global_burden_ disease/estimates/en/index1.html, accessed 22 March 2017). Conflict deaths include deaths due to collective violence and exclude deaths due to legal intervention. WHO Member States with estimated conflict deaths exceeding 5 per 100 000 population in 2011–2015 or 10 per 100 000 population in earlier five-year periods. The death rate is an average over each five year period. Confidence intervals are shown as the black horizontal lines.

DEATH REGISTRATION

SDG Target 17.19
By 2030, build on existing initiatives to develop measurements of progress on sustainable development that complement gross domestic product, and support statistical capacity-building in developing countries

Indicator 17.19.2: Proportion of countries that (a) have conducted at least one population and housing census in the last 10 years; and (b) have achieved 100 per cent birth registration and 80 per cent death registration

Completeness[1] (%) and quality[2] of cause-of-death data, 2005–2015 | Quality | ■ High | ▫ Medium | ▨ Low | ■ Very low

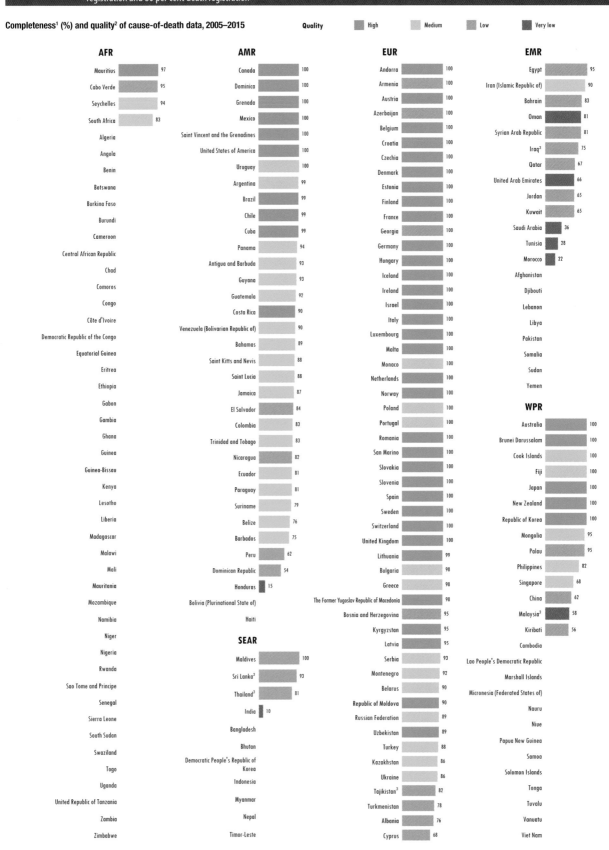

AFR		AMR		EUR		EMR	
Mauritius	97	Canada	100	Andorra	100	Egypt	95
Cabo Verde	95	Dominica	100	Armenia	100	Iran (Islamic Republic of)	90
Seychelles	94	Grenada	100	Austria	100	Bahrain	83
South Africa	83	Mexico	100	Azerbaijan	100	Oman	81
Algeria		Saint Vincent and the Grenadines	100	Belgium	100	Syrian Arab Republic	81
Angola		United States of America	100	Croatia	100	Iraq[3]	75
Benin		Uruguay	100	Czechia	100	Qatar	67
Botswana		Argentina	99	Denmark	100	United Arab Emirates	66
Burkina Faso		Brazil	99	Estonia	100	Jordan	65
Burundi		Chile	99	Finland	100	Kuwait	65
Cameroon		Cuba	99	France	100	Saudi Arabia	36
Central African Republic		Panama	94	Georgia	100	Tunisia	28
Chad		Antigua and Barbuda	93	Germany	100	Morocco	22
Comoros		Guyana	93	Hungary	100	Afghanistan	
Congo		Guatemala	92	Iceland	100	Djibouti	
Côte d'Ivoire		Costa Rica	90	Ireland	100	Lebanon	
Democratic Republic of the Congo		Venezuela (Bolivarian Republic of)	90	Israel	100	Libya	
Equatorial Guinea		Bahamas	89	Italy	100	Pakistan	
Eritrea		Saint Kitts and Nevis	88	Luxembourg	100	Somalia	
Ethiopia		Saint Lucia	88	Malta	100	Sudan	
Gabon		Jamaica	87	Monaco	100	Yemen	
Gambia		El Salvador	84	Netherlands	100		
Ghana		Colombia	83	Norway	100	**WPR**	
Guinea		Trinidad and Tobago	83	Poland	100	Australia	100
Guinea-Bissau		Nicaragua	82	Portugal	100	Brunei Darussalam	100
Kenya		Ecuador	81	Romania	100	Cook Islands	100
Lesotho		Paraguay	81	San Marino	100	Fiji	100
Liberia		Suriname	79	Slovakia	100	Japan	100
Madagascar		Belize	76	Slovenia	100	New Zealand	100
Malawi		Barbados	75	Spain	100	Republic of Korea	100
Mali		Peru	62	Sweden	100	Mongolia	95
Mauritania		Dominican Republic	54	Switzerland	100	Palau	95
Mozambique		Honduras	15	United Kingdom	100	Philippines	82
Namibia		Bolivia (Plurinational State of)		Lithuania	99	Singapore	68
Niger		Haiti		Bulgaria	98	China	62
Nigeria				Greece	98	Malaysia[3]	58
Rwanda		**SEAR**		The Former Yugoslav Republic of Macedonia	98	Kiribati	56
Sao Tome and Principe		Maldives	100	Bosnia and Herzegovina	95	Cambodia	
Senegal		Sri Lanka[3]	93	Kyrgyzstan	95	Lao People's Democratic Republic	
Sierra Leone		Thailand[3]	81	Latvia	95	Marshall Islands	
South Sudan		India	10	Serbia	93	Micronesia (Federated States of)	
Swaziland		Bangladesh		Montenegro	92	Nauru	
Togo		Bhutan		Belarus	90	Niue	
Uganda		Democratic People's Republic of Korea		Republic of Moldova	90	Papua New Guinea	
United Republic of Tanzania		Indonesia		Russian Federation	89	Samoa	
Zambia		Myanmar		Uzbekistan	89	Solomon Islands	
Zimbabwe		Nepal		Turkey	88	Tonga	
		Timor-Leste		Kazakhstan	86	Tuvalu	
				Ukraine	86	Vanuatu	
				Tajikistan[3]	82	Viet Nam	
				Turkmenistan	78		
				Albania	76		
				Cyprus	68		

[1] Figures shown for completeness refer to the latest available value (2005–2015). Completeness was assessed relative to the de facto resident populations. Global Health Estimates 2015: Deaths by cause, age, sex, by country and by region, 2000–2015. Geneva: World Health Organization; 2016 (http://www.who.int/healthinfo/global_burden_disease/estimates/en/index1.html, accessed 22 March 2017).

[2] See section 1.1. The colour represents the assessment of data quality for the period 2005–2015.

[3] Completeness refers to year prior to 2010.

ANNEX B

Tables of health statistics by country, WHO region and globally

Explanatory notes

The statistics shown in Annex B represent official WHO statistics based on the evidence available in early 2017. They have been compiled primarily using publications and databases produced and maintained by WHO or United Nations groups of which WHO is a member. A number of statistics have been derived from data produced and maintained by other international organizations. In some cases, as indicator definitions are being refined and baseline data are being collected, proxy indicators are presented. All such proxy indicators appearing in this annex are clearly indicated as such through the use of accompanying footnotes.

Wherever possible, estimates have been computed using standardized categories and methods in order to enhance cross-national comparability. This approach may result in some cases in differences between the estimates presented here and the official national statistics prepared and endorsed by individual WHO Member States. It is important to stress that these estimates are also subject to considerable uncertainty, especially for countries with weak statistical and health information systems where the quality of underlying empirical data is limited.

For indicators with a reference period expressed as a range, figures refer to the latest available year in the range unless otherwise noted.

Unless otherwise stated, the WHO regional and global aggregates for rates and ratios are weighted averages when relevant, while for absolute numbers they are the sums. Aggregates are shown only if data are available for at least 50% of the population (or other denominator) within an indicated group. For indicators with a reference period expressed as a range, aggregates are for the reference period shown in the heading unless otherwise noted. Some WHO regional and global aggregates may include country estimates that are not available for reporting.

More details on the indicators and estimates presented here are available at the WHO Global Health Observatory.[1]

Note: – indicates data not available or not applicable.

---

[1] The Global Health Observatory (GHO) is WHO's portal providing access to data and analyses for monitoring the global health situation. See: http://www.who.int/gho/en/, accessed 18 March 2017.

ANNEX B
Part 1

Member State	Total population[a] (000s)	Life expectancy at birth[b] (years) Male	Life expectancy at birth[b] (years) Female	Life expectancy at birth[b] (years) Both sexes	Healthy life expectancy at birth[b] (years)	3.1 Maternal mortality ratio[c] (per 100 000 live births)	Proportion of births attended by skilled health personnel[d] (%)	3.2 Under-five mortality rate[e] (per 1000 live births)	Neonatal mortality rate[e] (per 1000 live births)	3.3 New HIV infections among adults 15–49 years old[f] (per 1000 uninfected population)
	2015	2015			2015	2015	2005–2016	2015	2015	2015
Afghanistan	32 527	59.3	61.9	60.5	52.2	396	51[ac]	91.1	35.5	0.06
Albania	2 897	75.1	80.7	77.8	68.8	29	99	14.0	6.2	–
Algeria	39 667	73.8	77.5	75.6	66.0	140	97	25.5	15.5	0.02
Andorra	70	–	–	–	–	–	–	2.8	1.4	–
Angola	25 022	50.9	54.0	52.4	45.8	477	47[ac]	156.9	48.7	1.86
Antigua and Barbuda	92	74.1	78.6	76.4	67.5	–	100[ac]	8.1	4.9	–
Argentina	43 417	72.7	79.9	76.3	67.6	52	100	12.5	6.3	0.23
Armenia	3 018	71.6	77.7	74.8	66.8	25	100[ac]	14.1	7.4	0.26
Australia	23 969	80.9	84.8	82.8	71.9	6	99[ac]	3.8	2.2	0.10
Austria	8 545	79.0	83.9	81.5	72.0	4	99[ac]	3.5	2.1	–
Azerbaijan	9 754	69.6	75.8	72.7	64.7	25	100[ac]	31.7	18.2	0.20
Bahamas	388	72.9	79.1	76.1	66.6	80	98[ac]	12.1	6.9	2.26
Bahrain	1 377	76.2	77.9	76.9	67.0	15	100[ac]	6.2	1.1	–
Bangladesh	160 996	70.6	73.1	71.8	62.3	176	42[ac]	37.6	23.3	0.01
Barbados	284	73.1	77.9	75.5	66.6	27	99[ac]	13.0	8.0	1.19
Belarus	9 496	66.5	78.0	72.3	65.1	4	100	4.6	1.9	1.05
Belgium	11 299	78.6	83.5	81.1	71.1	7	–	4.1	2.2	–
Belize	359	67.5	73.1	70.1	62.3	28	94[ac]	16.5	8.3	0.82
Benin	10 880	58.8	61.1	60.0	52.5	405	77[ac]	99.5	31.8	0.69
Bhutan	775	69.5	70.1	69.8	61.2	148	75[ac]	32.9	18.3	–
Bolivia (Plurinational State of)	10 725	68.2	73.3	70.7	62.2	206	85	38.4	19.6	0.24
Bosnia and Herzegovina	3 810	75.0	79.7	77.4	68.6	11	100	5.4	4.0	–
Botswana	2 262	63.3	68.1	65.7	56.9	129	100[ac]	43.6	21.9	9.37
Brazil	207 848	71.4	78.7	75.0	65.5	44	99[ac]	16.4	8.9	0.39
Brunei Darussalam	423	76.3	79.2	77.7	70.4	23	100[ac]	10.2	4.3	–
Bulgaria	7 150	71.1	78.0	74.5	66.4	11	100[ac]	10.4	5.6	–
Burkina Faso	18 106	59.1	60.5	59.9	52.6	371	66	88.6	26.7	0.45
Burundi	11 179	57.7	61.6	59.6	52.2	712	60	81.7	28.6	0.18
Cabo Verde	521	71.3	75.0	73.3	64.4	42	92	24.5	12.2	0.60
Cambodia	15 578	66.6	70.7	68.7	58.9	161	89[ac]	28.7	14.8	0.08
Cameroon	23 344	55.9	58.6	57.3	50.3	596	65[ac]	87.9	25.7	3.57
Canada	35 940	80.2	84.1	82.2	72.3	7	98[ac]	4.9	3.2	–
Central African Republic	4 900	50.9	54.1	52.5	45.9	882	40	130.1	42.6	2.40
Chad	14 037	51.7	54.5	53.1	46.1	856	20	138.7	39.3	1.02
Chile	17 948	77.4	83.4	80.5	70.4	22	100	8.1	4.9	0.19
China	1 383 925	74.6	77.6	76.1	68.5	27	100[ac]	10.7	5.5	–
Colombia	48 229	71.2	78.4	74.8	65.1	64	99	15.9	8.5	0.39
Comoros	788	61.9	65.2	63.5	55.9	335	82	73.5	34.0	–
Congo	4 620	63.2	66.3	64.7	56.6	442	94[ac]	45.0	18.0	–
Cook Islands	21	–	–	–	–	–	100[ac]	8.1	4.4	–
Costa Rica	4 808	77.1	82.2	79.6	69.7	25	99	9.7	6.2	0.24
Côte d'Ivoire	22 702	52.3	54.4	53.3	47.0	645	59	92.6	37.9	1.88
Croatia	4 240	74.7	81.2	78.0	69.4	8	100	4.3	2.6	–
Cuba	11 390	76.9	81.4	79.1	69.2	39	99	5.5	2.3	0.48
Cyprus	1 165	78.3	82.7	80.5	71.3	7	97[ac]	2.7	1.5	–
Czechia	10 543	75.9	81.7	78.8	69.4	4	100[ac]	3.4	1.8	–
Democratic People's Republic of Korea	25 155	67.0	74.0	70.6	64.0	82	100	24.9	13.5	–
Democratic Republic of the Congo	77 267	58.3	61.5	59.8	51.7	693	80	98.3	30.1	0.34
Denmark	5 669	78.6	82.5	80.6	71.2	6	98[ac]	3.5	2.5	–
Djibouti	888	61.8	65.3	63.5	55.8	229	87[ac]	65.3	33.4	1.09
Dominica	73	–	–	–	–	–	100[ac]	21.2	15.6	–
Dominican Republic	10 528	70.9	77.1	73.9	65.1	92	98[ac]	30.9	21.7	0.36

	3.3				3.4		3.5	3.6	3.7		
TB incidence[g] (per 100 000 population)	Malaria incidence[h] (per 1000 population at risk)	Infants receiving three doses of hepatitis B vaccine[i] (%)	Reported number of people requiring interventions against NTDs[j]	Probability of dying from any of CVD, cancer, diabetes, CRD between age 30 and exact age 70[k] (%)	Suicide mortality rate[k] (per 100 000 population)	Total alcohol per capita (≥15 years of age) consumption (litres of pure alcohol), projected estimates[l]	Road traffic mortality rate[m] (per 100 000 population)	Proportion of married or in-union women of reproductive age who have their need for family planning satisfied with modern methods[n] (%)	Adolescent birth rate[o] (per 1000 women aged 15–19 years)	Member State
2015	2015	2015	2015	2015	2015	2016	2013	2005–2015	2005–2014	
189	23.6	78	13 765 392	31.0	5.5	0.5	15.5	–	51.9	Afghanistan
19	–	98	0	14.7	4.3	5.7	15.1	12.9	19.7	Albania
75	<0.1	95	7 561	15.0	3.1	1.0	23.8	77.2	12.4	Algeria
6.5	–	94	0	–	–	10.5	7.6	–	4.4	Andorra
370	124.0	64	18 534 219	24.8	20.5	10.8	26.9	–	190.9	Angola
7.5	–	99	158	15.6	0.0	5.4	6.7	–	–	Antigua and Barbuda
25	0.0	94	634	17.1	14.2	9.1	13.6	–	68.1	Argentina
41	–	94	39 044	23.2	5.4	5.4	18.3	39.2	22.7	Armenia
6.0	–	93	17 476	8.9	11.8	11.2	5.4	–	14.2	Australia
7.6	–	98	8	11.2	16.4	10.6	5.4	–	7.9	Austria
69	0.0	96	1 699 962	23.8	3.3	4.0	10.0	21.5	47.2	Azerbaijan
18	–	95	4 127	16.8	1.8	5.4	13.8	–	34.6	Bahamas
18	–	98	6	15.5	6.5	0.9	8.0	–	13.8	Bahrain
225	0.8	94	49 839 493	21.5	5.5	0.2	13.6	72.5	113.0	Bangladesh
0.0	–	97	97	16.2	0.4	7.8	6.7	70.0	49.7	Barbados
55	–	99	0	28.6	22.8	16.4	13.7	74.2	21.6	Belarus
9.4	–	98	6	11.6	20.5	13.2	6.7	–	7.2	Belgium
25	0.1	94	7 300	22.5	7.3	8.2	24.4	73.1	64.0	Belize
60	293.7	79	7 029 345	22.2	9.3	2.6	27.7	24.5	94.0	Benin
155	0.1	99	227 111	23.1	11.7	0.5	15.1	84.6	28.4	Bhutan
117	3.9	99	1 883 582	16.0	18.7	5.9	23.2	42.8	115.6	Bolivia (Plurinational State of)
37	–	82	0	17.6	6.0	5.9	17.7	21.9	11.0	Bosnia and Herzegovina
356	0.9	95	257 169	18.6	9.7	8.2	23.6	–	39.0	Botswana
41	7.9	96	11 067 291	16.9	6.3	8.9	23.4	89.3	64.8	Brazil
58	–	99	9 239	12.6	1.3	1.3	8.1	–	16.6	Brunei Darussalam
24	–	92	313	23.8	15.9	13.6	8.3	–	40.8	Bulgaria
52	389.2	91	11 658 638	23.0	9.2	7.6	30.0	37.1	130.0	Burkina Faso
122	126.3	94	5 601 304	21.6	8.0	6.9	31.3	32.6	85.0	Burundi
139	0.2	93	136 792	16.1	8.5	8.2	26.1	73.2	–	Cabo Verde
380	13.0	89	5 610 240	23.3	11.9	5.3	17.4	56.4	57.0	Cambodia
212	264.2	84	20 630 132	22.4	11.9	9.9	27.6	40.2	119.0	Cameroon
5.1	–	55	0	9.8	12.3	10.0	6.0	–	12.6	Canada
391	289.5	47	4 096 089	23.6	17.4	3.8	32.4	28.7	229.0	Central African Republic
152	163.2	55	10 688 191	23.0	8.7	5.2	24.1	17.5	203.4	Chad
16	–	97	7	11.5	9.9	9.0	12.4	–	51.5	Chile
67	<0.1	99	26 100 630	18.1	10.0	7.8	18.8	–	6.2	China
31	12.3	91	3 846 506	14.6	6.1	5.2	16.8	83.7	84.0	Colombia
35	5.0	80	525 978	22.6	7.4	0.2	28.0	27.8	70.0	Comoros
379	173.3	80	1 346 327	17.8	9.6	7.9	26.4	38.5	147.0	Congo
7.8	–	99	765	–	–	5.1	24.2	–	56.0	Cook Islands
11	0.0	92	11 684	11.1	7.7	4.1	13.9	89.1	61.2	Costa Rica
159	348.8	83	18 738 388	28.4	18.1	5.2	24.2	30.9	125.0	Côte d'Ivoire
13	–	94	11	17.1	17.5	13.6	9.2	–	11.8	Croatia
7.0	–	96	43 862	16.4	14.0	5.4	7.5	88.4	52.5	Cuba
6.2	–	97	2	11.5	4.7	9.3	5.2	–	4.2	Cyprus
5.2	–	97	3	15.6	13.7	13.7	6.1	85.7	11.1	Czechia
561	1.0	96	6 082 191	26.5	15.8	3.9	20.8	76.7	0.7	Democratic People's Republic of Korea
324	246.0	81	52 564 709	20.3	9.8	3.0	33.2	15.6	138.0	Democratic Republic of the Congo
6.0	–	–	0	11.6	12.2	10.1	3.5	–	2.4	Denmark
378	25.4	84	108 810	19.4	8.6	0.4	24.7	–	20.6	Djibouti
11	–	98	7 546	–	–	5.0	15.3	–	47.2[ad]	Dominica
60	0.3	81	989 731	18.7	6.8	6.6	29.3	84.1	90.0	Dominican Republic

ANNEX B
Part 1

Member State	Total population[a] (000s)	Life expectancy at birth[b] (years) Male	Life expectancy at birth[b] (years) Female	Life expectancy at birth[b] (years) Both sexes	Healthy life expectancy at birth[b] (years)	3.1 Maternal mortality ratio[c] (per 100 000 live births)	3.1 Proportion of births attended by skilled health personnel[d] (%)	3.2 Under-five mortality rate[e] (per 1000 live births)	3.2 Neonatal mortality rate[e] (per 1000 live births)	3.3 New HIV infections among adults 15–49 years old[f] (per 1000 uninfected population)
	2015	2015	2015	2015	2015	2015	2005–2016	2015	2015	2015
Ecuador	16 144	73.5	79.0	76.2	67.0	64	96	21.6	10.8	0.15
Egypt	91 508	68.8	73.2	70.9	62.2	33	92	24.0	12.8	0.03
El Salvador	6 127	68.8	77.9	73.5	64.1	54	98[ac]	16.8	8.3	0.15
Equatorial Guinea	845	56.6	60.0	58.2	51.2	342	68[ac]	94.1	33.1	0.24
Eritrea	5 228	62.4	67.0	64.7	55.9	501	34	46.5	18.4	0.21
Estonia	1 313	72.7	82.0	77.6	68.9	9	99[ac]	2.9	1.5	–
Ethiopia	99 391	62.8	66.8	64.8	56.1	353	28[ac]	59.2	27.7	–
Fiji	892	67.0	73.1	69.9	62.9	30	99	22.4	9.6	–
Finland	5 503	78.3	83.8	81.1	71.0	3	100[ac]	2.3	1.3	–
France	64 395	79.4	85.4	82.4	72.6	8	98[ac]	4.3	2.2	–
Gabon	1 725	64.7	67.2	66.0	57.2	291	89[ac]	50.8	23.2	1.39
Gambia	1 991	59.8	62.5	61.1	53.8	706	57	68.9	29.9	1.24
Georgia	4 000	70.3	78.3	74.4	66.5	36	100	11.9	7.2	0.50
Germany	80 689	78.7	83.4	81.0	71.3	6	99[ac]	3.7	2.1	–
Ghana	27 410	61.0	63.9	62.4	55.3	319	71	61.6	28.3	0.77
Greece	10 955	78.3	83.6	81.0	71.9	3	–	4.6	2.9	0.19
Grenada	107	71.2	76.1	73.6	65.0	27	99[ac]	11.8	6.0	–
Guatemala	16 343	68.5	75.2	71.9	62.1	88	66	29.1	13.4	0.41
Guinea	12 609	58.2	59.8	59.0	51.7	679	45[ac]	93.7	31.3	1.18
Guinea-Bissau	1 844	57.2	60.5	58.9	51.5	549	45[ac]	92.5	39.7	–
Guyana	767	63.9	68.5	66.2	58.9	229	86	39.4	22.8	0.88
Haiti	10 711	61.5	65.5	63.5	55.4	359	49	69.0	25.4	0.21
Honduras	8 075	72.3	77.0	74.6	64.9	129	83	20.4	11.0	0.10
Hungary	9 855	72.3	79.1	75.9	67.4	17	99[ac]	5.9	3.5	–
Iceland	329	81.2	84.1	82.7	72.7	3	–	2.0	0.9	–
India	1 311 051	66.9	69.9	68.3	59.5	174	81[ac]	47.7	27.7	0.11
Indonesia	257 564	67.1	71.2	69.1	62.2	126	87	27.2	13.5	0.50
Iran (Islamic Republic of)	79 109	74.5	76.6	75.5	66.6	25	96	15.5	9.5	0.14
Iraq	36 423	66.2	71.8	68.9	60.0	50	91	32.0	18.4	–
Ireland	4 688	79.4	83.4	81.4	71.5	8	100[ac]	3.6	2.3	–
Israel	8 064	80.6	84.3	82.5	72.8	5	–	4.0	2.1	–
Italy	59 798	80.5	84.8	82.7	72.8	4	100[ac]	3.5	2.1	0.16
Jamaica	2 793	73.9	78.6	76.2	66.9	89	99[ac]	15.7	11.6	1.07
Japan	126 573	80.5	86.8	83.7	74.9	5	100[ac]	2.7	0.9	–
Jordan	7 595	72.5	75.9	74.1	65.0	58	100	17.9	10.6	–
Kazakhstan	17 625	65.7	74.7	70.2	63.3	12	100[ac]	14.1	7.0	0.36
Kenya	46 050	61.1	65.8	63.4	55.6	510	62	49.4	22.2	3.52
Kiribati	112	63.7	68.8	66.3	59.1	90	98[ac]	55.9	23.7	–
Kuwait	3 892	73.7	76.0	74.7	65.8	4	99[ac]	8.6	3.2	–
Kyrgyzstan	5 940	67.2	75.1	71.1	63.8	76	98	21.3	11.5	0.28
Lao People's Democratic Republic	6 802	64.1	67.2	65.7	57.9	197	40	66.7	30.1	–
Latvia	1 971	69.6	79.2	74.6	67.1	18	98[ac]	7.9	5.2	0.53
Lebanon	5 851	73.5	76.5	74.9	65.7	15	–	8.3	4.8	0.05
Lesotho	2 135	51.7	55.4	53.7	46.6	487	78	90.2	32.7	18.80
Liberia	4 503	59.8	62.9	61.4	52.7	725	61	69.9	24.1	0.56
Libya	6 278	70.1	75.6	72.7	63.8	9	100[ac]	13.4	7.2	–
Lithuania	2 878	68.1	79.1	73.6	66.0	10	100[ac]	5.2	2.5	–
Luxembourg	567	79.8	84.0	82.0	71.8	10	100[ac]	1.9	0.9	–
Madagascar	24 235	63.9	67.0	65.5	56.9	353	44	49.6	19.7	0.50
Malawi	17 215	56.7	59.9	58.3	51.2	634	90[ac]	64.0	21.8	3.82
Malaysia	30 331	72.7	77.3	75.0	66.5	40	99[ac]	7.0	3.9	0.27
Maldives	364	76.9	80.2	78.5	69.6	68	96	8.6	4.9	–
Mali	17 600	58.2	58.3	58.2	51.1	587	49	114.7	37.8	1.05
Malta	419	79.7	83.7	81.7	71.7	9	100[ac]	6.4	4.4	–
Marshall Islands	53	–	–	–	–	–	90	36.0	16.7	–

	3.3			3.4		3.5	3.6	3.7		
TB incidence[g] (per 100 000 population)	Malaria incidence[h] (per 1000 population at risk)	Infants receiving three doses of hepatitis B vaccine[i] (%)	Reported number of people requiring interventions against NTDs[j]	Probability of dying from any of CVD, cancer, diabetes, CRD between age 30 and exact age 70[k] (%)	Suicide mortality rate[k] (per 100 000 population)	Total alcohol per capita (≥15 years of age) consumption (litres of pure alcohol), projected estimates[l]	Road traffic mortality rate[m] (per 100 000 population)	Proportion of married or in-union women of reproductive age who have their need for family planning satisfied with modern methods[n] (%)	Adolescent birth rate[o] (per 1000 women aged 15–19 years)	Member State
2015	2015	2015	2015	2015	2015	2016	2013	2005–2015	2005–2014	
52	0.1	78	1 943 932	13.1	7.5	5.1	20.1	80.7	–	Ecuador
15	–	93	1 640 557	23.5	2.6	0.4	12.8	80.0	56.0	Egypt
43	<0.1	91	702 992	14.2	11.1	3.4	21.1	81.9	72.0	El Salvador
172	215.1	16	466 357	25.0	22.6	11.6	22.9	20.5	176.0	Equatorial Guinea
65	14.5	95	1 441 264	25.4	6.7	1.2	24.1	19.6	76.0	Eritrea
18	–	91	0	17.2	18.9	12.8	7.0	–	15.6	Estonia
192	58.6	86	75 106 161	19.3	8.4	4.6	25.3	57.6	71.2	Ethiopia
51	–	99	898 821	31.4	8.5	3.3	5.8	–	27.5	Fiji
5.6	–	–	2	10.1	16.2	10.9	4.8	–	7.3	Finland
8.2	–	83	48	10.9	16.9	11.7	5.1	95.5	6.2	France
465	232.4	80	1 560 166	16.3	10.9	10.8	22.9	33.7	115.0	Gabon
174	208.8	97	171 850	20.4	6.2	5.0	29.4	23.9	88.0	Gambia
99	0.0	94	65	22.2	6.7	8.1	11.8	52.8	41.5	Georgia
8.1	–	88	147	12.0	13.4	11.4	4.3	–	7.8	Germany
160	266.4	88	15 536 903	21.3	6.9	4.4	26.2	44.6	65.0	Ghana
4.5	–	96	13	12.3	4.3	8.5	9.1	–	8.3	Greece
5.4	–	92	11	25.3	0.5	8.1	–	–	–	Grenada
25	1.4	74	3 321 447	15.5	2.5	3.1	19.0	65.5	91.0[ad]	Guatemala
177	367.8	51	9 213 212	20.3	7.7	0.8	27.3	15.7	146.0	Guinea
373	89.3	80	1 731 541	18.8	6.3	5.4	27.5	37.6	136.7	Guinea-Bissau
93	40.7	95	747 901	27.8	29.0	8.7	17.3	52.5	101.0	Guyana
194	8.4	60	9 831 829	24.3	11.2	6.3	15.1	44.8	66.0	Haiti
43	2.6	85	2 399 777	13.9	3.5	3.8	17.4	76.0	101.0	Honduras
9.3	–	–	2	22.9	21.6	12.3	7.7	–	19.8	Hungary
2.4	–	–	0	8.3	13.1	7.5	4.6	–	7.1	Iceland
217	18.6	87	497 396 247	23.3	15.7	5.0	16.6	63.9	28.1	India
395	26.1	81	111 437 132	26.6	2.9	0.6	15.3	78.8	47.0	Indonesia
16	0.5	98	18 692	14.8	3.6	1.0	32.1	68.6	37.7	Iran (Islamic Republic of)
43	0.0	56	2 107 072	22.0	3.0	0.4	20.2	59.3	82.0	Iraq
7.2	–	95	0	10.3	11.7	10.9	4.1	–	9.2	Ireland
4.0	–	97	2	9.5	5.5	3.0	3.6	–	10.2	Israel
5.8	–	93	0	9.4	7.9	7.6	6.1	–	5.8	Italy
4.6	–	91	343 044	15.2	1.4	5.5	11.5	83.0	45.7	Jamaica
17	–	–	10	8.8	19.6	7.8	4.7	–	4.4	Japan
7.0	–	99	258	19.6	3.2	0.5	26.3	58.0	26.0	Jordan
89	–	98	0	28.6	27.5	8.7	24.2	79.6	36.4	Kazakhstan
233	166.0	89	13 642 040	17.8	6.5	4.4	29.1	75.4	96.0	Kenya
551	–	87	33 294	28.2	14.3	2.7	2.9	35.8	49.9	Kiribati
22	–	99	0	18.0	4.0	0.2	18.7	–	7.1	Kuwait
144	0.0	97	111 901	24.0	7.4	5.5	22.0	62.1	42.1	Kyrgyzstan
182	20.9	89	2 183 066	25.8	12.3	7.3	14.3	61.3	94.0	Lao People's Democratic Republic
41	–	94	10	22.9	21.7	12.3	10.0	–	15.3	Latvia
13	–	81	5	18.4	3.1	1.6	22.6	–	–	Lebanon
788	–	93	523 534	23.6	10.4	5.7	28.2	76.1	94.0	Lesotho
308	246.2	52	4 048 546	17.1	6.3	5.4	33.7	37.2	147.0	Liberia
40	–	94	8	20.3	5.5	0.1	24.2[k]	29.6	6.0	Libya
56	–	94	33	20.4	32.7	18.2	10.6	–	13.9	Lithuania
6.1	–	99	0	9.7	11.1	11.1	8.7	–	6.4	Luxembourg
236	104.2	69	21 298 533	23.7	4.6	1.8	28.4	49.6	148.0	Madagascar
193	188.8	88	11 426 323	20.2	5.5	2.4	35.0	73.6	143.0	Malawi
89	1.9	99	174 457	17.1	5.8	1.5	24.0	–	12.7	Malaysia
53	–	99	1 892	12.4	8.6	1.7	3.5	42.7	13.7	Maldives
57	448.6	68	18 291 866	24.4	5.7	1.2	25.6	27.3	172.0	Mali
8.8	–	95	0	10.5	6.0	7.5	5.1	–	13.1	Malta
344	–	85	239 476	–	–	–	5.7	80.5	85.0	Marshall Islands

Member State	Total population[a] (000s) 2015	Life expectancy at birth[b] (years) 2015			Healthy life expectancy at birth[b] (years) 2015	3.1 Maternal mortality ratio[c] (per 100 000 live births) 2015	Proportion of births attended by skilled health personnel[d] (%) 2005–2016	3.2 Under-five mortality rate[e] (per 1000 live births) 2015	Neonatal mortality rate[e] (per 1000 live births) 2015	3.3 New HIV infections among adults 15–49 years old[f] (per 1000 uninfected population) 2015
		Male	Female	Both sexes						
Mauritania	4 068	61.6	64.6	63.1	55.1	602	65	84.7	35.7	0.28
Mauritius	1 273	71.4	77.8	74.6	66.8	53	100[ac]	13.5	8.4	0.42
Mexico	127 017	73.9	79.5	76.7	67.4	38	96	13.2	7.0	0.16
Micronesia (Federated States of)	104	68.1	70.6	69.4	62.5	100	100[ac]	34.7	18.8	–
Monaco	38	–	–	–	–	–	–	3.5	1.9	–
Mongolia	2 959	64.7	73.2	68.8	62.0	44	99	22.4	11.1	0.03
Montenegro	626	74.1	78.1	76.1	67.9	7	99	4.7	3.1	–
Morocco	34 378	73.3	75.4	74.3	64.9	121	74	27.6	17.6	0.07
Mozambique	27 978	55.7	59.4	57.6	49.6	489	54[ac]	78.5	27.1	7.07
Myanmar	53 897	64.6	68.5	66.6	59.2	178	60[ac]	50.0	26.4	0.41
Namibia	2 459	63.1	68.3	65.8	57.5	265	88	45.4	15.9	6.79
Nauru	10	–	–	–	–	–	97[ac]	35.4	22.7	–
Nepal	28 514	67.7	70.8	69.2	61.1	258	56[ac]	35.8	22.2	0.08
Netherlands	16 925	80.0	83.6	81.9	72.2	7	–	3.8	2.4	–
New Zealand	4 529	80.0	83.3	81.6	71.6	11	97[ac]	5.7	3.1	–
Nicaragua	6 082	71.5	77.9	74.8	63.7	150	88[ac]	22.1	9.8	0.23
Niger	19 899	60.9	62.8	61.8	54.2	553	40	95.5	26.8	0.19
Nigeria	182 202	53.4	55.6	54.5	47.7	814	35	108.8	34.3	–
Niue	2	–	–	–	–	–	100[ac]	23.0	12.5	–
Norway	5 211	79.8	83.7	81.8	72.0	5	99[ac]	2.6	1.5	–
Oman	4 491	75.0	79.2	76.6	66.7	17	99[ac]	11.6	5.2	–
Pakistan	188 925	65.5	67.5	66.4	57.8	178	52[ac]	81.1	45.5	0.16
Palau	21	–	–	–	–	–	100	16.4	9.0	–
Panama	3 929	74.7	81.1	77.8	68.1	94	94	17.0	9.6	0.48
Papua New Guinea	7 619	60.6	65.4	62.9	56.4	215	53	57.3	24.5	0.54
Paraguay	6 639	72.2	76.0	74.0	65.2	132	96[ac]	20.5	10.9	0.30
Peru	31 377	73.1	78.0	75.5	65.6	68	90	16.9	8.2	0.17
Philippines	100 699	65.3	72.0	68.5	61.1	114	73	28.0	12.6	0.12
Poland	38 612	73.6	81.3	77.5	68.7	3	100[ac]	5.2	3.1	–
Portugal	10 350	78.2	83.9	81.1	71.4	10	99[ac]	3.6	2.0	–
Qatar	2 235	77.4	80.0	78.2	67.7	13	100	8.0	3.8	–
Republic of Korea	50 293	78.8	85.5	82.3	73.2	11	100[ac]	3.4	1.6	–
Republic of Moldova	4 069	67.9	76.2	72.1	64.8	23	100[ac]	15.8	11.9	0.55
Romania	19 511	71.4	78.8	75.0	66.8	31	99[ac]	11.1	6.3	–
Russian Federation	143 457	64.7	76.3	70.5	63.3	25	100[ac]	9.6	5.0	–
Rwanda	11 610	61.9	67.4	64.8	55.5	290	91[ac]	41.7	18.7	1.41
Saint Kitts and Nevis	56	–	–	–	–	–	100[ac]	10.5	6.5	–
Saint Lucia	185	72.6	77.9	75.2	66.1	48	99	14.3	9.3	–
Saint Vincent and the Grenadines	109	71.3	75.2	73.2	64.6	45	99[ac]	18.3	11.5	–
Samoa	193	70.9	77.5	74.0	66.6	51	83[ac]	17.5	9.5	–
San Marino	32	–	–	–	–	–	–	2.9	0.7	–
Sao Tome and Principe	190	65.6	69.4	67.5	59.1	156	93[ac]	47.3	17.1	–
Saudi Arabia	31 540	73.2	76.0	74.5	64.5	12	98[ac]	14.5	7.9	–
Senegal	15 129	64.6	68.6	66.7	58.3	315	53	47.2	20.8	0.14
Serbia	8 851	72.9	78.4	75.6	67.7	17	100[ac]	6.7	4.2	–
Seychelles	96	69.1	78.0	73.2	65.5	–	99[ac]	13.6	8.6	–
Sierra Leone	6 453	49.3	50.8	50.1	44.4	1 360	60	120.4	34.9	0.69
Singapore	5 604	80.0	86.1	83.1	73.9	10	100[ac]	2.7	1.0	–
Slovakia	5 426	72.9	80.2	76.7	68.1	6	99[ac]	7.3	4.2	–
Slovenia	2 068	77.9	83.7	80.8	71.1	9	100[ac]	2.6	1.4	–
Solomon Islands	584	67.9	70.8	69.2	62.1	114	86[ac]	28.1	12.2	–
Somalia	10 787	53.5	56.6	55.0	47.8	732	9	136.8	39.7	0.48
South Africa	54 490	59.3	66.2	62.9	54.5	138	94	40.5	11.0	14.40
South Sudan	12 340	56.1	58.6	57.3	49.9	789	19[ac]	92.6	39.3	–

	3.3				3.4		3.5	3.6	3.7		
TB incidence[g] (per 100 000 population)	Malaria incidence[h] (per 1000 population at risk)	Infants receiving three doses of hepatitis B vaccine[i] (%)	Reported number of people requiring interventions against NTDs[j]	Probability of dying from any of CVD, cancer, diabetes, CRD between age 30 and exact age 70[k] (%)	Suicide mortality rate[k] (per 100 000 population)	Total alcohol per capita (≥15 years of age) consumption (litres of pure alcohol), projected estimates[l]	Road traffic mortality rate[m] (per 100 000 population)	Proportion of married or in-union women of reproductive age who have their need for family planning satisfied with modern methods[n] (%)	Adolescent birth rate[o] (per 1000 women aged 15–19 years)	Member State
2015	2015	2015	2015	2015	2015	2016	2013	2005–2015	2005–2014	
107	74.2	73	690 268	18.5	5.9	0.1	24.5	23.8	71.0	Mauritania
22	–	97	0	22.5	9.3	4.0	12.2	40.8	29.4	Mauritius
21	0.2	82	9 923 501	15.2	5.0	7.1	12.3	81.9	70.9	Mexico
124	–	78	72 590	25.9	11.2	2.4	1.9	–	32.6	Micronesia (Federated States of)
0.0	–	99	0	–	–	–	0.0	–	–	Monaco
428	–	99	43	29.9	28.3	7.8	21.0	68.3	26.7	Mongolia
21	–	82	0	22.0	11.0	9.6	11.9	34.2	13.4	Montenegro
107	–	99	2 742	16.7	4.8	0.8	20.8	74.8	32.0	Morocco
551	297.7	80	23 150 013	22.9	8.4	2.3	31.6	28.2	167.0	Mozambique
365	11.8	75	41 292 086	24.5	4.3	2.2	20.3	–	30.3	Myanmar
489	14.0	92	1 073 269	18.6	7.6	11.8	23.9	75.1	82.0	Namibia
113	–	91	2	–	–	3.6	–	42.5	105.3[ad]	Nauru
156	3.3	91	18 850 311	21.8	6.0	2.5	17.0	56.0	71.0	Nepal
5.8	–	94	64	11.0	11.9	8.7	3.4	–	4.5	Netherlands
7.4	–	92	3	10.4	12.6	10.1	6.0	–	19.1	New Zealand
51	2.9	98	933 780	16.3	9.5	5.1	15.3	84.0	92.0	Nicaragua
95	356.5	65	15 779 050	17.8	4.1	0.5	26.4	40.8	206.0	Niger
322	380.8	56	140 541 791	20.8	9.9	9.1	20.5	28.8	122.0	Nigeria
8.1	–	99	0	–	–	7.1	–	–	14.3	Niue
6.3	–	–	2	9.6	10.9	7.8	3.8	–	5.0	Norway
8.4	–	99	5	17.8	5.6	0.5	25.4	19.1	13.5	Oman
270	8.6	72	31 056 287	24.7	2.1	0.2	14.2	47.0	44.0	Pakistan
76	–	90	15	–	–	–	4.8	–	27.0	Palau
50	3.7	73	437 597	13.7	5.5	7.9	10.0	75.9	91.1	Panama
432	122.2	62	6 425 746	36.1	10.3	2.4	16.8	40.6	–	Papua New Guinea
41	0.0	93	795 686	17.8	10.2	6.3	20.7	84.1	63.0	Paraguay
119	21.2	90	2 831 613	12.7	5.8	8.9	13.9	62.7	65.0	Peru
322	0.4	60	43 430 927	28.6	3.4	5.6	10.5	51.5	57.0	Philippines
19	–	96	47	18.4	22.3	12.3	10.3	–	14.0	Poland
23	–	98	6	11.3	13.6	10.6	7.8	–	10.5	Portugal
34	–	99	26	14.2	6.4	1.0	15.2	68.9	13.4	Qatar
80	0.8	98	2	8.3	28.3[ae]	11.9	12.0	–	1.7	Republic of Korea
152	–	88	0	23.1	14.8	15.9	12.5	60.4	26.7	Republic of Moldova
84	–	90	19	21.3	11.7	13.7	8.7	–	38.9	Romania
80	–	97	0	29.3	20.1	13.9	18.9	72.4	26.6	Russian Federation
56	301.3	98	5 065 110	20.4	8.5	11.5	32.1	65.0	45.0	Rwanda
5.1	–	94	2	–	–	6.9	–	–	–	Saint Kitts and Nevis
8.8	–	99	33 729	19.7	6.8	7.6	18.1	72.4	42.5	Saint Lucia
7.4	–	98	1	24.4	2.7	7.6	8.2	–	70.0	Saint Vincent and the Grenadines
11	–	59	61 325	22.0	5.7	2.8	15.8	39.4	44.0	Samoa
2.5	–	75	0	–	–	–	3.2	–	1.3[ad]	San Marino
97	17.8	96	199 686	18.0	2.0	8.8	31.1	50.3	92.0	Sao Tome and Principe
12	0.1	98	3	16.4	3.4	0.2	27.4	–	17.6	Saudi Arabia
139	97.6	89	11 849 373	17.9	6.1	0.5	27.2	46.3	80.0	Senegal
21	–	94	0	20.4	17.0	11.8	7.7	25.1	22.0	Serbia
9.5	–	98	0	21.7	9.3	10.8	8.6	–	61.2	Seychelles
307	302.8	86	7 500 446	30.3	15.3	5.7	27.3	37.5	125.0	Sierra Leone
44	–	96	10 473	10.1	9.9	1.9	3.6	–	2.7	Singapore
6.5	–	96	5	17.6	12.5	12.3	6.6	–	21.2	Slovakia
7.2	–	–	7	13.2	21.4	11.3	6.4	–	4.6	Slovenia
89	67.0	98	534 850	26.4	7.9	1.4	19.2	60.0	62.0	Solomon Islands
274	85.5	42	5 015 936	20.2	5.4	0.5	25.4	–	64.0	Somalia
834	3.1	71	6 696 701	26.5	10.7	11.2	25.1	–	54.0	South Africa
146	156.0	31	9 706 562	20.3	6.4	–	27.9	5.6	158.0	South Sudan

ANNEX B
Part 1

Member State	Total population[a] (000s)	Life expectancy at birth[b] (years)			Healthy life expectancy at birth[b] (years)	Maternal mortality ratio[c] (per 100 000 live births)	Proportion of births attended by skilled health personnel[g] (%)	Under-five mortality rate[e] (per 1000 live births)	Neonatal mortality rate[e] (per 1000 live births)	New HIV infections among adults 15–49 years old[f] (per 1000 uninfected population)
		Male	Female	Both sexes		3.1		3.2		3.3
	2015	2015			2015	2015	2005–2016	2015	2015	2015
Spain	46 122	80.1	85.5	82.8	72.4	5	–	4.1	2.8	0.14
Sri Lanka	20 715	71.6	78.3	74.9	67.0	30	99	9.8	5.4	0.05
Sudan	40 235	62.4	65.9	64.1	55.9	311	78[ac]	70.1	29.8	–
Suriname	543	68.6	74.7	71.6	63.1	155	90	21.3	11.5	0.62
Swaziland	1 287	56.6	61.1	58.9	50.9	389	88[ac]	60.7	14.2	23.60
Sweden	9 779	80.7	84.0	82.4	72.0	4	–	3.0	1.6	–
Switzerland	8 299	81.3	85.3	83.4	73.1	5	–	3.9	2.7	–
Syrian Arab Republic	18 502	59.9	69.9	64.5	56.1	68	96[ac]	12.9	7.0	–
Tajikistan	8 482	66.6	73.6	69.7	62.1	32	90[ac]	44.8	20.5	0.33
Thailand	67 959	71.9	78.0	74.9	66.8	20	100[ac]	12.3	6.7	0.20
The former Yugoslav Republic of Macedonia	2 078	73.5	77.8	75.7	67.5	8	100[ac]	5.5	3.5	–
Timor-Leste	1 185	66.6	70.1	68.3	60.7	215	29	52.6	22.3	–
Togo	7 305	58.6	61.1	59.9	52.8	368	45	78.4	26.7	1.21
Tonga	106	70.6	76.4	73.5	66.0	124	96	16.7	6.9	–
Trinidad and Tobago	1 360	67.9	74.8	71.2	63.3	63	100[ac]	20.4	13.2	0.52
Tunisia	11 254	73.0	77.8	75.3	66.7	62	74	14.0	8.2	0.04
Turkey	78 666	72.6	78.9	75.8	66.2	16	97[ac]	13.5	7.1	–
Turkmenistan	5 374	62.2	70.5	66.3	59.8	42	100	51.4	22.6	–
Tuvalu	10	–	–	–	–	–	93	27.1	17.6	–
Uganda	39 032	60.3	64.3	62.3	54.0	343	57	54.6	18.7	5.12
Ukraine	44 824	66.3	76.1	71.3	64.1	24	100[ac]	9.0	5.5	0.68
United Arab Emirates	9 157	76.4	78.6	77.1	67.9	6	–	6.8	3.5	–
United Kingdom	64 716	79.4	83.0	81.2	71.4	9	–	4.2	2.4	–
United Republic of Tanzania	53 470	59.9	63.8	61.8	54.1	398	49	48.7	18.8	2.11
United States of America	321 774	76.9	81.6	79.3	69.1	14	99	6.5	3.6	–
Uruguay	3 432	73.3	80.4	77.0	67.9	15	100	10.1	5.1	0.27
Uzbekistan	29 893	66.1	72.7	69.4	62.4	36	100[ac]	39.1	20.4	0.02
Vanuatu	265	70.1	74.0	72.0	64.6	78	89[ac]	27.5	11.6	–
Venezuela (Bolivarian Republic of)	31 108	70.0	78.5	74.1	65.2	95	100[ac]	14.9	8.9	0.33
Viet Nam	93 448	71.3	80.7	76.0	66.6	54	94	21.7	11.4	0.28
Yemen	26 832	64.3	67.2	65.7	57.7	385	45[ac]	41.9	22.1	0.07
Zambia	16 212	59.0	64.7	61.8	53.6	224	63	64.0	21.4	8.55
Zimbabwe	15 603	59.0	62.3	60.7	52.3	443	78	70.7	23.5	8.84

WHO region

African Region	989 173	58.2	61.7	60.0	52.3	542	53	81.3	28.0	2.72
Region of the Americas	986 705	74.0	79.9	77.0	67.3	52	96	14.7	7.7	0.30
South-East Asia Region	1 928 174	67.3	70.7	68.9	60.5	164	78	42.5	24.3	0.16
European Region	910 053	73.2	80.2	76.8	68.0	16	99	11.3	6.0	0.47
Eastern Mediterranean Region	643 784	67.4	70.4	68.8	60.1	166	71	52.0	26.6	0.13
Western Pacific Region	1 855 126	74.5	78.7	76.6	68.7	41	96	13.5	6.7	0.09
Global	7 313 015	69.1	73.7	71.4	63.1	216	78	42.5	19.2	0.50

3.3				3.4		3.5	3.6	3.7		
TB incidence[g] (per 100 000 population)	Malaria incidence[h] (per 1000 population at risk)	Infants receiving three doses of hepatitis B vaccine[i] (%)	Reported number of people requiring interventions against NTDs[j]	Probability of dying from any of CVD, cancer, diabetes, CRD between age 30 and exact age 70[k] (%)	Suicide mortality rate[k] (per 100 000 population)	Total alcohol per capita (≥15 years of age) consumption (litres of pure alcohol), projected estimates[l]	Road traffic mortality rate[m] (per 100 000 population)	Proportion of married or in-union women of reproductive age who have their need for family planning satisfied with modern methods[n] (%)	Adolescent birth rate[o] (per 1000 women aged 15–19 years)	Member State
2015	2015	2015	2015	2015	2015	2016	2013	2005–2015	2005–2014	
12	–	97	91	10.0	8.5	9.2	3.7	–	8.4	Spain
65	0.0	99	33 229	17.7	35.3	4.1	17.4	69.4	20.3	Sri Lanka
88	36.6	93	26 533 962	25.7	10.2	3.3	24.3	30.2	87.0	Sudan
33	1.7	89	56 918	20.9	26.6	8.0	19.1	73.2	65.3	Suriname
565	1.4	98	331 005	25.1	14.7	6.0	24.2	80.6	87.0	Swaziland
9.2	–	53	26	9.1	15.4	8.8	2.8	–	5.1	Sweden
7.4	–	–	0	8.7	15.1	10.0	3.3	–	2.0	Switzerland
20	–	41	50 995	23.9	2.7	0.8	20.0	53.3	54.0	Syrian Arab Republic
87	0.0	96	123 178	25.8	4.0	2.9	18.8	50.8	54.0	Tajikistan
172	2.7	99	145 141	16.2	16.0	7.2	36.2	89.2	60.0	Thailand
13	–	92	0	22.2	8.0	2.8	9.4	22.3	18.7	The former Yugoslav Republic of Macedonia
498	0.2	76	1 170 044	20.7	7.1	1.0	16.6	38.3	50.0	Timor-Leste
52	345.1	88	5 586 475	22.4	9.5	2.6	31.1	32.2	85.0	Togo
15	–	82	36 871	24.1	3.5	1.4	7.6	47.9	30.0	Tonga
17	–	90	19 323	25.6	14.5	7.9	14.1	55.1	35.5	Trinidad and Tobago
37	–	98	6 773	16.8	5.5	1.6	24.4	73.2	6.7[ad]	Tunisia
18	0.0	96	0	16.8	8.7	1.9	8.9	59.7	29.0	Turkey
70	–	99	0	34.5	10.0	5.5	17.4	–	21.0	Turkmenistan
232	–	96	10 550	–	–	1.9	–	41.0	42.0	Tuvalu
202	218.3	78	23 239 105	21.6	7.1	11.8	27.4	44.7	140.0	Uganda
91	–	22	0	28.9	20.1	12.8	10.6	68.0	27.2	Ukraine
1.6	–	94	0	17.4	2.9	3.0	10.9	–	34.2	United Arab Emirates
10	–	–	30	11.0	8.5	12.3	2.9	–	19.3	United Kingdom
306	113.9	98	33 064 128	17.8	7.0	6.3	32.9	45.9	72.1	United Republic of Tanzania
3.2	–	92	754	13.6	14.3	9.3	10.6	83.4	26.6	United States of America
30	–	95	6	16.7	17.0	6.8	16.6	–	63.5	Uruguay
79	0.0	99	399 873	26.9	9.3	5.1	11.2	–	29.5	Uzbekistan
63	3.3	64	266 041	22.3	5.8	1.3	16.6	50.7	78.0	Vanuatu
29	68.4	87	280 243	17.9	3.0	7.1	45.1	–	94.5	Venezuela (Bolivarian Republic of)
137	0.3	97	4 468 764	17.3	7.4	8.6	24.5	69.7	36.0	Viet Nam
48	22.2	69	5 840 695	30.9	8.2	0.2	21.5	47.0	67.0	Yemen
391	173.7	90	11 830 416	17.2	6.4	3.9	24.7	63.8	145.0	Zambia
242	114.2	87	10 346 543	18.4	10.5	8.5	28.2	86.0	120.0	Zimbabwe
										WHO region
275	244.9	76	632 923 079	20.9	8.8	6.0	26.6	49.6	100.3	African Region
27	10.0	89	52 468 604	14.7	9.6	8.2	15.9	82.5	51.7	Region of the Americas
246	17.9	87	726 474 894	23.2	12.9	4.0	17.0	73.5	33.9	South-East Asia Region
36	0.0	81	2 378 913	17.8	14.1	10.3	9.3	72.9	17.6	European Region
116	19.0	80	86 152 675	21.8	3.8	0.7	19.9	61.1	46.1	Eastern Mediterranean Region
86	3.1	90	90 710 965	17.1	10.8	7.8	17.3	89.7	15.3	Western Pacific Region
142	94.0	84	1 591 109 130	18.8	10.7	6.4	17.4	76.7	44.1	**Global**

Member State	3.9 Mortality rate attributed to household and ambient air pollution[p] (per 100 000 population) 2012	3.9 Mortality rate attributed to exposure to unsafe WASH services[q] (per 100 000 population) 2012	Mortality rate attributed to unintentional poisoning[k] (per 100 000 population) 2015	3.a Age-standardized prevalence of tobacco smoking among persons 15 years and older[r] (%) Male 2015	3.a Female 2015	3.b Diphtheria-tetanus-pertussis (DTP3) immunization coverage among 1-year-olds[i] (%) 2015	3.b Total net official development assistance to medical research and basic health per capita[s] (constant 2014 US$), by recipient country 2014	3.c Skilled health professional density[t] (per 10 000 population) 2005–2015	3.d Average of 13 International Health Regulations core capacity scores[u] 2010–2016	1.a General government health expenditure as % of general government expenditure[v] 2014
Afghanistan	114.8	34.6	1.6	–	–	78	8.26	6.6	42	12.0
Albania	166.1	0.2	0.3	51.2	7.6	98	0.76	–	–	9.4
Algeria	30.6	2.4	1.1	–	–	95	<0.01	31.2	73	9.9
Andorra	–	–	–	37.2	27.8	97	–	81.3	29	27.9
Angola	105.8	111.2	5.7	–	–	64	1.94	15.9	18	5.0
Antigua and Barbuda	–	–	0.6	–	–	99	–	–	81	18.1
Argentina	24.6	0.7	0.8	29.5	18.4	94	0.02	–	76	6.9
Armenia	93.2	1.1	0.7	52.3	1.5	94	2.03	78.0	96	7.0
Australia	0.4	<0.1	0.5	16.7	13.1	93	–	157.2	100	17.3
Austria	34.2	0.1	0.4	–	–	98	–	133.2	87	16.3
Azerbaijan	47.0	2.1	0.7	46.5	0.4	96	0.88	97.5	84	3.9
Bahamas	20.3	0.1	0.3	–	–	95	–	67.1	75	14.8
Bahrain	11.1	0.1	0.3	48.8	7.6	98	–	33.8	96	10.5
Bangladesh	68.6	6.0	0.3	39.8	0.7	94	1.02	6.0	76	5.7
Barbados	17.3	0.2	0.5	13.1	0.9	97	–	65.7	84	10.9
Belarus	100.8	0.2	3.6	46.2	10.6	99	0.63	149.7	90	13.8
Belgium	30.2	0.5	0.5	26.5	20.0	99	–	127.8	82	15.1
Belize	17.1	1.2	0.8	–	–	94	3.30	25.8	55	13.8
Benin	92.6	32.2	3.2	17.7	1.0	79	6.23	7.5	28	9.6
Bhutan	58.9	7.1	0.9	–	–	99	4.55	13.4	76	8.0
Bolivia (Plurinational State of)	48.9	7.0	4.5	30.5	17.1	99	1.69	14.8	77	11.8
Bosnia and Herzegovina	230.6	<0.1	1.9	47.2	30.0	82	3.06	74.8	57	14.1
Botswana	39.1	9.2	1.5	–	–	95	1.75	31.1	62	8.8
Brazil	15.8	1.1	0.2	19.3	11.3	96	0.01	93.0	97	6.8
Brunei Darussalam	0.2	<0.1	0.2	29.3	3.1	99	–	96.6	92	6.5
Bulgaria	217.3	<0.1	0.8	42.4	28.2	91	–	88.6	69	11.0
Burkina Faso	96.5	40.9	3.1	36.0	4.5	91	4.88	6.8	50	11.2
Burundi	106.5	68.4	5.6	–	–	94	4.27	–	62	13.2
Cabo Verde	56.1	4.5	0.5	22.2	3.5	93	3.81	8.7	62	11.7
Cambodia	71.4	5.6	0.9	44.1	2.8	89	4.27	11.2	55	6.1
Cameroon	91.8	40.9	3.1	43.8	0.9	84	3.23	6.0	54	4.3
Canada	5.4	0.6	0.6	17.7	12.2	91	–	119.5	100	18.8
Central African Republic	97.0	102.3	4.9	–	–	47	8.43	3.0	29	14.2
Chad	124.2	92.8	5.0	–	–	55	3.51	3.5	40	9.0
Chile	19.3	0.2	0.3	40.0	36.0	96	0.03	11.8	79	15.9
China	161.1	0.4	1.6	47.6	1.8	99	0.06	31.5	98	10.4
Colombia	22.0	0.8	0.3	16.0	6.2	91	0.20	22.2	89	18.1
Comoros	73.5	28.6	3.7	23.1	6.0	80	6.03	–	29	8.7
Congo	93.2	48.1	1.8	43.2	1.7	80	1.38	10.5	44	8.7
Cook Islands	–	–	–	–	–	99	2.90	69.5	56	6.1
Costa Rica	16.9	0.7	0.4	18.5	8.3	92	0.09	19.5	86	23.3
Côte d'Ivoire	90.7	44.1	4.0	–	–	83	3.64	6.2	78	7.3
Croatia	79.9	<0.1	0.3	39.4	33.5	94	–	92.7	71	14.0
Cuba	66.0	0.7	0.4	52.7	17.8	99	0.29	155.0	99	18.0
Cyprus	19.8	0.3	0.3	–	–	97	–	64.0	93	7.6
Czechia	58.0	0.5	0.5	37.4	29.0	99	–	120.0	91	14.9
Democratic People's Republic of Korea	238.4	1.4	2.3	–	–	96	1.13	68.7	73	–
Democratic Republic of the Congo	118.5	107.8	3.6	–	–	81	6.18	10.5	71	11.1
Denmark	20.3	0.8	0.4	17.6	16.4	93	–	204.6	89	16.8
Djibouti	81.8	26.4	3.0	–	–	84	4.87	7.9	46	14.1
Dominica	–	–	–	–	–	98	–	–	62	10.5
Dominican Republic	26.1	1.9	0.4	18.8	9.4	85	0.58	28.3	71	17.4

	2.2		6.1	6.2	7.1	11.6	13.1	16.1	17.19	
Prevalence of stunting in children under 5[w] (%)	Prevalence of wasting in children under 5[w] (%)	Prevalence of overweight in children under 5[w] (%)	Proportion of population using improved drinking-water sources[x] (%)	Proportion of population using improved sanitation[x] (%)	Proportion of population with primary reliance on clean fuels[y] (%)	Annual mean concentrations of fine particulate matter (PM$_{2.5}$) in urban areas[z] (µg/m^3)	Average death rate due to natural disasters[k] (per 100 000 population)	Mortality rate due to homicide[k] (per 100 000 population)	Estimated direct deaths from major conflicts[k,aa] (per 100 000 population)	Completeness of cause-of-death data[ab] (%)	
2005–2016	2005–2016	2005–2016	2015	2015	2014	2014	2011–2015	2015	2011–2015	2005–2015	Member State
40.9	9.5	5.4	55	32	17	63.4	0.8	7.0	40.9	–	Afghanistan
23.1	9.4	23.4	95	93	67	17.1	0.0	4.1	<0.1	76	Albania
11.7	4.1	12.4	84	88	>95	25.1	<0.1	4.2	1.0	–	Algeria
–	–	–	100	100	>95[af]	10.5	–	–	–	100	Andorra
37.6	4.9	3.3	49	52	48	42.4	0.1	9.6	0.0	–	Angola
–	–	–	98	–	>95	13.0	0.0	4.8	0.0	93	Antigua and Barbuda
8.2	1.2	9.9	99	96	>95	14.4	0.1	4.7	0.0	99	Argentina
9.4	4.2	13.6	100	90	>95	25.0	0.0	1.7	0.0	100	Armenia
2.0	0.0	7.7	100	100	>95[af]	5.8	0.1	0.9	<0.1	100	Australia
–	–	–	100	100	>95[af]	17.1	0.2	1.0	<0.1	100	Austria
18.0	3.1	13.0	87	89	>95	26.3	0.0	2.2	0.3	100	Azerbaijan
–	–	–	98	92	>95[af]	12.6	0.0	23.7	0.0	89	Bahamas
–	–	–	100	99	>95[af]	60.1	0.0	0.7	2.0	83	Bahrain
36.1	14.3	1.4	87	61	10	88.8	0.1	2.9	<0.1	–	Bangladesh
7.7	6.8	12.2	100	96	>95	14.0	0.0	10.1	0.0	75	Barbados
4.5	2.2	9.7	100	94	>95	18.0	0.0	6.2	<0.1	90	Belarus
–	–	–	100	100	>95[af]	15.9	<0.1	1.1	<0.1	100	Belgium
15.0	1.8	7.3	100	91	87	20.7	0.0	37.2	0.0	76	Belize
34.0	4.5	1.7	78	20	7	27.9	<0.1	6.0	0.0	–	Benin
33.6	5.9	7.6	100	50	68	39.0	0.0	1.5	0.0	–	Bhutan
18.1	1.6	8.7	90	50	79	31.6	0.5	13.6	0.0	–	Bolivia (Plurinational State of)
8.9	2.3	17.4	100	95	40	55.1	0.1	3.1	<0.1	95	Bosnia and Herzegovina
31.4	7.2	11.2	96	63	63	19.2	0.1	10.8	0.0	–	Botswana
7.1	1.6	7.3	98	83	93	11.3	0.2	30.5	0.2	99	Brazil
19.7	2.9	8.3	–	–	>95[af]	5.4	0.0	1.3	0.0	100	Brunei Darussalam
–	–	–	99	86	79	30.3	0.1	1.5	<0.1	98	Bulgaria
27.3	7.6	1.2	82	20	7	36.8	<0.1	9.8	<0.1	–	Burkina Faso
57.5	6.1	2.9	76	48	<5	48.9	0.2	6.2	0.1	–	Burundi
–	–	–	92	72	71	–	0.0	5.9	0.0	95	Cabo Verde
32.4	9.6	2.0	76	42	13	25.0	0.7	2.2	<0.1	–	Cambodia
31.7	5.2	6.7	76	46	18	63.6	<0.1	11.5	1.2	–	Cameroon
–	–	–	100	100	>95[af]	7.2	0.1	1.8	<0.1	100	Canada
40.7	7.1	1.8	69	22	<5	55.9	0.0	13.1	25.6	–	Central African Republic
39.9	13.0	2.5	51	12	<5	61.3	<0.1	9.0	0.1	–	Chad
1.8	0.3	9.3	99	99	>95	25.0	0.1	4.6	<0.1	99	Chile
9.4	2.3	6.6	96	77	57	59.5	0.1	0.9	<0.1	62	China
12.7	0.9	4.8	91	81	91	18.1	0.3	48.8	0.8	83	Colombia
32.1	11.1	10.9	90	36	7	16.0	0.1	7.6	0.0	–	Comoros
21.2	8.2	5.9	77	15	18	56.9	0.1	10.1	0.0	–	Congo
–	–	–	100	98	80	–	–	–	–	100	Cook Islands
5.6	1.0	8.1	98	95	>95	19.1	0.1	9.2	0.0	90	Costa Rica
29.6	7.6	3.2	82	23	18	19.2	<0.1	11.8	0.5	–	Côte d'Ivoire
–	–	–	100	97	94	20.3	0.1	1.0	0.0	100	Croatia
–	–	–	95	93	87	16.5	0.2	4.9	0.0	99	Cuba
–	–	–	100	100	>95[af]	17.2	0.0	2.2	0.0	68	Cyprus
–	–	–	100	99	>95	20.7	0.2	0.9	<0.1	100	Czechia
27.9	4.0	0.0	100	82	7	31.4	0.2	4.4	0.0	–	Democratic People's Republic of Korea
42.6	8.1	4.4	52	29	6	60.7	<0.1	13.4	1.8	–	Democratic Republic of the Congo
–	–	–	100	100	>95[af]	10.5	<0.1	1.1	<0.1	100	Denmark
33.5	21.5	8.1	90	47	10	46.0	0.0	6.8	0.1	–	Djibouti
–	–	–	–	–	92	13.0	–	–	–	100	Dominica
7.1	2.4	7.6	85	84	92	17.0	<0.1	30.2	0.0	54	Dominican Republic

ANNEX B
Part 2

Member State	3.9 Mortality rate attributed to household and ambient air pollution[p] (per 100 000 population) 2012	3.9 Mortality rate attributed to exposure to unsafe WASH services[q] (per 100 000 population) 2012	Mortality rate attributed to unintentional poisoning[k] (per 100 000 population) 2015	3.a Age-standardized prevalence of tobacco smoking among persons 15 years and older[r] (%) Male 2015	Female 2015	3.b Diphtheria-tetanus-pertussis (DTP3) immunization coverage among 1-year-olds[i] (%) 2015	3.b Total net official development assistance to medical research and basic health per capita[s] (constant 2014 US$), by recipient country 2014	3.c Skilled health professional density[t] (per 10 000 population) 2005–2015	3.d Average of 13 International Health Regulations core capacity scores[u] 2010–2016	1.a General government health expenditure as % of general government expenditure[v] 2014
Ecuador	12.8	1.8	0.8	14.0	3.3	78	0.44	37.5	81	10.2
Egypt	50.9	1.6	0.5	49.9	0.3	93	0.08	22.5	94	5.6
El Salvador	42.7	2.4	0.4	–	–	91	0.45	24.1	94	16.7
Equatorial Guinea	99.3	57.3	2.9	–	–	16	0.86	–	27	7.0
Eritrea	84.9	34.9	3.6	–	–	95	3.10	–	49	3.6
Estonia	47.0	<0.1	0.9	41.2	24.9	93	–	92.9	71	13.5
Ethiopia	57.4	29.6	2.5	8.9	0.5	86	4.67	2.8	79	15.7
Fiji	95.1	3.0	0.5	38.7	12.4	99	12.04	27.3	98	9.2
Finland	6.0	0.2	0.6	23.2	18.5	98	–	174.5	96	12.4
France	17.2	0.5	0.8	29.8	25.6	98	–	138.3	89	15.7
Gabon	50.1	28.1	1.5	–	–	80	1.38	–	52	7.4
Gambia	71.2	21.0	2.6	–	–	97	11.44	10.0	33	15.3
Georgia	204.9	0.2	0.9	57.7	5.7	94	1.91	86.0	82	5.0
Germany	32.5	0.9	0.2	32.4	28.3	96	–	176.0	99	19.6
Ghana	80.0	20.0	1.6	13.1	0.4	88	4.98	10.2	74	6.8
Greece	45.1	<0.1	0.3	52.6	32.7	99	–	96.9	76	10.0
Grenada	–	–	0.8	–	–	92	–	45.2	66	9.2
Guatemala	37.3	9.2	1.2	–	–	74	1.65	17.6	55	17.8
Guinea	89.3	40.7	2.9	–	–	51	8.35	–	57	9.0
Guinea-Bissau	106.5	48.9	2.8	–	–	80	6.70	7.3	49	7.8
Guyana	84.7	4.0	1.0	–	–	95	1.51	7.4	85	9.4
Haiti	115.2	28.5	2.8	22.1	2.5	60	4.34	–	56	6.1
Honduras	54.6	7.9	0.6	33.3	2.1	85	3.66	15.2	83	15.4
Hungary	122.8	<0.1	0.4	32.0	24.8	99	–	98.8	85	10.1
Iceland	6.4	<0.1	0.7	17.0	15.1	92	–	201.4	72	15.7
India	133.7	27.4	1.9	20.4	1.9	87	0.20	27.5	98	5.0
Indonesia	85.0	3.6	0.5	76.2	3.6	81	0.32	15.7	99	5.7
Iran (Islamic Republic of)	35.2	0.9	1.4	21.5	0.7	98	0.06	30.4	85	17.5
Iraq	33.5	3.9	0.5	–	–	58	0.34	26.6	91	6.5
Ireland	14.6	0.3	0.4	22.4[ag]	21.9[ag]	95	–	150.9	78	13.4
Israel	15.8	0.5	0.2	41.2	19.3	94	–	88.8	71	11.6
Italy	35.2	0.1	0.5	28.3	19.7	93	–	104.2	90	13.7
Jamaica	35.6	1.9	0.5	29.9	5.9	91	0.03	14.8	83	8.1
Japan	24.2	0.1	0.5	33.7[ag]	10.6[ag]	96	–	130.9	100	20.3
Jordan	21.2	1.0	0.7	70.2	10.7	99	3.72	55.1	72	13.7
Kazakhstan	90.0	1.2	2.8	43.9	9.3	98	0.52	111.4	78	10.9
Kenya	60.0	32.5	2.0	24.6	2.1	89	4.74	10.7	69	12.8
Kiribati	–	–	2.0	63.9	40.9	87	8.15	48.2	60	5.8
Kuwait	14.2	<0.1	0.2	–	–	99	–	66.8	85	5.8
Kyrgyzstan	87.1	1.8	0.9	50.4	3.6	97	4.30	77.1	50	11.9
Lao People's Democratic Republic	108.3	13.9	1.3	56.6	9.1	89	5.65	10.4	75	3.4
Latvia	101.6	<0.1	1.4	48.9	24.3	95	–	82.5	91	9.8
Lebanon	29.1	0.4	0.4	45.4	31.0	81	8.40	49.4	76	10.7
Lesotho	80.4	28.3	3.1	55.1	0.4	93	1.81	–	74	13.1
Liberia	71.3	25.0	2.1	27.6	2.4	52	29.13	2.8	26	11.9
Libya	33.2	0.6	0.8	–	–	94	0.02	90.0	64	4.9
Lithuania	73.5	<0.1	1.2	38.1	22.2	93	–	122.8	82	13.4
Luxembourg	19.8	0.1	0.3	25.8	21.4	99	–	152.5	88	13.6
Madagascar	85.2	26.6	2.4	–	–	69	3.72	3.6	29	10.2
Malawi	72.7	26.1	2.7	25.4	6.0	88	7.88	3.5	40	16.8
Malaysia	21.6	0.4	0.6	43.0	1.4	99	0.02	46.8	100	6.4
Maldives	15.3	0.6	0.6	–	–	99	1.65	72.0	60	26.6
Mali	117.1	61.1	3.2	36.8	3.2	68	6.11	5.3	55	7.0
Malta	31.1	<0.1	0.2	29.7	20.2	97	–	125.8	79	15.6
Marshall Islands	–	–	–	–	–	85	3.21	40.1	51	23.8
Mauritania	64.6	28.9	2.4	44.0	3.7	73	3.63	7.8	29	6.0

	2.2		6.1	6.2	7.1	11.6	13.1	16.1		17.19	
Prevalence of stunting in children under 5[w] (%)	Prevalence of wasting in children under 5[w] (%)	Prevalence of overweight in children under 5[w] (%)	Proportion of population using improved drinking-water sources[c] (%)	Proportion of population using improved sanitation[x] (%)	Proportion of population with primary reliance on clean fuels[y] (%)	Annual mean concentrations of fine particulate matter (PM$_{2.5}$) in urban areas[z] (µg/m³)	Average death rate due to natural disasters[k] (per 100 000 population)	Mortality rate due to homicide[k] (per 100 000 population)	Estimated direct deaths from major conflicts[k,aa] (per 100 000 population)	Completeness of cause-of-death data[ab] (%)	
2005–2016	2005–2016	2005–2016	2015	2015	2014	2014	2011–2015	2015	2011–2015	2005–2015	Member State
25.2	2.3	7.5	87	85	>95	13.3	0.2	10.2	<0.1	81	Ecuador
22.3	9.5	15.7	99	95	>95	100.6	0.0	5.0	0.4	95	Egypt
13.6	2.1	6.4	94	75	83	37.0	0.1	63.2	0.0	84	El Salvador
26.2	3.1	9.7	48	75	22	32.0	0.0	3.2	0.0	–	Equatorial Guinea
50.3	15.3	1.9	58	16	14	35.7	0.0	7.5	0.1	–	Eritrea
–	–	–	100	97	92	8.4	0.0	4.4	<0.1	100	Estonia
38.4	9.9	2.8	57	28	<5	36.2	0.0	7.6	0.2	–	Ethiopia
–	–	–	96	91	37	6.0	0.4	2.5	0.0	100	Fiji
–	–	–	100	98	>95[af]	7.1	0.0	1.6	<0.1	100	Finland
–	–	–	100	99	>95[af]	12.6	0.2	0.9	<0.1	100	France
17.5	3.4	7.7	93	42	73	35.8	0.0	9.0	0.0	–	Gabon
25.0	11.1	3.2	90	59	<5	43.0	<0.1	9.1	0.0	–	Gambia
11.3	1.6	19.9	100	86	55	23.0	0.2	4.2	<0.1	100	Georgia
1.3	1.0	3.5	100	99	>95[af]	14.4	0.1	0.7	<0.1	100	Germany
18.8	4.7	2.6	89	15	21	22.1	0.2	10.0	0.0	–	Ghana
–	–	–	100	99	>95[af]	12.6	<0.1	2.0	<0.1	98	Greece
–	–	–	97	98	>95	14.0	0.0	6.4	0.0	100	Grenada
46.5	0.7	4.7	93	64	36	33.4	0.2	36.2	0.2	92	Guatemala
31.3	9.9	3.8	77	20	6	19.4	0.0	8.5	0.2	–	Guinea
27.2	5.9	2.3	79	21	<5	28.9	0.0	9.2	<0.1	–	Guinea-Bissau
12.0	6.4	5.3	98	84	61	16.1	0.0	18.8	0.0	93	Guyana
21.9	5.2	3.6	58	28	9	24.6	0.4	28.1	0.0	–	Haiti
22.7	1.4	5.2	91	83	48	39.6	0.1	85.7	<0.1	15	Honduras
–	–	–	100	98	>95[af]	22.7	0.0	1.2	0.0	100	Hungary
–	–	–	100	99	>95[af]	7.7	0.0	1.3	0.0	100	Iceland
38.4	21.0	1.9	94	40	34	65.7	0.2	4.0	0.1	10	India
36.4	13.5	11.5	87	61	57	17.8	0.1	4.3	<0.1	–	Indonesia
6.8	4.0	0.0	96	90	>95	40.2	0.1	4.1	0.1	90	Iran (Islamic Republic of)
22.1	6.5	11.4	87	86	>95	51.3	<0.1	12.7	83.6	75	Iraq
–	–	–	98	91	>95[af]	9.9	<0.1	0.9	<0.1	100	Ireland
–	–	–	100	100	>95[af]	19.2	<0.1	2.0	0.3	100	Israel
–	–	–	100	100	>95[af]	18.2	0.1	0.9	0.0	100	Italy
5.7	3.0	7.8	94	82	93	17.1	0.0	35.2	0.0	87	Jamaica
7.1	2.3	1.5	100	100	>95[af]	12.9	4.2	0.3	<0.1	100	Japan
7.8	2.4	4.7	97	99	>95	37.7	0.0	3.0	<0.1	65	Jordan
8.0	3.1	9.3	93	98	92	21.1	<0.1	9.0	<0.1	86	Kazakhstan
26.0	4.0	4.1	63	30	6	16.8	0.1	8.2	0.6	–	Kenya
–	–	–	67	40	<5	–	0.0	9.1	0.0	56	Kiribati
4.9	3.1	6.0	99	100	>95[af]	78.4	0.0	2.5	0.1	65	Kuwait
12.9	2.8	7.0	90	93	76	15.4	0.0	7.7	<0.1	95	Kyrgyzstan
43.8	6.4	2.0	76	71	<5	33.5	0.2	6.9	0.0	–	Lao People's Democratic Republic
–	–	–	99	88	>95	20.1	0.0	6.7	0.0	95	Latvia
–	–	–	99	81	>95	31.2	0.0	4.2	3.8	–	Lebanon
33.2	2.8	7.4	82	30	32	21.7	0.2	29.7	0.0	–	Lesotho
32.1	5.6	3.2	76	17	<5	6.0	0.0	10.4	0.0	–	Liberia
21.0	6.5	22.4	–	97	–	58.2	0.1	2.5	19.6	–	Libya
–	–	–	97	92	>95[af]	19.4	0.0	6.8	0.0	99	Lithuania
–	–	–	100	98	>95[af]	16.6	0.0	0.4	0.0	100	Luxembourg
49.2	15.2	0.0	52	12	<5	32.0	0.2	7.7	<0.1	–	Madagascar
42.4	3.8	5.1	90	41	<5	25.6	0.2	1.7	0.0	–	Malawi
17.7	8.0	7.1	98	96	>95	16.6	<0.1	3.8	0.1	58	Malaysia
20.3	10.2	6.5	99	98	>95	–	0.0	3.5	0.0	100	Maldives
38.5	15.3	4.7	77	25	<5	34.5	<0.1	10.8	3.7	–	Mali
–	–	–	100	100	>95[af]	14.4	0.0	2.9	0.0	100	Malta
–	–	–	95	77	41	–	–	–	–	–	Marshall Islands
27.9	14.8	1.3	58	40	45	86.2	<0.1	10.2	0.3	–	Mauritania

Member State	3.9 Mortality rate attributed to household and ambient air pollution (per 100 000 population) 2012	3.9 Mortality rate attributed to exposure to unsafe WASH services (per 100 000 population) 2012	Mortality rate attributed to unintentional poisoning (per 100 000 population) 2015	3.a Age-standardized prevalence of tobacco smoking among persons 15 years and older (%) Male 2015	3.a Female 2015	3.b Diphtheria-tetanus-pertussis (DTP3) immunization coverage among 1-year-olds (%) 2015	3.b Total net official development assistance to medical research and basic health per capita (constant 2014 US$), by recipient country 2014	3.c Skilled health professional density (per 10 000 population) 2005–2015	3.d Average of 13 International Health Regulations core capacity scores 2010–2016	1.a General government health expenditure as % of general government expenditure 2014
Mauritius	20.3	0.9	0.1	40.1	3.3	97	0.07	–	70	10.0
Mexico	23.5	1.1	0.5	20.8	6.6	87	0.01	45.8	97	11.6
Micronesia (Federated States of)	–	–	1.1	–	–	72	4.13	38.0	86	21.2
Monaco	–	–	–	–	–	99	–	266.3	79	18.8
Mongolia	132.4	3.1	2.2	47.7	5.3	99	2.37	65.6	86	6.7
Montenegro	137.6	<0.1	0.7	–	–	89	0.34	76.9	56	9.8
Morocco	25.1	3.4	0.7	45.4	1.4	99	0.31	14.9	95	6.0
Mozambique	65.7	37.9	3.3	31.4	5.9	80	9.56	4.6	69	8.8
Myanmar	128.2	10.4	1.8	31.6	6.4	75	3.00	15.0	84	3.6
Namibia	48.0	9.8	2.0	38.9	11.4	92	3.95	31.3	81	13.9
Nauru	–	–	–	43.0	52.0	91	9.83	78.8	42	5.2
Nepal	103.2	12.9	0.6	37.1	11.1	91	4.32	–	72	11.2
Netherlands	24.0	0.2	0.2	26.2	23.3	95	–	116.9	94	20.9
New Zealand	0.5	0.6	0.3	17.2	15.4	92	–	135.7	96	23.4
Nicaragua	63.9	3.5	0.6	–	–	98	3.79	23.0	88	24.0
Niger	111.7	69.2	3.6	18.6	0.2	65	4.83	1.6	75	5.6
Nigeria	99.0	50.9	3.1	17.4	1.1	56	2.68	18.3	64	8.2
Niue	–	–	–	20.3	11.4	99	6.21	116.3	61	5.9
Norway	12.7	0.5	1.1	22.4	22.1	95	–	218.3	98	18.2
Oman	14.5	0.4	0.2	21.0	1.0	99	–	48.9	95	6.8
Pakistan	87.2	20.7	1.5	41.9	3.0	72	1.00	14.1	53	4.7
Palau	–	–	–	–	–	90	1.42	72.8	91	18.1
Panama	22.9	4.1	0.6	10.6	2.6	73	0.27	38.5	71	14.6
Papua New Guinea	46.3	12.4	2.0	–	–	62	3.41	5.9	64	9.5
Paraguay	54.5	2.3	0.5	28.3	7.9	93	0.55	23.3	79	11.9
Peru	33.0	1.3	1.1	21.5	5.9	90	0.35	26.1	70	15.0
Philippines	88.7	5.1	0.2	43.0	8.5	60	0.59	–	87	10.0
Poland	68.9	<0.1	0.4	32.4	23.7	98	–	80.1	74	10.7
Portugal	16.8	0.1	0.3	31.5	13.7	98	–	108.0	93	11.9
Qatar	8.9	<0.1	0.3	–	–	99	–	76.6	97	5.8
Republic of Korea	23.2	0.2	0.6	49.8 [ag]	4.2 [ag]	98	–	79.0	100	12.3
Republic of Moldova	101.4	<0.1	1.5	45.7	5.4	87	3.38	78.5	81	13.3
Romania	129.5	<0.1	0.7	36.9	22.7	89	–	89.1	77	12.8
Russian Federation	98.6	0.2	2.1	59.0	22.8	97	–	78.8	99	9.5
Rwanda	68.6	19.4	2.7	–	–	98	9.90	7.3	46	9.9
Saint Kitts and Nevis	–	–	–	–	–	93	–	–	60	6.9
Saint Lucia	–	–	0.3	–	–	99	2.89	19.6	77	11.5
Saint Vincent and the Grenadines	–	–	0.5	–	–	98	1.92	–	65	14.8
Samoa	–	–	0.7	41.0	18.9	66	5.47	23.6	75	15.1
San Marino	–	–	–	–	–	76	–	149.1	40	13.2
Sao Tome and Principe	–	–	1.4	–	–	96	28.76	–	16	12.4
Saudi Arabia	27.5	0.2	0.9	27.9	2.9	98	–	77.7	97	8.2
Senegal	45.7	25.4	2.1	23.4	0.7	89	7.84	4.9	30	8.0
Serbia	137.3	0.3	0.5	43.6	39.7	95	0.25	75.1	37	13.9
Seychelles	–	–	0.5	43.0	8.8	97	1.77	54.2	88	9.7
Sierra Leone	143.8	90.4	4.7	60.0	12.0	86	17.70	3.4	47	10.8
Singapore	20.7	0.1	0.1	28.0	5.0	96	–	75.6	99	14.1
Slovakia	64.0	<0.1	0.5	39.7	17.6	96	–	94.6	95	15.0
Slovenia	36.7	<0.1	0.4	22.3	18.1	95	–	113.8	74	12.8
Solomon Islands	54.3	10.4	1.3	–	–	98	9.40	22.1	57	12.5
Somalia	116.9	98.8	3.7	–	–	42	6.70	1.1	6	–
South Africa	51.6	12.1	1.2	31.4	6.5	69	0.58	58.8	100	14.2
South Sudan	95.1	50.0	3.9	–	–	31	8.70	–	50	4.0
Spain	14.7	0.3	0.4	31.3	27.1	97	–	91.8	95	14.5
Sri Lanka	125.4	3.3	0.4	28.4	0.4	99	1.21	24.8	79	11.2

	2.2			6.1	6.2	7.1	11.6	13.1	16.1	17.19	
Prevalence of stunting in children under 5[w] (%)	Prevalence of wasting in children under 5[w] (%)	Prevalence of overweight in children under 5[w] (%)	Proportion of population using improved drinking-water sources[x] (%)	Proportion of population using improved sanitation[x] (%)	Proportion of population with primary reliance on clean fuels[y] (%)	Annual mean concentrations of fine particulate matter (PM$_{2.5}$) in urban areas[z] (μg/m^3)	Average death rate due to natural disasters[k] (per 100 000 population)	Mortality rate due to homicide[k] (per 100 000 population)	Estimated direct deaths from major conflicts[k,aa] (per 100 000 population)	Completeness of cause-of-death data[ab] (%)	
2005–2016	2005–2016	2005–2016	2015	2015	2014	2014	2011–2015	2015	2011–2015	2005–2015	Member State
–	–	–	100	93	>95	14.3	0.2	2.7	0.0	97	Mauritius
12.4	1.0	5.2	96	85	86	20.1	0.2	19.0	1.1	100	Mexico
–	–	–	89	57	25	6.0	1.3	4.7	0.0	–	Micronesia (Federated States of)
–	–	–	100	100	>95[af]	9.2	–	–	–	100	Monaco
10.8	1.0	10.5	64	60	32	32.1	0.0	8.2	0.0	95	Mongolia
9.4	2.8	22.3	100	96	74	24.3	0.0	2.6	0.0	92	Montenegro
14.9	2.3	10.7	85	77	>95	18.9	<0.1	1.6	<0.1	22	Morocco
43.1	6.1	7.9	51	21	<5	22.3	0.2	3.0	0.1	–	Mozambique
29.2	7.0	1.3	81	80	9	56.6	0.1	3.9	1.6	–	Myanmar
23.1	7.1	4.1	91	34	46	18.4	0.9	14.6	0.0	–	Namibia
24.0	1.0	2.8	97	66	>95	–	–	–	–	–	Nauru
37.1	11.3	2.1	92	46	26	74.3	7.2	3.3	<0.1	–	Nepal
–	–	–	100	98	>95[af]	14.9	<0.1	0.7	0.0	100	Netherlands
–	–	–	100	–	>95[af]	5.3	0.9	1.2	0.0	100	New Zealand
23.0	1.5	6.2	87	68	49	26.0	0.2	15.0	<0.1	82	Nicaragua
43.0	18.7	3.0	58	11	<5	51.5	0.2	10.0	0.2	–	Niger
32.9	7.2	1.6	69	29	<5	37.6	0.1	9.8	3.1	–	Nigeria
–	–	–	99	100	91	–	–	–	–	–	Niue
–	–	–	100	98	>95[af]	9.1	0.1	0.7	0.3	100	Norway
14.1	7.5	4.4	93	97	>95[af]	47.4	0.1	5.0	0.0	81	Oman
45.0	10.5	4.8	91	64	45	67.7	0.4	9.5	4.2	–	Pakistan
–	–	–	–	100	58	–	–	–	–	95	Palau
19.1	1.2	0.0	95	75	86	12.8	0.3	18.7	0.0	94	Panama
49.5	14.3	13.8	40	19	31	12.0	0.2	12.2	0.2	–	Papua New Guinea
10.9	2.6	11.7	98	89	64	16.9	<0.1	7.5	0.1	81	Paraguay
14.6	0.6	7.2	87	76	68	35.7	0.1	14.6	<0.1	62	Peru
30.3	7.9	5.0	92	74	45	27.1	2.5	11.6	1.1	82	Philippines
–	–	–	98	97	>95[af]	25.4	<0.1	0.9	0.0	100	Poland
–	–	–	100	100	>95[af]	9.6	0.1	1.1	0.0	100	Portugal
–	–	–	100	98	>95	104.6	0.0	8.1	0.0	67	Qatar
2.5	1.2	7.3	–	100	>95	27.8	0.3	2.0	0.0	100	Republic of Korea
6.4	1.9	4.9	88	76	93	17.1	0.0	5.5	0.0	90	Republic of Moldova
–	–	–	100	79	82	20.2	0.6	1.5	0.0	100	Romania
–	–	–	97	72	>95	16.6	<0.1	10.3	0.5	89	Russian Federation
37.9	2.2	7.7	76	62	<5	50.6	<0.1	5.1	0.7	–	Rwanda
–	–	–	98	–	>95[af]	–	–	–	–	88	Saint Kitts and Nevis
2.5	3.7	6.3	96	91	>95	15.0	0.7	13.5	0.0	88	Saint Lucia
–	–	–	95	–	>95	–	2.2	21.7	0.0	100	Saint Vincent and the Grenadines
–	–	–	99	92	27	–	2.4	3.1	0.0	–	Samoa
–	–	–	–	–	>95[af]	–	–	–	–	100	San Marino
17.2	4.0	2.4	97	35	30	–	0.0	6.4	0.0	–	Sao Tome and Principe
9.3	11.8	6.1	97	100	>95	127.1	<0.1	5.8	<0.1	36	Saudi Arabia
20.5	7.8	1.0	79	48	36	43.2	<0.1	7.3	0.1	–	Senegal
6.0	3.9	13.9	99	96	71	21.4	0.1	1.7	<0.1	93	Serbia
7.9	4.3	10.2	96	98	>95	13.0	0.0	10.2	0.0	94	Seychelles
37.9	9.4	8.9	63	13	<5	16.8	0.1	13.2	0.0	–	Sierra Leone
–	–	–	100	100	>95[af]	17.0	0.0	2.7	0.0	68	Singapore
–	–	–	100	99	>95	20.2	0.0	1.3	0.0	100	Slovakia
–	–	–	100	99	>95	19.4	<0.1	0.6	0.0	100	Slovenia
32.8	4.3	2.5	81	30	9	5.0	2.0	4.1	0.0	–	Solomon Islands
25.3	15.0	3.0	–	–	9	16.9	0.4	5.6	35.8	–	Somalia
23.9	4.7	10.9	93	66	82	31.3	<0.1	26.2	<0.1	83	South Africa
31.1	22.4	6.0	59	7	<5	32.1	0.3	4.5	21.1	–	South Sudan
–	–	–	100	100	>95[af]	9.9	0.1	0.8	<0.1	100	Spain
14.7	21.4	0.6	96	95	19	28.5	0.4	3.1	<0.1	93	Sri Lanka

ANNEX B
Part 2

Member State	3.9 Mortality rate attributed to household and ambient air pollution[p] (per 100 000 population) 2012	3.9 Mortality rate attributed to exposure to unsafe WASH services[q] (per 100 000 population) 2012	Mortality rate attributed to unintentional poisoning[k] (per 100 000 population) 2015	3.a Age-standardized prevalence of tobacco smoking among persons 15 years and older[r] (%) Male 2015	3.a Female 2015	3.b Diphtheria-tetanus-pertussis (DTP3) immunization coverage among 1-year-olds[i] (%) 2015	3.b Total net official development assistance to medical research and basic health per capita[s] (constant 2014 US$), by recipient country 2014	3.c Skilled health professional density[t] (per 10 000 population) 2005–2015	3.d Average of 13 International Health Regulations core capacity scores[u] 2010–2016	1.a General government health expenditure as % of general government expenditure[v] 2014
Sudan	64.5	34.6	4.2	–	–	93	2.47	42.2	71	11.6
Suriname	22.1	0.8	0.7	–	–	89	1.41	–	72	11.8
Swaziland	62.6	22.7	3.3	19.0	2.2	90	2.66	15.3	56	16.6
Sweden	0.4	1.1	0.6	20.4	20.8	98	–	160.0	93	19.0
Switzerland	18.5	0.3	0.2	26.9	19.7	97	–	219.3	92	22.7
Syrian Arab Republic	30.0	1.8	0.7	–	–	41	0.29	38.5	63	4.8
Tajikistan	92.0	7.5	1.9	–	–	96	3.88	64.4	94	6.8
Thailand	64.0	1.9	0.5	41.4	2.3	99	0.49	24.7	98	13.3
The former Yugoslav Republic of Macedonia	137.5	<0.1	0.4	–	–	91	0.31	70.1	90	12.9
Timor-Leste	91.6	10.3	1.0	–	–	76	10.77	12.7	66	2.4
Togo	81.1	37.9	2.5	–	–	88	3.13	3.6	74	7.8
Tonga	–	–	1.4	47.3	13.0	82	6.53	44.1	74	13.5
Trinidad and Tobago	26.8	0.2	0.4	–	–	96	–	47.5	73	8.2
Tunisia	42.6	0.8	0.6	–	–	98	0.19	48.4	55	14.2
Turkey	51.0	0.8	0.5	39.5	12.4	96	0.03	42.7	78	10.5
Turkmenistan	70.9	5.8	1.2	–	–	99	0.88	68.5	84	8.7
Tuvalu	–	–	–	–	–	96	11.12	77.5	89	16.9
Uganda	70.5	30.3	3.1	16.4	2.9	78	5.33	14.6	73	11.0
Ukraine	140.4	0.4	3.0	49.4	14.0	23	0.75	96.8	99	10.8
United Arab Emirates	7.3	<0.1	0.3	–	–	94	–	46.2	91	8.7
United Kingdom	25.7	0.4	0.4	19.9[ag]	18.4[ag]	96	–	112.4	88	16.5
United Republic of Tanzania	51.4	27.6	2.4	27.5	3.8	98	5.77	4.6	67	12.3
United States of America	12.1	0.6	1.2	19.5[ag]	15.0[ag]	95	–	117.8	96	21.3
Uruguay	21.4	0.3	0.7	26.7	19.4	95	0.09	97.9	82	20.8
Uzbekistan	76.5	2.4	1.5	24.9	1.3	99	1.09	141.0	83	10.7
Vanuatu	–	–	0.9	–	–	64	22.25	24.0	43	17.9
Venezuela (Bolivarian Republic of)	20.5	1.3	0.3	–	–	87	0.01	–	94	5.8
Viet Nam	83.2	2.0	1.0	47.1	1.3	97	1.05	24.1	99	14.2
Yemen	61.3	13.0	2.9	–	–	69	4.36	10.7	46	3.9
Zambia	65.4	24.5	2.9	26.5	4.6	90	4.58	8.3	92	11.3
Zimbabwe	52.9	27.1	2.1	31.2	2.1	87	4.30	12.7	73	8.5

WHO region

African Region	80.2	43.1	2.8	–	–	76	4.54	14.1	56	9.9
Region of the Americas	20.3	1.5	0.8	–	–	91	0.32	84.6	79	13.6
South-East Asia Region	119.9	20.1	1.5	–	–	87	0.47	24.6	80	9.3
European Region	64.2	0.6	1.0	–	–	93	–	106.4	81	13.2
Eastern Mediterranean Region	58.8	13.1	1.4	–	–	80	1.46	26.3	72	8.8
Western Pacific Region	133.5	0.8	1.4	–	–	94	0.24	42.0	79	12.3

Global	92.4	12.4	1.5	–	–	86	1.16	45.6	73	11.7

2.2			6.1	6.2	7.1	11.6	13.1	16.1		17.19	
Prevalence of stunting in children under 5[w] (%)	Prevalence of wasting in children under 5[w] (%)	Prevalence of overweight in children under 5[w] (%)	Proportion of population using improved drinking-water sources[x] (%)	Proportion of population using improved sanitation[x] (%)	Proportion of population with primary reliance on clean fuels[y] (%)	Annual mean concentrations of fine particulate matter (PM$_{2.5}$) in urban areas[z] (µg/m³)	Average death rate due to natural disasters[k] (per 100 000 population)	Mortality rate due to homicide[k] (per 100 000 population)	Estimated direct deaths from major conflicts[k,aa] (per 100 000 population)	Completeness of cause-of-death data[ab] (%)	
2005–2016	2005–2016	2005–2016	2015	2015	2014	2014	2011–2015	2015	2011–2015	2005–2015	Member State
38.2	16.3	3.0	–	–	23	52.7	0.1	6.5	7.0	–	Sudan
8.8	5.0	4.0	95	79	91	16.3	0.0	10.7	0.0	79	Suriname
25.5	2.0	9.0	74	58	35	19.8	0.2	20.0	0.0	–	Swaziland
–	–	–	100	99	>95[af]	5.9	0.1	1.2	0.0	100	Sweden
–	–	–	100	100	>95[af]	12.5	<0.1	0.6	0.0	100	Switzerland
27.5	11.5	17.9	90	96	>95	34.1	0.0	2.5	309.0	81	Syrian Arab Republic
26.8	9.9	6.6	74	95	72	50.7	0.1	1.3	0.1	82	Tajikistan
16.3	6.7	10.9	98	93	76	27.3	0.3	4.0	0.7	81	Thailand
4.8	1.8	12.4	99	91	61	42.7	0.0	1.4	0.3	98	The former Yugoslav Republic of Macedonia
50.2	11.0	1.5	72	41	<5	15.0	0.0	4.4	0.0	–	Timor-Leste
27.5	6.7	2.0	63	12	6	25.9	0.0	9.1	0.0	–	Togo
8.1	5.2	17.3	100	91	63	–	0.0	3.8	0.0	–	Tonga
–	–	–	95	92	>95	12.7	0.0	32.8	0.0	83	Trinidad and Tobago
10.2	2.8	14.3	98	92	>95	35.2	0.0	1.6	0.3	28	Tunisia
9.5	1.7	10.9	100	95	–	35.2	0.2	2.4	0.8	88	Turkey
11.5	4.2	5.9	–	–	>95	26.2	0.0	4.2	<0.1	78	Turkmenistan
10.0	3.3	6.3	98	–	30	–	–	–	–	–	Tuvalu
34.2	4.3	5.8	79	19	<5	79.6	<0.1	13.1	1.9	–	Uganda
–	–	–	96	96	>95	16.9	<0.1	6.0	6.2	86	Ukraine
–	–	–	100	98	>95	64.4	0.0	3.7	<0.1	66	United Arab Emirates
–	–	–	100	99	>95[af]	12.4	0.1	1.3	<0.1	100	United Kingdom
34.4	4.5	3.6	56	16	<5	23.9	<0.1	7.6	<0.1	–	United Republic of Tanzania
2.1	0.5	6.0	99	100	>95[af]	8.4	0.4	5.3	<0.1	100	United States of America
10.7	1.3	7.2	100	96	>95	11.5	0.0	7.6	0.0	100	Uruguay
19.6	4.5	12.8	–	100	90	38.3	0.1	3.0	0.0	89	Uzbekistan
28.5	4.4	4.6	95	58	16	7.0	0.9	2.1	0.0	–	Vanuatu
13.4	4.1	6.4	93	94	>95	24.0	<0.1	51.7	<0.1	90	Venezuela (Bolivarian Republic of)
24.6	6.4	5.3	98	78	51	27.6	0.1	3.9	0.0	–	Viet Nam
46.5	16.3	2.0	–	–	62	42.0	<0.1	6.1	14.3	–	Yemen
40.0	6.3	6.2	65	44	16	29.5	0.0	9.7	0.0	–	Zambia
27.6	3.3	3.6	77	37	31	23.9	0.2	28.5	<0.1	–	Zimbabwe
											WHO region
33.5	7.4	4.1	68	32	16	37.4	0.1	10.3	1.4	5	African Region
6.6	0.9	7.1	96	89	91	14.7	0.2	18.6	0.2	94	Region of the Americas
33.8	15.3	5.3	92	49	35	58.8	0.3	4.0	0.1	11	South-East Asia Region
6.1	1.5	12.8	99	93	>95	19.1	0.1	3.3	0.5	95	European Region
25.1	9.1	6.7	91	78	71	62.9	0.2	6.5	19.5	32	Eastern Mediterranean Region
7.0	2.4	5.2	95	79	61	49.8	0.5	1.7	0.1	64	Western Pacific Region
22.9	7.7	6.0	91	68	57	43.1	0.3	6.4	2.0	48	**Global**

[a] World Population Prospects, the 2015 revision (WPP2015). New York (NY): United Nations DESA, Population Division.

[b] WHO life expectancy. http://www.who.int/gho/mortality_burden_disease/life_tables/en/

[c] WHO, UNICEF, UNFPA, World Bank Group and the United Nations Population Division. Trends in maternal mortality: 1990 to 2015. Estimates by WHO, UNICEF, UNFPA, World Bank Group and the United Nations Population Division. Geneva: World Health Organization; 2015 (http://www.who.int/reproductivehealth/publications/monitoring/maternal-mortality-2015/en/, accessed 17 March 2017). WHO Member States with a population of less than 100 000 in 2015 were not included in the analysis.

[d] WHO/UNICEF joint Global Database 2017. (http://www.who.int/gho/maternal_health/en/ and https://data.unicef.org/topic/maternal-health/delivery-care). The data are extracted from public available sources and have not undergone country consultation. WHO regional and global figures are for the period 2010–2016.

[e] Levels & Trends in Child Mortality. Report 2015. Estimates Developed by the UN Inter-agency Group for Child Mortality Estimation. New York (NY), Geneva and Washington (DC): United Nations Children's Fund, World Health Organization, World Bank and United Nations; 2015 (http://www.unicef.org/publications/files/Child_Mortality_Report_2015_Web_9_Sept_15.pdf, accessed 17 March 2017).

[f] UNAIDS/WHO estimates; 2016. (http://www.who.int/gho/hiv/epidemic_status/incidence/en/)

[g] Global tuberculosis report 2016. Geneva: World Health Organization; 2016 (http://apps.who.int/iris/bitstream/10665/250441/1/9789241565394-eng.pdf?ua=1, accessed 17 April 2017).

[h] World Malaria Report 2016. Geneva: World Health Organization; 2016 (http://www.who.int/malaria/publications/world-malaria-report-2016/report/en/, accessed 17 March 2017).

[i] WHO/UNICEF coverage estimates revision. July 2016 (see: http://www.who.int/immunization/monitoring_surveillance/routine/coverage/en/index4.html). This indicator is used here as a proxy for the SDG indicator.

[j] Neglected tropical diseases [online database]. Global Health Observatory (GHO) data. Geneva: World Health Organization (http://www.who.int/gho/neglected_diseases/en/).

[k] Global Health Estimates 2015: Deaths by cause, age, sex, by country and by region, 2000–2015. Geneva, World Health Organization; 2016. (http://www.who.int/healthinfo/global_burden_disease/estimates/en/index1.html, accessed 22 March 2017). WHO Member States with a population of less than 90 000 in 2015 were not included in this analysis.

[l] WHO Global Information System on Alcohol and Health [online database]. Geneva: World Health Organization; 2017 (http://apps.who.int/gho/data/node.main.GISAH?showonly=GISAH).

[m] Global status report on road safety 2015. Geneva: World Health Organization; 2015 (http://www.who.int/violence_injury_prevention/road_safety_status/2015/en/, accessed 22 March 2017). WHO Member States with a population of less than 90 000 in 2015 who did not participate in the survey for the report were not included in the analysis.

[n] World Contraceptive Use 2016 [online database]. New York (NY): United Nations, Department of Economic and Social Affairs, Population Division; 2016. Regional aggregates are estimates for the year 20165 from: United Nations, Department of Economic and Social Affairs, Population Division (2016). Model-based Estimates and Projections of Family Planning Indicators 2016. New York: United Nations. (http://www.un.org/en/development/desa/population/theme/family-planning/cp_model.shtml)

[o] World Fertility Data 2015. New York (NY): United Nations, Department of Economic and Social Affairs, Population Division; 2015. (http://www.un.org/en/development/desa/population/publications/dataset/fertility/wfd2015.shtml) Regional aggregates are the average of two five-year periods, 2010–2015 and 2015–2020, taken from: World Population Prospects: The 2015 Revision. DVD Edition. New York (NY): United Nations, Department of Economic and Social Affairs, Population Division; 2015 (http://esa.un.org/unpd/wpp/Download/Standard/Fertility/, accessed 13 April 2016).

[p] Public health and environment [online database]. Global Health Observatory (GHO) data. Geneva: World Health Organization (http://www.who.int/gho/phe/en/). WHO Member States with a population of less than 250 000 population in 2012 were not included in the analysis.

[q] Preventing disease through healthy environments. A global assessment of the burden of disease from environmental risks. Geneva: World Health Organization; 2016 (http://apps.who.int/iris/bitstream/10665/204585/1/9789241565196_eng.pdf?ua=1, accessed 23 March 2017); and: Preventing diarrhoea through better water, sanitation and hygiene. Exposures and impacts in low- and middle-income countries. Geneva: World Health Organization; 2014 (http://apps.who.int/iris/bitstream/10665/150112/1/9789241564823_eng.pdf?ua=1&ua=1, accessed 23 March 2017). WHO Member States with a population of less than 250 000 in 2012 were not included in the analysis.

[r] WHO global report on trends in prevalence of tobacco smoking 2015. Geneva: World Health Organization; 2015 (http://apps.who.int/iris/bitstream/10665/156262/1/9789241564922_eng.pdf, accessed 22 March 2017).

[s] United Nations' SDG indicators global database (https://unstats.un.org/sdgs/indicators/database/?indicator=3.b.2, accessed 6 April 2017). Based on the Creditor Reporting System database of the Organisation for Economic Co-operation and Development, 2016.

[t] Skilled health professionals refer to the latest available values (2005–2015) in the WHO Global Health Workforce Statistics database (http://who.int/hrh/statistics/hwfstats/en/) aggregated across physicians and nurses/midwives. Refer to the source for the latest values, disaggregation and metadata descriptors.

[u] International Health Regulations (2005) Monitoring Framework [online database]. Geneva: WHO (http://www.who.int/gho/ihr/en/).

[v] Global Health Expenditure Database [online database]. Geneva. World Health Organization. 2017 (http://apps.who.int/nha/database/Select/Indicators/en, accessed March 23, 2017). WHO regional and global figures represent unweighted averages. This indicator reflects the health-related portion of the SDG indicator.

[w] United Nations Children's Fund, World Health Organization, the World Bank Group. Levels and trends in child malnutrition. UNICEF/WHO/World Bank Group Joint Child Malnutrition Estimates. UNICEF, New York; WHO, Geneva; the World Bank Group, Washington (DC); May 2017. WHO regional and global estimates are for the year 2016.

[x] Progress on sanitation and drinking water – 2015 update and MDG assessment. New York (NY): UNICEF; and Geneva: World Health Organization; 2015 (http://apps.who.int/iris/bitstream/10665/177752/1/9789241509145_eng.pdf?ua=1, accessed 23 March 2017). This indicator is used here as a proxy for the SDG indicator.

[y] Burning opportunity: clean household energy for health, sustainable development, and wellbeing of women and children. Geneva: World Health Organization; 2016 (http://apps.who.int/iris/bitstream/10665/204717/1/9789241565233_eng.pdf, accessed 23 March 2017).

[z] Ambient air pollution: a global assessment of exposure and burden of disease. Geneva: World Health Organization; 2016 (see: http://who.int/phe/publications/air-pollution-global-assessment/en/, accessed 23 March 2017).

[aa] Conflict deaths include deaths due to collective violence and exclude deaths due to legal intervention. The death rate is an average over the five year period.

[ab] Global Health Estimates 2015: Deaths by cause, age, sex, by country and by region, 2000–2015. Geneva, World Health Organization; 2016. (http://www.who.int/healthinfo/global_burden_disease/estimates/en/index1.html, accessed 22 March 2017). Completeness was assessed relative to the de facto resident populations. WHO regional and global figures are for 2015.

[ac] Non-standard definition. For more details see the WHO/UNICEF joint Global Database 2017. (http://www.who.int/gho/maternal_health/en/ and https://data.unicef.org/topic/maternal-health/delivery-care)

[ad] Updated estimate.

[ae] The estimate of total suicide mortality for the Republic of Korea has been updated using data published in the WHO Mortality Database after the closure date for the Global Health Estimates 2015.

[af] For high-income countries with no information on clean fuel use, usage is assumed to be >95%.

[ag] Cigarette smoking only.

ANNEX C
WHO regional groupings[1]

WHO African Region: Algeria, Angola, Benin, Botswana, Burkina Faso, Burundi, Cabo Verde, Cameroon, Central African Republic, Chad, Comoros, Congo, Côte d'Ivoire, Democratic Republic of the Congo, Equatorial Guinea, Eritrea*, Ethiopia, Gabon, Gambia, Ghana, Guinea, Guinea-Bissau, Kenya, Lesotho, Liberia, Madagascar, Malawi, Mali, Mauritania, Mauritius, Mozambique, Namibia, Niger, Nigeria, Rwanda, Sao Tome and Principe, Senegal, Seychelles, Sierra Leone, South Africa, South Sudan*, Swaziland, Togo, Uganda, United Republic of Tanzania, Zambia, Zimbabwe.

WHO Region of the Americas: Antigua and Barbuda, Argentina, Bahamas, Barbados, Belize, Bolivia (Plurinational State of), Brazil, Canada, Chile, Colombia, Costa Rica, Cuba, Dominica, Dominican Republic, Ecuador, El Salvador, Grenada, Guatemala, Guyana, Haiti, Honduras, Jamaica, Mexico, Nicaragua, Panama, Paraguay, Peru, Saint Kitts and Nevis, Saint Lucia, Saint Vincent and the Grenadines, Suriname, Trinidad and Tobago, the United States of America, Uruguay, Venezuela (Bolivarian Republic of).

WHO South-East Asia Region: Bangladesh, Bhutan, Democratic People's Republic of Korea, India, Indonesia, Maldives, Myanmar, Nepal, Sri Lanka, Thailand, Timor-Leste*.

WHO European Region: Albania, Andorra*, Armenia*, Austria, Azerbaijan*, Belarus, Belgium, Bosnia and Herzegovina*, Bulgaria, Croatia*, Cyprus, Czechia*, Denmark, Estonia*, Finland, France, Georgia*, Germany, Greece, Hungary, Iceland, Ireland, Israel, Italy, Kazakhstan*, Kyrgyzstan*, Latvia*, Lithuania*, Luxembourg, Malta, Monaco, Montenegro*, Netherlands, Norway, Poland, Portugal, Republic of Moldova*, Romania, Russian Federation, San Marino, Serbia*, Slovakia*, Slovenia*, Spain, Sweden, Switzerland, Tajikistan*, The former Yugoslav Republic of Macedonia*, Turkey, Turkmenistan*, Ukraine, the United Kingdom, Uzbekistan*.

WHO Eastern Mediterranean Region: Afghanistan, Bahrain, Djibouti, Egypt, Iran (Islamic Republic of), Iraq, Jordan, Kuwait, Lebanon, Libya, Morocco, Oman, Pakistan, Qatar, Saudi Arabia, Somalia, Sudan, Syrian Arab Republic, Tunisia, United Arab Emirates, Yemen.

WHO Western Pacific Region: Australia, Brunei Darussalam, Cambodia, China, Cook Islands, Fiji, Japan, Kiribati, Lao People's Democratic Republic, Malaysia, Marshall Islands*, Micronesia (Federated States of)*, Mongolia, Nauru*, New Zealand, Niue*, Palau*, Papua New Guinea, Philippines, Republic of Korea, Samoa, Singapore, Solomon Islands, Tonga, Tuvalu*, Vanuatu, Viet Nam.

---

[1] Member States indicated with an * may have data for periods prior to their official membership of WHO.

Notes